Ronald L. Cramer

Sister Gilmary Beagle, SS.C.M.

Lida Lim

John Prejza, Jr.

Norman C. Najimy

Donna Ogle

Robert E. Quackenbush

Joan Smutny

DeWayne Triplett

Language

Skills and Use

Special Populations Author   Dale R. Jordan

Reader Consultants   Mildred G. Gersh
Bessie Williams

Scott, Foresman and Company
Editorial Offices: Glenview, Illinois

Regional Sales Offices: Palo Alto, California •
Tucker, Georgia • Glenview, Illinois •
Oakland, New Jersey • Dallas, Texas

Program Author

E. Brooks Smith

Book Authors

Readiness — Book Eight

Sister Gilmary Beagle, SS.C.M.

Harold Cafone

Ronald L. Cramer

Beverly Dryden

Janet Hamerman

Lida Lim

Barbara McDermitt

Carol A. Mejia

Virginia Mickish

Norman C. Najimy

Donna Ogle

Mary Sue Ordway

John Prejza, Jr.

Robert E. Quackenbush

E. Brooks Smith

Joan Smutny

DeWayne Triplett

ISBN: 0-673-12756-7

Copyright © 1980,
Scott, Foresman and Company, Glenview, Illinois
All Rights Reserved.
Printed in the United States of America

2345678910-VHP-8887868584838281 8079

Acknowledgments

Text

page 11: Untitled haiku poem by Lisa Kelly. Copyright © 1980 by Scott, Foresman and Company

page 27: "To Look at Any Thing". © 1961 by John Moffitt. Reprinted from his volume *The Living Seed* by permission of Harcourt Brace Jovanovich, Inc.

pages 38–39: From *Gone-Away Lake,* © 1957 by Elizabeth Enright. Reprinted by permission of Harcourt Brace Jovanovich, Inc. and Russell & Volkening, Inc.

page 63: "The Time We Climbed Snake Mountain" by Leslie Silko. Copyright © 1972 by Leslie Silko. Reprinted by permission of the author.

page 74: Andrew Schiller and William A. Jenkins. *In Other Words,* A Junior Thesaurus. Copyright © 1977, Scott, Foresman and Company.

page 97: "74th Street" from *The Malibu and Other Poems* by Myra Cohn Livingston (A Margaret K. McElderry Book). Copyright © 1972 by Myra Cohn Livingston. Use by permission of Atheneum Publishers and McIntosh and Otis, Inc.

page 106: Excerpt from p. 15 "Take 'mo' as in motor . . . own design and its own purpose." in *Mopeding* by Charles Coombs. Copyright © 1978 by Charles Coombs. By permission of William Morrow & Company.

page 107: From the book *Lurkers of the Deep* by Bruce Robison. Copyright © 1978 by Bruce Robison. Reprinted by permission of the David McKay Company, Inc.

page 114: Lewis Carroll, *The Complete Works of Lewis Carroll.* New York: Random House, Inc., p. 754.

page 133: "New Excavations". From *Fiddler's Farewell,* by Leonora Speyer. Copyright 1926 by Alfred A. Knopf, Inc. and renewed 1954 by Leonora Speyer. Reprinted by permission of Alfred A. Knopf, Inc.

pages 136, 137: Adapted from *The World Book Encyclopedia.* © 1978 World Book-Childcraft International, Inc. Reprinted by permission.

page 140: Reprinted by permission of G.P. Putnam's Sons and Barthold Fles, Literary Agent from *The San Francisco Earthquake and Fire* by Helen Markley Miller. Copyright © 1970 by Helen Markley Miller.

page 142: Abridged from *Disaster 1906: The San Francisco Earthquake and Fire* by Edward F. Dolan, Jr. Copyright © 1967 by Edward F. Dolan, Jr. Reprinted by permission of Julian Messner, a Simon & Schuster division of Gulf & Western Corporation.

page 171: "Letterslot" as it appears in *Verse* by John Updike (Crest, 1965). British title: "Cheerful Alphabet of Pleasant Objects" in *Hoping for Hoopoe* by John Updike. Copyright © 1958 by John Updike. Reprinted by permission of Harper and Row, Publishers, Inc., and Victor Gollancz, Ltd.

page 207: "Primer Lesson" from *Slabs of the Sunburnt West* by Carl Sandburg. Copyright 1922 by Harcourt Brace Jovanovich, Inc., copyright 1950 by Carl Sandburg. Reprinted by permission of the publisher.

Continued on page 384.

CONTENTS

UNIT THREE

UNIT SIX

UNIT SEVEN

UNIT TEN

Unit One

A haiku is a three-line poem of seventeen syllables.
The following haiku, written by a sixth-grader,
praises the treasures of the earth.

A Haiku

Our great mother Earth
Still holds precious jewels and stones
Yet to be treasured.

Lisa Kelly

Words are also precious jewels, and the ability to use them
well is a gift to be treasured. In this unit, you will review
ways in which language can serve you.

What Are Surveys and Interviews?

You can gather information for an interview or survey by questioning people.

Information about bicycle problems was gathered in the survey and interview below.

Survey

Bike Problems
Which is your most common bike problem?

Bad brakes	||	2
Loose chain	++++	5
Flat tire	++++ ++++ ||||	14
Broken gears	||||	4

Interview

Q: How should bicycle riders take care of the tires on their bikes?
A: Put the proper amount of air in them.
Q: How can bicycle riders keep from getting flat tires?
A: Don't ride over curbs. Don't ride double or make skidding stops.

In the survey, many people were asked the question: Which bicycle problem happens to you most often? The survey shows that flat tires happen most often.

The interview shows questions about tires that were asked and notes that were written. The notes contain the important information learned during the interview.

A. Answer the following questions. Use the survey and interview above.
   1. What is the second most common bicycle problem?
   2. What information was gathered about how to keep from getting flat tires?

B. Write three other questions that could be asked in an interview with a bicycle expert. They can be about taking care of, buying, or riding a bicycle.

C. Make up a survey form for one of the following topics: Watching TV, Allowances, Getting Exercise, Household Chores, Homework, Reading.

Review 2   **What Do You Know About Words?**

Some words or groups of words have special meanings. The words in our language come from many different sources.

Idioms

Do you know the special meanings of the underlined words?

> Keep your eye on that tiger!
> The zoo official announced, "The tiger flew the coop."

The underlined words above are called **idioms.** Idioms are expressions that have special meanings all their own. The idiom *keep your eye on* does not mean "to put your eye on," as the separate words suggest. It means "to watch carefully."

The idiom *flew the coop* also has a special meaning. The picture on the right shows an exact meaning of the phrase. As an idiom, *flew the coop* means "to leave suddenly."

A. Choose one of the idioms below. Write a sentence that shows the special meaning of the idiom. Then make a picture that shows what one might think the idiom means.

1. hit the ceiling
2. cross one's mind
3. keep a stiff upper lip
4. put heads together

B. Read the sentences below. Tell what the meaning of each underlined idiom is.

1. Our team did well at the beginning of the season. Now we have gone downhill.
2. The bell rang suddenly so the teacher cut the lesson short.
3. My little brother cried all morning long. He really got on my nerves.
4. Don tried to make the pieces of the puzzle fit. Finally he had to throw in the towel.
5. Their escape was a close one. They made it by the skin of their teeth.

13

Word Histories

Words enter our language from many different sources. A word history tells what languages a word came from and what the spellings and meanings of the word were.

magazine

Magazine came into English about 400 years ago from French *magazin*, and can be traced back to Arabic *makhzan*, meaning "storehouse."

1. From what language did the English word *magazine* come?

2. From what language did the French word *magazin* come?

3. How is the current meaning of *magazine* similar to the Arabic meaning?

Word Families

Some groups of words in our language come from the same ancestor word in another language. These groups of words are called *word families*.

legible

Below are words related to *legible*. They can all be traced back to the Latin word *legere* (le′ge re), meaning "to read, choose, select."

coil	intellect	lesson
collect	intelligent	lignite
cull	intelligible	neglect
diligent	lecture	negligence
elect	legend	recollect
eligible	legion	sacrilege
elite	legume	select

C. Read the word family for *legible*.

1. This sentence will help you remember the meaning of *legible*: Make sure your handwriting is *legible*. How is the meaning of *legible* related to the Latin meaning of *legere*?

2. How are these words related to the meaning of *legere: elect? intelligent?*

Coined Words

Words also enter our language when people coin words, or make them up. Often a coined word is a blend, or combination of two familiar words. For example, a meal eaten at midmorning that combines breakfast and lunch is called *brunch*.

D. Try coining words for the things below.

1. a half-smile and half-frown

2. a tiny elephant

3. a sad rabbit

4. a skinny hippo

14

Review 3   What Are Complete Sentences?

A complete sentence has a subject and a predicate.

Read the sentences below and notice the two parts.

> The sixth-graders are planning a surprise.
> They will bring a picnic lunch for the teachers.

The subjects in the sentences are *The sixth-graders* and *They*. The words *are planning a surprise* and *will bring a picnic lunch for the teachers* are the predicates. The sentences would not make sense if either the subject or the predicate was missing.

A. Add a subject to complete each of the items. Use a different word in each.
1. was reading a good mystery story at the beach
2. wanted her brother to help her find some shells
3. gathered some tiny snail shells
4. strung the shells together
5. admired the lovely shell necklace

B. Add a predicate to complete each item.
1. In the distance a log cabin
2. A faint trail of smoke
3. The darkness of night
4. Just then a glowing lantern
5. Perhaps the lost youth

C. There are 3 complete sentences below. Make the other groups of words into complete sentences.
1. Jefferson School had a carnival.
2. Sold tickets to their friends.
3. Posters all over town.
4. The gym was decorated with balloons.
5. Cool drinks and popcorn.
6. Were exhausted at the end of the day.
7. Sherry won a goldfish at the ring toss.

What Are Nouns and Verbs?

A noun is a word that names a person, place, or thing. A verb shows action or links the subject to the predicate. Nouns and verbs have special forms.

Nouns

The underlined words in the sentences below are nouns.

Singular Nouns (name one person, place, or thing):
The man parked his car in his garage.
Plural Nouns (name more than one person, place, or thing):
The men parked their cars in their garages.
Proper Nouns (name a particular person, place, or thing):
Lupe visited the Lincoln Memorial in Washington, D.C.

Proper nouns name a particular person, place, or thing and begin with a capital letter. All other nouns are called common nouns.

A. There are 14 nouns in the sentences below. Draw one line under the 7 singular nouns. Draw a circle around the 7 plural nouns.

1. This land is ruled by a king and queen.
2. The castle is surrounded by high walls of stone.
3. Men and women work in a nearby field.
4. The older children watch over all the sheep.
5. Knights on horses compete in a tournament.

B. Write a proper noun for each common noun.
Example: ocean   Atlantic Ocean

1. river   3. state   5. friend
2. teacher   4. building   6. school

C. Copy the list. Capitalize the proper nouns.

1. mark twain   5. golden gate bridge
2. a high mountain   6. the largest city
3. two students   7. paris, france
4. lake michigan   8. an easy game

Verbs

Verbs have different tenses to show whether something happens in the present, past, or future.

Look at the action verbs in the sentences below.

Present Tense (happening now):

The boys <u>play</u> tennis here today.

Past Tense (happened in the past):

The boys <u>played</u> last Sunday.

Future Tense (will happen in the future):

The boys <u>will play</u> tomorrow.

Linking verbs join the subject to the predicate. Look at the linking verbs in the sentences below.

Present Tense: She <u>is</u> our gym coach.

Past Tense: She <u>was</u> a good athlete years ago.

Future Tense: She <u>will be</u> our coach again next year.

D. Fill in the blanks with an action verb of your own or a linking verb from the chart.

Tense	Linking Verbs
Present	am is are
Past	was were
Future	will be

1. Colts _____ young horses.
2. In some cities police officers ____ horses.
3. A palomino ____ a golden-colored horse.
4. I ____ my horse apples and carrots.
5. The wild mustangs ____ across the fields.
6. During a hunt, horses often ____ fences.
7. Tomorrow Leroy ____ the winner of a blue ribbon.

E. Write the verb in each sentence. Then tell what tense it is by writing *present*, *past*, or *future*.

1. There is a rodeo in this town today.
2. The riders brushed their horses yesterday.
3. Some contestants will receive prize money.
4. In this event, the cowgirls gallop on their horses around three large barrels.
5. The cowgirls were skillful riders.
6. Rodeo clowns will entertain after the next event.
7. That cowboy stayed on the bull for eight seconds.

17

What Are Adverbs and Adjectives?

An adjective tells more about a noun, and an adverb tells more about a verb. Adjectives and adverbs can be used to make comparisons.

Adjectives

Look at the underlined adjectives below.

What Kind	How Many	Which One
ugly monster	twenty cats	that book
red rose	one country	this city
huge feet	thirteen pens	sixth grade

Adjectives describe nouns. They tell *what kind, how many,* or *which one.*

A. Fill in the blanks with adjectives.
1. Do not pick the ____ apples on ____ tree.
2. You will need a ____ ladder to reach ____ branches.
3. I counted ____ baskets of ____ apples.
4. Did Lisa work ____ hours in ____ orchard?

B. List the 10 adjectives in the sentences below. Beside each adjective show whether it tells *what kind, how many,* or *which one.*
1. The fifth grade toured this museum.
2. Enormous statues of prehistoric animals fill these halls.
3. One room has bronze tools.
4. Two guards watch over that exhibit of ancient jewelry.

Adverbs

Adverbs tell more about verbs. Read the sentences below.

Paul played his trombone loudly. (how?)
He always (when?) practices here. (where?)

Adverbs tell *how, when,* or *where.*

C. Add an adverb from the box to each sentence.

1. This river flows (how?) in some places.
2. Canoes tip (when?) in these rapids.
3. Andy's hat floated (where?) and disappeared.
4. They covered ten miles (when?).
5. They paddled (how?) all afternoon.
6. The bottom (where?) is rocky.

Adverbs	
how?	hard, swiftly
when?	often, today
where?	here, away

D. Write the adverb in each sentence. Then show whether the adverb tells *how, when,* or *where.*

1. The sky suddenly darkened.
2. Kimiko raced inside.
3. She quickly shut the window.
4. Lightning flashed brightly in the sky.
5. Storms always frighten her.

Making Comparisons

Look at the forms of the adjectives *smart* and *obedient* and the adverbs *fast* and *carefully* in the sentences below.

Comparing Two Things or Actions:
My dog is <u>smarter</u> and <u>more obedient</u> than your dog.
Jeff works <u>faster</u> and <u>more carefully</u> than Tom.

Comparing Three or More Things or Actions:
My dog is the <u>smartest</u> and <u>most obedient</u> dog in the neighborhood.
Jeff works the <u>fastest</u> and <u>most carefully</u> of the three.

The endings *-er* and *-est* or the words *more* and *most* are used with adjectives and adverbs to make comparisons.

E. Write the following sentences. Use the correct form of the adjective or adverb in parentheses.

1. Fall is the (colorful) season of all.
2. Paula works (patiently) than Nora.
3. The ocean is the home of the (large) animals that ever lived.
4. Of the five players, Stephen can run the (fast).
5. Who is (old), Carmella or Joy?
6. This is the (difficult) problem on the test.

What Is a Card Catalog?

A card catalog contains cards that have information about the books in the library. The cards are arranged in alphabetical order.

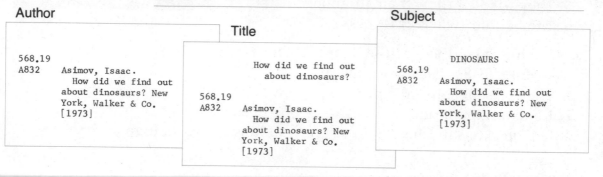

Most books in the library have three cards filed in the card catalog—an author card, a title card, and a subject card. The example above shows three cards for the book *How Did We Find Out About Dinosaurs?* All three cards contain the same information arranged in different ways. Author Isaac Asimov's name appears at the top of the author card (last name first). The title *How Did We Find Out About Dinosaurs?* appears at the top of the title card. The subject DINOSAURS appears in capital letters at the top of the subject card.

All cards are filed alphabetically according to the first word in the first line of the card (unless the word is *a, an,* or *the*).

A. Write the letter of the alphabet under which you would look in the card catalog to find each item listed below.
 1. poems by Gwendolyn Brooks
 2. *A Wrinkle in Time*
 3. a book about scuba diving
 4. stories by N. Scott Momaday
 5. the author of *The Chocolate War*

B. Write the kind of card—author, title, or subject—that you would look at first in the card catalog to find each item listed below.
 1. stories by Juan Ramón Jiménez
 2. the author of *The Red Pony*
 3. a book by Langston Hughes
 4. a book about presidents
 5. *Please Don't Eat the Daisies*

Review 7 How Do You Use Punctuation?

Use end punctuation, commas, and apostrophes correctly to make your sentences clear.

End Punctuation

Statement:	Pelé is a famous soccer player.
Question:	Have you ever seen him play?
Exclamation:	What a great athlete he is!

Different kinds of sentences have different end punctuation.

A. Rewrite each sentence. Add the correct end punctuation.

1. Do you want to go to the movies
2. Look out for the falling rocks
3. Antonia is a graceful ice skater
4. Have you met your new neighbor
5. Jennifer wants to become a geologist

Commas

Compound Sentences:	I turned the corner, and I jumped over a mud puddle.
Words in a Series:	What is big, brown, and cuddly?
City and State:	He was born in Dayton, Ohio.
In a Date:	The party is on March 7, 1979.

B. Rewrite the sentences. Add commas where necessary. You should add 8 commas.

1. Mrs. Andrews ordered the van in Orlando Florida.
2. She picked it up on May 10 1979.
3. The van was painted green white and black.
4. The family drove to Denver Colorado.
5. The van was comfortable and the trip was pleasant.
6. Clark took pictures of mountains rivers and wild flowers with his camera.

Apostrophes with Possessives

One use of apostrophes is to show ownership, or possession.

Singular Possessive: I need to see <u>Peter's</u> book.

ending in _s_: Please find <u>Bess's</u> notes.

Plural Possessive: Where are the <u>children's</u> hats?

ending in _s_: Did you see the <u>ponies'</u> saddles?

C. Rewrite the sentences below. Add an apostrophe (') or an apostrophe and the letter _s_ ('s) where necessary.

1. What is your friend address?
2. Yesterday it rained on Chris glove.
3. Both trees leaves have changed to bright colors.
4. What were those women names?
5. The daisies petals were wilted.
6. Where is your boss office?

Apostrophes with Contractions

Another use for apostrophes is to form contractions.

1. Verb + Not	Contraction	2. Pronoun + Verb	Contraction
do + not	don't	I + am	I'm
is + not	isn't	I + have	I've
was + not	wasn't	it + is	it's
has + not	hasn't	we + are	we're
will + not	won't	you + are	you're
should + not	shouldn't	they + will	they'll

D. Use an apostrophe to write a contraction for two words in each sentence.

1. They are weeding the garden.
2. Billy has not decided what to do for vacation.
3. The plans will not be set for a few weeks yet.
4. I am still working on that assignment.
5. Do not take my things.
6. It is too hot in here.
7. I have never seen such a storm!

Review 8   How Can You Show Order in a Paragraph?

Signal words are often used in the sentences of a paragraph to show the order.

Read the paragraph below.

> To begin with, Iris gathered all the things she needed for her overnight camp out. She placed everything on her bed. Then she checked each item off her list. She checked off a waterproof sheet, a bedroll, extra clothing, a towel, and insect lotion. She realized she had forgotten her toothbrush and toothpaste. Finally, Iris neatly packed everything in her bedroll. The bedroll was compact and easy to carry. Iris was ready when her ride arrived.

The first part of the paragraph starts with the signal words *To begin with*. The middle and last parts of the paragraph use the words *Then* and *Finally*. These signal words help show the order of the paragraph.

A. Write one paragraph using each sentence below. Include signal words to make the order clear.
1. Ken folded the wrapping paper at the corners.
2. Ken wrapped paper around the box.
3. Ken put the present in a box.
4. He tied ribbon around the present.
5. He taped a card to the present.

B. Choose an idea below. Write a paragraph, using signal words to make the order clear.
1. putting on a costume
2. safely changing a light bulb
3. fixing lunch
4. using a pay telephone
5. giving a large dog a bath

Evaluation

A. Write the letter that tells what the underlined part of each sentence is.

1. The sky <u>is full of clouds</u>.
   a. subject   **b.** predicate
2. <u>A spring forest</u> smells good.
   a. subject   **b.** predicate
3. <u>The speeding car</u> hit a post.
   a. subject   **b.** predicate
4. Juan <u>will meet us at the gym</u>.
   a. subject   **b.** predicate

5. Aiko's bike <u>had a flat tire</u>.
   a. subject   **b.** predicate
6. <u>The juicy orange</u> was good.
   a. subject   **b.** predicate
7. The child <u>rocked the boat</u>.
   a. subject   **b.** predicate
8. <u>The steep road</u> wound upward.
   a. subject   **b.** predicate

D. Write the letter that tells which of the following the underlined word in each sentence is.

a. a singular noun   **c.** a singular possessive
b. a plural noun   **d.** a plural possessive

1. The <u>birds</u> sang every morning.
2. The <u>boy's</u> family left early.
3. Who put the <u>cats'</u> food here?
4. We need eggs for this <u>cake</u>.
5. What is your <u>book</u> about?

6. The <u>tree's</u> leaves have fallen.
7. The <u>peas</u> were almost cooked.
8. The <u>apples'</u> taste is sweet.
9. He enjoyed the <u>flower's</u> smell.
10. These <u>bananas</u> are on sale.

C. Write the letter of the response that tells what the tense of the underlined verb is.

1. Today Shigeo <u>races</u> me home.
   a. present   **b.** past   **c.** future
2. We <u>will play</u> ball tomorrow.
   a. present   **b.** past   **c.** future
3. I <u>am</u> in the sixth grade.
   a. present   **b.** past   **c.** future
4. Juana <u>is</u> our class secretary.
   a. present   **b.** past   **c.** future
5. Tell us when it <u>happened</u>.
   a. present   **b.** past   **c.** future

6. The game <u>will be</u> exciting.
   a. present   **b.** past   **c.** future
7. We <u>were</u> at the store.
   a. present   **b.** past   **c.** future
8. They <u>are</u> both my dogs.
   a. present   **b.** past   **c.** future
9. Dad <u>will cook</u> the dinner.
   a. present   **b.** past   **c.** future
10. Aliki <u>joined</u> our club.
    a. present   **b.** past   **c.** future

D. Write the letter of the response that tells what the underlined word in the sentence is.

1. We've visited <u>this</u> city.
   a. adjective   **b.** adverb
2. They will come over <u>later</u>.
   a. adjective   **b.** adverb
3. <u>Quietly</u> Chin shut the door.
   a. adjective   **b.** adverb
4. The <u>sleepy</u> dog lay down.
   a. adjective   **b.** adverb

5. A door creaked <u>upstairs</u>.
   a. adjective   **b.** adverb
6. The clock struck <u>ten</u> times.
   a. adjective   **b.** adverb
7. Adela is going to move <u>away</u>.
   a. adjective   **b.** adverb
8. Mine is the <u>third</u> picture.
   a. adjective   **b.** adverb

E. Some of the sentences below contain mistakes in comparing things. Write the letter of any underlined part of a sentence that is wrong.

1. <u>Of</u> <u>all</u> <u>the</u> <u>seasons,</u> <u>fall</u> <u>is</u> <u>better</u>.
    a   b   c   d   e   f   g
2. <u>This</u> <u>job</u> <u>is</u> <u>harder</u> <u>than</u> <u>that</u> <u>one</u>.
    a   b   c   d   e   f   g
3. <u>Who</u> <u>is</u> <u>youngest,</u> <u>you</u> <u>or</u> <u>Pedro?</u>
    a   b   c   d   e   f
4. <u>This</u> <u>book</u> <u>is</u> <u>more</u> <u>exciting</u> <u>than</u> <u>mine</u>.
     a   b   c d   e   f   g
5. <u>Of</u> <u>all</u> <u>the</u> <u>racers,</u> <u>Aiko</u> <u>runs</u> <u>faster</u>.
    a   b   c   d   e   f   g
6. <u>Of</u> <u>the</u> <u>two</u> <u>dogs,</u> <u>this</u> <u>one</u> <u>moves</u> <u>most</u> <u>gracefully</u>.
    a   b   c   d   e   f   g   h   i

F. Write the letter of each underlined part of the sentence that should be followed by a comma.

1. <u>It</u> <u>was</u> <u>a</u> <u>hot</u> <u>dusty</u> <u>and</u> <u>lonely</u> <u>spot</u> <u>in</u> <u>the</u> <u>desert</u>.
    a b c d   e   f   g   h   i   j   k
2. <u>Dale</u> <u>gathered</u> <u>some</u> <u>wood</u> <u>and</u> <u>I</u> <u>put</u> <u>up</u> <u>the</u> <u>tent</u>.
     a   b   c   d   e f g h   i   j
3. <u>The</u> <u>spacecraft</u> <u>reached</u> <u>Jupiter</u> <u>on</u> <u>March</u> <u>16</u> <u>1982</u>.
     a   b   c   d   e   f   g   h
4. <u>They</u> <u>spent</u> <u>the</u> <u>winter</u> <u>in</u> <u>Tucson</u> <u>Arizona</u>.
     a   b   c   d   e   f   g

Unit Two

How closely do you look at things? Do you really take the time to see them?

To Look at Any Thing

To look at any thing,
If you would know that thing,
You must look at it long:
To look at this green and say,
'I have seen spring in these
Woods,' will not do—you must
Be the thing you see:
You must be the dark snakes of
Stems and ferny plumes of leaves,
You must enter in
To the small silences between
The leaves,
You must take your time
And touch the very peace
They issue from.

John Moffitt

No spring is just a spring, the poet reminds us. Even the stems and leaves of spring carry their own vivid pictures for those who look closely. Like a poet, a painter, or any artist, a writer must observe a subject with care and imagination. In this unit you will learn how to create your own word pictures— pictures that can make your writing as unique as you.

Lesson 1　Creating Word Pictures

Using specific words will help you create vivid pictures for your readers.

Thinking It Through

As you read the following sentence, try to form a picture of the car in your mind.

> A nice car went down the road.

- How did the car go down the road?
- What kind of road was the car on?

General words like *nice*, *car*, *went*, and *road* tell what is happening but don't give a vivid picture.

Notice how your mental pictures change as you read these sentences:

> A sleek limousine sped down the boulevard.
> A shiny racer zoomed down the freeway.
> An antique convertible putt-putted down the lane.

These sentences use exact words to communicate the writer's idea to the reader. Each sentence gives the reader a clear mental picture. In the first sentence, *sleek* and *limousine* describe the car; *sped* indicates how the car moved; *boulevard* tells what kind of road the car was on.

- What specific words are used in the other sentences?

Rewrite each of the following sentences 3 ways,
answering the questions differently each time. Change the
underlined general words to specific words or add specific
words to modify the general words.

1. The <u>man</u> <u>ate</u> his <u>meal</u>.

  a. *Who* was the man—a lumberjack,
    a patient, or someone else?
  b. *How* did the man eat?
  c. *What* was the meal?

2. <u>Someone</u> <u>came</u> into the <u>room</u>.

  a. *Who* came into the room?
  b. *How* did the person move?
  c. *What room* was it?

3. The wind <u>blew</u> through the
<u>trees</u>.

  a. *How* did the wind sound?
  b. *What kinds* of trees?

4. <u>Many</u> <u>animals</u> <u>were</u> in the <u>place</u>.

  a. *How many* animals and *what kind*
    were there?
  b. *What* were the animals doing?
  c. *What* place were they in?

5. <u>They</u> live in a <u>house</u>.

  a. *Who* are they?
  b. *What kind* of house is it?

6. A <u>strange</u> <u>dog</u> <u>walked</u> toward us.

  a. *Why* was the dog strange?
  b. *What kind* of dog was it?
  c. *How* did the dog walk?

7. The <u>boy</u> set the <u>table</u>.

  a. *Who* was the boy?
  b. *What kind* of table was it?

Choose 2 of the topics below or 2 of your own. For each
topic list 3 specific details to create a word picture. Then
put the details together in related sentences.

  1. a suspicious stranger
  2. a street corner at
    rush hour

  3. a busy restaurant
  4. someone playing a game
  5. a child walking a big dog

Lesson 2 **Focusing on an Image**

Focusing on the features of a place or an object helps you write effective visual descriptions.

Thinking It Through

Imagine that you are on vacation in Arizona and have just seen a desert for the first time. You want to describe it to a friend back home.

First think about the distinctive features, or special qualities, of the desert.

● What attracted your attention—the plants? the sand? the sun?

Then list specific words and phrases to describe the features, such as:

treeless mountains against
the sky
sand patterns drawn by
the wind
fiery sun smeared across
the sky
towering, thorny plants
scurrying insects

The word *scurrying* gives you a mental picture of how the insects move. The phrase *fiery sun smeared across the sky* also creates a visual image.

● What has the wind done to the sand?
● How are the mountains described?
● Which words describe the desert plants?

Working It Through

A. Study the picture of the cactus.

1. Read the list of characteristics to describe the cactus.
2. Choose and list the 5 phrases you feel best describe the plant.

a round-looking plant
plump, spiny body
tough, green skin
green and sticky
shaped like a barrel
a coat of prickly fur
strange and unusual
a surprising burst of color

B. Look carefully at the picture of the desert iguana.

1. List 3 or 4 specific words or phrases to describe it.
2. Think about the visual image another person would have of the animal by using only your details as a description.

Trying It Out

Read all the directions below before you begin the activity.

1. Make a list of details to describe one of your favorite places or objects.
2. Choose the clearest and most vivid details to use in several sentences about the place or object.
3. Have a classmate guess what you have described by reading your sentences.

31

Lesson 3 **Observing Details**

Using your five senses to observe things closely will help you write good descriptions.

Thinking It Through

Imagine that you and your family are having a barbecue at a park on a warm summer afternoon.

- What do you see around you?
- What noises do you hear nearby? in the distance?
- What do you smell?

Now suppose that you have just heaped your plate with barbecued chicken, corn on the cob, and coleslaw. Take a few bites.

- What do you feel? What do you taste?

Even though you weren't really at a barbecue, you may have been able to remember times when you have been. You probably recalled the charcoal crispness of the chicken, the tangy flavor of the sauce, the buttery ooze of the corn on the cob, and the cool crunch of coleslaw. Perhaps you also remembered the sounds of children giggling and splashing in a nearby pool.

People who write good descriptions use their five senses to make close observations. They use specific words and phrases to describe the sensory images they notice around them. Such words and phrases are called **sensory details.**

Working It Through

A. Choose 4 of the following foods. First list at least 3 sensory details about each. Then put each group of details into sentences describing each food.

1. a hamburger
2. freshly baked bread
3. vegetable soup
4. strawberries
5. grapefruit juice
6. ham-and-lettuce sandwich
7. cheese and crackers
8. spaghetti

B. Improve the following paragraph by using specific words in place of general words and by adding sensory details.

We had a great meal at my grandparents' house last Sunday. We had hamburgers, rice, and salad. My favorite was the chicken. Gramps has a neat way of making it. It tastes delicious—especially with Grandma's special applesauce and homemade bread. Even though I was full, I had both desserts. I could never refuse Grandma's pie and cookies.

Trying It Out

Imagine 2 of the following activities, using as many of your senses as you can. Then list at least 3 details to describe each. Use the details in sentences about each.

1. walking in rain
2. playing a record
3. slicing raw onions
4. eating a peanut butter sandwich
5. diving into cold water

Take Another Look   Did you write more than one sentence for each activity you described? Did you use sensory details to make your description effective?

Describing a Place

When you describe a place, put the details in a clear order.

Thinking It Through

When you write a description of a place, one of your purposes is to help the reader visualize that place. One way to create an accurate mental picture is to present details so that the reader sees them in the same order as you did.

The following description of a museum shows one way to order details. Notice that each hall is described in a separate paragraph.

> In Hall A, I discovered several shriveled Egyptian mummies wrapped up in layers of cloth. Their stone coffins were covered with a kind of picture writing called *hieroglyphics*. These pictures also decorated pieces of pottery.
>
> Hall B contained semiprecious stones such as amethyst and jade. Glass cases displayed gold bracelets and earrings with turquoise stones.
>
> Walking through Hall C, I saw Native American pottery and hand-woven baskets, which were used to store food and belongings. Beaded leather clothing and necklaces made of shells or turquoise stones were also on display.

- What would you expect to see first in the museum?
- What mental picture do you have of the writer's route through the museum?

Working It Through

A. Write a description of a baseball park using the details below plus any additional details you feel are important. Arrange the items in the order in which you think you would notice them.

the dugout at the side of the field
the flashing lights of the scoreboard
pennants waving in the wind
organ music blaring over the loudspeaker
peanut vendors hawking in the stands
rows of hard benches in the bleachers
the black-and-white striped uniforms of the home team
screaming fans cheering for their favorite team

B. Write a description of one of the places listed below or of a place you choose. Arrange the details in order so that the reader can follow details from one point to the next. Remember to start a new paragraph whenever you move from a description of one important part of the place to another.

1. a restaurant
2. a barber shop
3. an amusement park
4. a dentist's office
5. a grocery store
6. a hobby shop
7. a county fair
8. a shopping mall
9. your classroom
10. your favorite spot
11. a farm
12. the scene from a window in your classroom or your home

Trying It Out

Imagine that you were given the power to create your own place, exactly as you would wish it to be.

1. Write a description of your imaginary place.
2. Ask a classmate to make a picture of what you have described.
3. See how well the drawing portrays the image you had in mind.

Lesson 5 Describing an Experience

When you describe an experience, use details that appeal to the senses and the emotions.

When describing an experience, a writer creates a mood by using sensory details and words that appeal to the emotions.

Think about the ways in which the following details appeal to your senses and emotions.

> low grumbling in the distance
> saplings hunched over in pain
> murky gray clouds
> drops of rain like tiny pounding hammers
> gusts of wind whipping around the house

- What do these details describe?
- How would you arrange these details if you were going to use them in a descriptive paragraph?

As you read the following paragraph about a thunderstorm, think about the mood it creates. Also notice how the writer has ordered the details listed above.

> Murky gray clouds rolled across the sky, and a low grumbling echoed in the distance. Saplings hunched over in pain as gusts of wind whipped around the house, rattling doors and windows and whisking away chairs and toys lying loose about the yard. Soon droplets of rain began to beat angrily against the windows like tiny pounding hammers. Hailstones struck the roof and immediately bounced to the ground.

- Which words and phrases in the paragraph help create an eerie feeling?
- What details were added to the original list?

Working It Through

A. Combine the following details to describe the excitement you feel while watching a parade. If you wish, add more descriptive words and phrases that express sensations and emotions.

acrobats performing somersaults in the street
the grandstand decorated with red-and-white banners
little children playfully tugging on balloon strings
the mayor smiling and waving from a limousine
the marching band's dark blue uniforms trimmed with
   gold braid
sad-faced clowns pulling multicolored scarfs from their
   coat sleeves

B. Write a description of one of the experiences listed below or another experience you have had.

1. finding a stray kitten or puppy
2. riding on a roller coaster
3. being stuck between floors in an elevator
4. forgetting your lines in a school play
5. competing in swimming, skating, or another sport
6. knowing your turn is next for an oral report

Trying It Out

1. Read the description on pages 38 and 39.
2. Write a description of one of your happiest or most exciting experiences.
3. Underline 5 words or phrases that express sensations or emotions.

Take Another Look
Use the following questions to improve your description.

1. Does it create a feeling or mood?
2. Did you use specific words to describe the experience?
3. Did you put the details in a clear order so that your readers could follow them easily?

The following is from a book titled *Gone-Away Lake*. The book tells about two cousins, Julian and Portia, and the marvelous discoveries they make while staying at their new summer home.

Julian had to mow the lawn in the morning, and Aunt Hilda needed Portia's help with the weeding. But the children didn't mind; home was a good, interesting place, the weather was perfect, and they had their secret to look forward to. The puppies had been brought out-of-doors to roll and tumble on the grass. They staggered about, their eyes sun-dazzled and their tongues hanging out. The great feathered peonies loomed over them like palm trees. Katy moved among her children with a worried, possessive air. One of them kept wandering away by himself, and she would go after him, take him up by the loose skin at the back of his neck, and bring him back where he belonged.

"We could call that one Gulliver," Portia suggested, "because he's always traveling."

"Excellent," said Aunt Hilda. "It suits him."

"Aunt Hilda, is this a weed I'm pulling?"

"Oh, no, heavens, that's a delphinium! I don't think you've disturbed it much, though; just press the earth back firmly. Now this beastly little thing with the fat stems *is* a weed. So is this one with the fancy leaves that looks as if it ought to be a flower."

The sun was warm, but a soft wind stirred among the trees as though it were stroking and turning the wealth of new leaves, counting them over. Julian's lawn mower made a sound of metal snoring back and forth across the lawn, and the little boys in their hollow tree were just as shrill as the shrill blue-jays. (Davey Gayson had arrived at seven o'clock that morning, sitting patiently on the kitchen doorstep, clicking his empty cap-pistol until the family came down for breakfast.)

Just now they were preparing to blast off again.

"Turn the nose east, path vertical," ordered Foster.

"What do you mean, vertical?" said Davey.

"Straight up, of course. We have to use the speed of the earth's rotation, don't we? We're going to the place the moon will be four days from now, aren't we?"

"I guess so," said Davey.

"My soul, the things children know these days—"
sighed Aunt Hilda.

"And Foster can't really read yet," said Portia.
"Only 'yow!' and 'wham!' and 'bop!'
Comic-book words. He can read all *those*."

In the huge swinging maple tree
the oriole stopped his work from
time to time and sang. The house
wrens sang, too, but their song
seemed more in the nature of
conversation, and in the woods a certain
red cardinal sounded like a little bottle being
filled up, up, up with some clear liquid.

"If you could just hold onto it," said Portia,
sitting back on the warm grass. Her knees
were stiff from kneeling.

"Onto what? The weather?"
Aunt Hilda sat back on the
grass, too, and pushed her
tumbled hair away from
her brow with the back
of her muddy hand.
She was a very pretty
woman.

"The weather, partly,
but mostly the time.
June like this, and
everything starting to be.
Summer starting to be.
Everything just exactly *right*."

"But if it were this way every day, all the time,
we'd get too used to it. We'd *toughen* to it," said
Aunt Hilda. "People do. It's just because it doesn't
and can't last that a day like this is so wonderful."

"Good things must have comparers, I suppose," said
Portia. "Or how would we know how good they are?"

"Exactly!" Aunt Hilda went back to her weeding; and
after a minute Portia did, too.

"But I bet *I'd* know it was good even if it lasted forever,"
she said.

39

Improving Your First Draft

You can improve your first draft of a description by using specific words and details that appeal to the senses.

Thinking It Through

Rick was writing a description of his room. In the first paragraph he described the physical appearance of the room. In the second paragraph he explained why his room was pleasant.

After reading the first draft to a few friends, Rick felt that it didn't give a very clear image. His friends didn't picture the room in the same way that he did.

Read Rick's description and think of ways in which you could improve it.

> My room has one big window, there are some rugs on the floor. My dresser has things like pictures and model cars on it. On the wall are some pictures of baseball players. I like to look at them. I like my room a lot.
>
> It is my hideout. I have a bed, a desk, a chair, and a bookcase. I like to sit on one of the rugs and read a book or listen to the radio. I also like to look out the window.

When you revise your first draft, use a question checklist similar to this:

1. Are there places where I can use more specific words to help my reader imagine the place?
2. Can I add details that appeal to the senses?
3. Are there any details I should group together so that my reader can follow the order more easily?
4. Have I started each sentence with a capital letter and ended it with the correct punctuation?

Working It Through

Rewrite and improve the first draft about Rick's room. The checklist in Thinking It Through and questions like the following will help you.

1. What color is Rick's room?
2. What do the rugs look like?
3. Is any of the furniture special? Why?
4. What kinds of pictures and model cars are on Rick's dresser?
5. Which baseball players does Rick have pictures of?
6. Why does Rick like to look at baseball pictures?
7. What kind of books does Rick like to read?
8. Which radio station does he listen to?
9. Who is his favorite disk jockey?
10. Which two sentences are separated by a comma instead of a period? Which word should be capitalized?
11. Does the statement *I like my room a lot* describe something in the room or does it help create a feeling that the room is pleasant? Does this statement belong at the end of the first paragraph?
12. Does the sentence *I have a bed, a desk, a chair, and a bookcase* belong in the second paragraph or does it add to the physical description of the room given in the first paragraph?

Trying It Out

1. Write a description of one of your favorite places or choose a description you wrote in an earlier lesson.
2. Ask a classmate to read your description and write 2 questions that will help you make the word picture even sharper and more vivid.
3. Use the checklist in Thinking It Through to improve your first draft.
4. Revise your description, using your classmate's questions to improve the word picture.

Review • Descriptive Details

A. Rewrite the sentences. Change the underlined general words to specific words or add specific words to modify the general words. The questions will help you.

1. The <u>horse</u> <u>came</u> toward us.
   What kind of horse was it?
   How did the horse move?

2. The <u>woman</u> <u>spoke</u> to the <u>children</u>.
   Who was the woman—a teacher, a neighbor?
   How did she speak?
   What kind of children were they?

3. The <u>man</u> <u>cut</u> the <u>food</u>.
   Who was the man—a chef, a butcher?
   How was the food cut—peeled, carved, or cut in some other way?
   What kind of food was it?

4. The <u>detective</u> <u>looked</u> at the <u>marks</u>.
   What kind of detective was the person—smart, clever?
   How did the detective look at the marks?
   What kind of marks were they?

5. The <u>girl</u> <u>moves</u> to the <u>music</u>.
   Who is the girl—a teenager, a dancer, or someone else?
   How does she move?
   What kind of music?

B. Write a description of one of the following topics:
   1. exploring a cave
   2. foggy night at the ocean
   3. safari trip through a jungle
   4. Halloween party
   5. attic
   6. service station

C. Think about the following questions:
   1. Did you use specific words to create a vivid picture?
   2. Did you use details that appeal to the senses?
   3. Did you use details that create a feeling or mood?
   4. Did you start each sentence with a capital letter and end it with the correct punctuation?

Evaluation • Descriptive Details

A. Improve the paragraphs below for the following items.
Then rewrite the paragraphs.
1. Specific words that create a picture
2. Details that appeal to the senses
3. Details that create a mood or feeling
4. Capital letters and end punctuation

> I like to go down to the harbor. It is a nice place. I watch the boats go. How pretty their sails are. The sails move in the wind. I like the sound of the motorboats. The motorboats move through the water, and the water goes up in the air.
>
> I also like it when the lake is quiet. The waves make nice lines. Often I look at the pretty sunsets.

B. Write a description of a circus. Use the picture below and the following ideas to help you: band, tigers, crowd, acrobats, trapeze artists, clowns, ringleader, popcorn.

Your paragraph will be evaluated on the following:
    specific words
    details that appeal to the senses
    details that create a mood or feeling
    capital letters and end punctuation

43

Conversations with a chimp? New words from a gorilla? Impossible? Recent experiments have shown that animals may be capable of using language to communicate with human beings.

Gorillas have trouble using their lips and vocal system, so they have been taught to use sign language. The same sign language has been used with human beings who are unable to talk.

One especially bright female gorilla, Koko, has learned to use nearly 400 sign-language words. According to her trainer, she not only can identify objects, but can also tease, lie, express emotions, and create new words. Some words Koko has made up are "eye hat" for mask, "white tiger" for zebra, and "elephant baby" to describe a Pinocchio doll.

Some animals have been taught to type statements into a computer. With the aid of a computer, a chimpanzee named Lana has been taught to read and write in a brand-new language called Yerkish. Each key on the computer has a special color and picture representing an English word. When Lana presses the key for chocolates, for example, the computer promptly gives her a piece of candy. She has enlarged her vocabulary to express sentences such as, "Please, machine, give juice."

Other animals have been taught to communicate with plastic symbols or gestures.

These recent experiments are raising a lot of questions. Can animals really talk when they use language? Are they thinking and expressing ideas? Or are they merely responding to get rewards, without understanding their actions? Further research may answer these questions.

How can language experiments such as those described here benefit animals? How can they benefit people?

Spotlight • Word Personalities

Have you ever thought of a word as having a personality? All words have a meaning, of course, but many words also make you feel or react in a certain way. Your reaction is based on what the word suggests to you, or its **connotation.** The connotation gives the word a kind of personality.

See for yourself. Look at the picture and words at the right. Imagine that you were a part of the audience being entertained by the comedian and that you heard the words showing different opinions about him. Decide which words suggest something pleasant to you, which suggest something unpleasant, and which cause no particular reaction.

Many words have the same connotations for most people, but some words suggest different things to different people. Sometimes a word causes a particular reaction because of a personal experience. Also, the way a word is used can give it different connotations.

Get together with 3 or 4 of your classmates and discuss the connotations of the words at the right. See what each word suggests to each of you. Try to think of additional words to use for the discussion.

mob	pop
sunset	snuggle
elderly	shriek
whisper	cheap
plump	tickle
rain	blue

45

The Sentence

A sentence is a group of words that expresses a complete thought. It contains a subject and a predicate.

Examples of the four kinds of sentences are given below. All begin with a capital letter.

A **statement** tells something. It ends with a period.

A **question** asks something. It ends with a question mark.

A **request** or **command** asks for or orders something. It ends with a period. The subject *you* is understood.

An **exclamation** is a statement or command made with emotion or strong feeling. It ends with an exclamation mark.

Now read the five word groups below.
- Which word group does not make sense by itself?
- What *kind* of sentence is each of the other examples?

> This morning was cloudy and rainy.
> Did you bring your raincoat and umbrella?
> This is quite a storm!
> Go.
> Into the gym.

The word group *Into the gym* is not a sentence. It does not make sense by itself. It needs a subject to tell you who or what the sentence is about. It needs a predicate to tell you what the subject did.

Notice the subject and the predicate in each of the following sentences.

> Our class filed into the gym.
> Everyone did exercises.
> Was Kate performing on the parallel bars?
> She was terrific!
> She is practicing for the Junior Olympics.

Working It Through

A. Make sentences out of the following word groups.

1. the assembly at four o'clock
2. was the speaker
3. applauded loudly
4. her speech was about
5. echoed in the hall
6. the awards for achievement
7. received for volleyball
8. her proud parents
9. for his science project, Luis
10. was over by six o'clock

B. Change each sentence below into the kind of sentence indicated in parentheses.

1. The mayor is standing on the platform.   (question)
2. Stand behind the curb, please.   (exclamation)
3. Are you going to the fireworks display?   (statement)
4. We saw some fantastic skyrockets!   (command)
5. Is the show over at ten?   (statement)
6. They'll give us a ride home.   (question)
7. Can we stop for something to eat?   (request)
8. I'm starved.   (exclamation)

Trying It Out

1. Get together with a classmate and interview each other.
2. Each of you make up a list of 5 questions you want to ask the other about himself or herself.
3. Exchange questions and write answers to the ones you receive. Make certain your 5 questions and 5 answers are complete sentences.

Lesson 8 Subjects and Predicates

A sentence has a simple and complete subject and a
simple and complete predicate.

The subject of a sentence tells who or what the sentence is
about. All the words in the subject are called the
complete subject, which is printed in blue below.

Several beautiful kites flew over the green meadow.

The most important word in the complete subject is the
word that names who or what the sentence is about. This
word is most often a noun or pronoun and is called the
simple subject.
- What is the simple subject in the complete subject
  Several beautiful kites?

The predicate usually tells what the subject does or is. All
the words in the predicate are called the **complete
predicate.** The complete predicate in the example above is
printed in red.

The most important word in the complete predicate is
the verb. The verb tells what action the subject does, or it
links the subject to another word. The verb is called the
simple predicate.
- What is the simple predicate in the complete predicate
  flew over the green meadow?

Working It Through
A. Write these sentences and draw a line between the
complete subject and the complete predicate in each.
  1. My cousin Pepe entered the model plane contest.
  2. The planes had to fly without engines.
  3. The best entry was Pepe's.
  4. He won an award for the most original design.
  5. Pepe wasn't very good as a pilot.

6. The plane crashed after soaring only four feet.

7. Pepe decided to be an architect after that.

8. He won't fly any more planes.

B. Write these sentences. Put one line under the simple subject and two lines under the simple predicate.

Example: Many people have dreamed of flying.

1. The Chinese invented kites.

2. Balloons were used for flying in the late 1700s.

3. In 1783, two Frenchmen made the first flight in a hot-air balloon.

4. Later, some people experimented with gliders.

5. Gasoline engines appeared in the last century.

6. Finally, Orville Wright succeeded in flying the first real airplane on December 17, 1903.

7. The world's first airline began in 1914.

8. It carried one passenger at a time.

9. The 22-mile trip cost five dollars.

10. Amelia Earhart was a pioneer flier over the Atlantic Ocean.

Trying It Out

Add words to the simple subject and to the simple predicate in each of these sentences.

1. Jets soar.

2. Sailboats floated.

3. A train was chugging.

4. One submarine is diving.

5. Passengers stood.

6. The captain will speak.

7. Wheels are spinning.

8. Fog was covering.

Take Another Look   Use these questions to improve your sentences.

1. Did you use specific words that appeal to the senses instead of vague, general words?

2. Did you begin each sentence with a capital letter and end it with a punctuation mark?

Correcting Sentence Fragments

A part of a sentence punctuated as if it were a complete sentence is called a sentence fragment.

Thinking It Through

Sometimes writers are in such a hurry to get their ideas down on paper that they punctuate a *part* of a sentence as a complete sentence.

Read these examples aloud.

> Beth likes to paint. And to play football.
> Some words have interesting histories. Such as *sandwich* and *diesel*.
> I like most sports. But not soccer.

The second part of each example is called a **sentence fragment.** A sentence fragment doesn't make sense or sound complete by itself. Some fragments are missing a subject or a predicate or both.

The first two examples should be written like this:

> Beth likes to paint and to play football.
> Some words have interesting histories, such as *sandwich* and *diesel*.

● How should the third example be written?

Working It Through

A. Write the following items, correcting the sentence fragments.

1. The rackets are important. In tennis and badminton.
2. Some players prefer metal rackets. Because of their light weight.
3. My friend and I like to jog. Through Elm Park.
4. The shoes you wear are important. When you run.
5. Our team plays on Mondays. After school.
6. Field hockey is fun. Though ice hockey is faster.

B. Find 8 fragments and add a word or words to make them 8 complete sentences.

1. A fantastic goal in the second period!
2. The playoff games start tomorrow.
3. To practice his slap shot from center ice.
4. Central's record is 9–0.
5. Since we lost our last two games.
6. We did end up in second place, however.
7. And scored the most goals.
8. The locker room's gloomy mood.
9. Looking forward to next year's season.
10. Most of the players.
11. Mr. Simms, our coach
12. We'll win the championship for sure!

Trying It Out

Write the paragraph below, correcting all sentence fragments. Your paragraph should contain 6 to 8 sentences.

Some words have interesting histories, such as *sandwich*, *diesel*, and *boycott*. Which are derived from people's names. *Hamburger*, *frankfurter*, and *limousine* are named after places. Still other words are blends. Combinations of words put together. *Chortle* comes from blending *chuckle* and *snort*. *Telecast* from *television* and *broadcast*. *Breakfast* and *lunch* are combined to produce *brunch*. A meal one eats late in the morning. Can you name any blends?

Correcting Run-On Sentences

Two or more sentences not separated by a period or joined by a comma and a connecting word are called a run-on sentence.

Thinking It Through

Read these examples aloud.

She used to play the guitar. Now she plays the violin.
Mike plays the cello he also plays the drums.
The band played the national anthem, Sheila sang it.

In the first example, there are two separate sentences. The second and third examples each contain two sentences also. But the ideas run on as though they were one sentence. This is called a **run-on sentence.** The two ideas should be separated.

One way to separate the two sentences is to use a period.

Mike plays the cello. He also plays the drums.
The band played the national anthem. Sheila sang it.

Another way to separate run-on sentences is to use a comma and a connecting word, such as *and, but,* or *or*.

Mike plays the cello, *but* he also plays the drums.
The band played the national anthem, *and* Sheila sang it.

One of the best ways to detect run-ons is to read your sentences aloud and listen for the way a sentence naturally ends. Then check to see if you have used the correct punctuation.

Working It Through

Read aloud each of the items below. Then write them, correcting those that are run-on sentences. You should correct 8 items.

1. Colleen's drum lessons are on Saturday mornings.
2. She also takes ballet, she likes the drums more.
3. There are thirty members in the band five of them are drummers.
4. Her first recital is next week, already she is nervous.
5. She will dance first then she will play in the band.
6. The new uniforms will be ready on time.
7. Mr. Lornberg is making them they are blue and gold.
8. He also made the costumes for our class play.
9. Mrs. Lornberg is the band leader, she also teaches math.
10. Should I volunteer to set up the chairs, should I help with the decorations?
11. I put up the streamers Jerry passed out the programs.
12. The lights dimmed. The concert began.

Trying It Out

Write the paragraph below, correcting all sentence fragments and run-ons. Your paragraph should contain 12 to 16 sentences.

I remember when I took trumpet lessons I was eight years old. When I practiced, everyone left the house. Except Moe, my dog. He would just curl up in the farthest corner of the room, he would cover his ears with his paws. At the first note, he would start whining I continued to try to learn "Lady of Spain." My least favorite song. No one appreciated good music. Especially the neighbors. I continued to practice the trumpet daily. So I could perform. With the band. It paid off I was a hit at the concert. Even my neighbors enjoyed my solo too bad Moe couldn't be there to help me celebrate.

Lesson 11 Subject-Verb Agreement

A plural verb form should be used in a sentence when two or more subjects are joined by *and* or *both . . . and.*

Thinking It Through

A singular verb must be used with a singular subject, and a plural verb must be used with a plural subject.

WINTHROP

by

Dick Cavalli

I'M NOT A GOOD GARDENER... ALL MY PLANTS IS DYING.

ALL MY PLANTS **ARE** DYING! ALL MY PLANTS **ARE** DYING!

WHY DOES EVERYBODY COME TO ME WITH THEIR TROUBLES?

4-19 DICK CAVALLI

Reprinted by permission. © 1978 NEA, Inc.

My <u>plant</u> <u><u>grows</u></u> in the yard.
My <u>plant</u> <u><u>is dying</u></u>.
All my <u>plants</u> <u><u>grow</u></u> in the yard.
All my <u>plants</u> <u><u>are dying</u></u>.

- Which verbs are singular?
- Which verbs are plural?

Sometimes a sentence has two or more subjects joined by *and.* This is called a **compound subject.** A plural verb form must be used with a compound subject joined by *and.*

My <u>lily and</u> my <u>rose</u> <u><u>are dying</u></u>.

Subjects joined by *both . . . and* are also compound subjects. They, too, require a plural verb.

<u>Both violets and roses</u> <u><u>wilt</u></u>.

Working It Through

A. Write the following sentences. Put one line under each compound subject and two lines under each verb.

1. Spices and herbs have shaped the course of history.
2. England, Spain, and Holland competed for spice routes.

54

3. Both Columbus and Cabot were searching for spices.

4. Malaysia and India are primary sources.

5. Nutmeg and mace have similar flavors.

6. Cinnamon and nutmeg are often used in the same recipe.

7. Are salt and pepper the most commonly used spices?

8. Oregano and hot pepper are used in many Italian dishes.

9. Curry and ginger are spices commonly used in India.

10. Mint and lavender are pleasant-smelling herbs.

11. Mint and other herbs are often used to make tea.

B. Write the following sentences, choosing the correct verb form in parentheses.

1. Both Jorge and I (likes, like) to cook.

2. Tacos and chili (is, are) my favorite dishes.

3. But peppers and hot sauce (upsets, upset) my stomach.

4. Chicken and dumplings (makes, make) his mouth water.

5. Eggs, sugar, and vanilla (is, are) used to make flan.

6. He and I (hates, hate) to clean up the dishes.

7. The garbage disposal and the dishwasher really (comes, come) in handy.

8. Refried beans and tostadas (is, are) on the menu for next week.

9. Both my father and mother (wants, want) to come.

10. What (is, are) Jorge and I going to make for dessert?

Trying It Out

Write the following paragraph, correcting the 5 errors in agreement between the compound subjects and the verbs.

Many legends and uses surrounds herbs and spices. Onions and garlic was believed to ward off evil spirits. Sage and rosemary was once used to prevent aging. To the ancient Greeks, both hatred and misfortune was symbolized by basil. Some tea and perfume is made with marjoram.

Lesson 12　More about Subject-Verb Agreement

When a compound subject is joined by *or, either . . . or,* or *neither . . . nor,* the verb agrees with the subject closer to it.

Thinking It Through

Notice what form of the verb is used in the following sentences.

> Kevin and Kelly feed the frog.
> Kevin or Kelly feeds the frog.

The plural verb *feed* is used when two singular subjects are joined by *and*. The singular verb *feeds* is used when two singular subjects are joined by *or*. In the second sentence *or* tells that only one of the subjects is doing the action, not both. The verb agrees with the subject closer to it.

Study the following sentences. Notice whether the subject closer to the verb in each is singular or plural.

> Either flies or spiders were fed to the frog.
> The gorillas or the orangutan is in that cage.
> Neither snakes, toads, nor lizards live in the Arctic.

In the first example, the compound subject is *flies or spiders*. Notice that *spiders,* the subject closer to the verb, is plural. The verb must be plural too.

Look again at the second and third examples.
- What is the compound subject in each?
- Is the subject closest to the verb singular or plural?
- Is the verb singular or plural?

Working It Through

A. Write each sentence, choosing the correct verb form in parentheses.

1. The dolphins or the seal (performs, perform) at noon.
2. Neither the mother nor the baby ducks (is, are) swimming.
3. The trainer or the zookeepers (cleans, clean) the cages.
4. Neither the bats nor the lemur (is, are) awake.
5. Either the biologist or the zoologist (gives, give) the lecture.
6. Neither the theater nor the auditorium (is, are) air conditioned.
7. The students or the teacher (files, file) in first.
8. Neither the weather nor the humidity (affects, affect) us.

B. Write the following sentences, correcting the errors in subject-verb agreement.

1. Neither a lender nor a borrower make a good friend.
2. Neither a stick nor stones breaks my bones.
3. Winning and losing is not important.
4. Those roses and that geranium is red.
5. Tom, Leo, or Chita bat first.
6. Neither thunder nor lightning scare me.

Trying It Out

Write sentences using the following compound subjects, or choose ten of your own.

1. fruits or vegetables
2. neither soccer nor rugby
3. either Gary or Tina
4. pens or a pencil
5. either the banjo or the guitars
6. knives and forks
7. both science and history
8. purple and yellow
9. breakfast and lunch
10. snow and sleet

Take Another Look
Did you check to make sure your verbs agree with your subjects?

Review • Sentences

A. Some of the groups of words below are complete sentences. Some are sentence fragments. Correct and rewrite each sentence fragment.

1. We had to decide how much sports equipment to take.
2. In a big dish.
3. Tomorrow is the big day!
4. Where can I sleep?
5. To the seashore.
6. Or my tennis racket.
7. Everyone making lists.
8. Mother forgot about lunch.

B. Rewrite the following sentences to correct the run-ons. Make certain that punctuation and capitalization are correct.

1. Pete went home he went upstairs.
2. Mariko can ski well, she also is an expert skater.
3. The air is warmer soon it will be spring.
4. I will rake the yard Pedro will fill the birdbath.
5. The sky got dark, soon the rain started.
6. Adela held out the apple the horse trotted up.
7. My grandmother left on Friday, I was in school.
8. The circus was a lot of fun we want to go again.

C. Complete each sentence with the correct verb.

1. My sister and I ____ to visit the ranch.   (want, wants)
2. Either Kevin or Polly ____ us about it every day. (tell, tells)
3. Neither Jim nor his parents ____ vacations.   (take, takes)
4. My parents and my sister ____ very anxious to go. (is, are)
5. Mom said, "Your uncles or your dad ____ these exciting summer vacations."   (plan, plans)

For extra practice turn to page 362.

Evaluation • Sentences

A. Some of the following groups of words are sentence fragments. Make each sentence fragment a complete sentence.

 1. Luci enjoyed her visit, but was glad to get home.
 2. What a party!
 3. Not to mention a huge piece of pie.
 4. It was a long hike, with steep hills to climb.
 5. With a beautiful view at the top.

B. Write the letter of the correct item.

 1. **a.** Fran is a gymnast, she is quite graceful.
  b. Fran is a gymnast. She is quite graceful.
  c. Fran is a gymnast she is quite graceful.
 2. **a.** Joe's vacation comes soon, he is going to Iowa.
  b. Joe's vacation comes soon he is going to Iowa.
  c. Joe's vacation comes soon, and he is going to Iowa.

 3. **a.** I like to play baseball my sister likes tennis.
  b. I like to play baseball, but my sister likes tennis.
  c. I like to play baseball, my sister likes tennis.
 4. **a.** We may go skating, or we may build a snow fort.
  b. We may go skating, we may build a snow fort.
  c. We may go skating we may build a snow fort.

C. Some, but not all, of the following sentences contain errors. If you find an error, write the number of the sentence and the letter of the underlined part in which the error occurs.

 1. <u>Both</u> Dad and <u>I</u> <u>like</u> baseball.
    a   b c
 2. <u>Either</u> milk or water <u>were</u> <u>added</u>.
    a   b   c
 3. A wasp and an <u>ant</u> <u>are</u> <u>insects</u>.
            a b   c
 4. Aiko <u>or</u> <u>Dolores</u> <u>is</u> in the play.
      a   b   c

 5. <u>Neither</u> Tomas <u>nor</u> Yukio <u>is</u> here.
    a   b   c
 6. <u>Both</u> <u>cake</u> and pie <u>is</u> fattening.
    a   b   c
 7. <u>Cinnamon</u> or nutmeg <u>are</u> good.
      a   b   c
 8. <u>Are</u> <u>Chiang</u> or Angela coming?
    a   b   c

Spotlight • Activities to Choose

1. Write from another point of view. Imagine that you are an object—for example, a rock, a pickle, or a drop of water. You have been given the ability to think and speak for one entire day. Write 8 sentences you would say, including 2 for each of the four kinds of sentences.

2. Create a word-shape picture. Choose a favorite object or animal and list specific, precise words and phrases to describe it. Then use the words and phrases to make an outline drawing of the object or animal. See the example below.

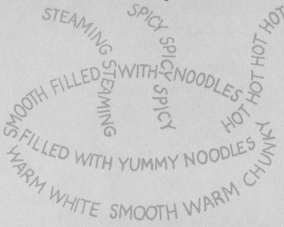

3. Guess who it is. Get together with a group of your classmates. Have each person write 6 sentences that tell about himself or herself. Use compound subjects in 3 of the sentences. (For example, *Stickball and Ping-Pong are the games I like most.*) Select someone to collect and read the sets of sentences. After a set has been read, members of the group guess who was described.

4. Have a listening session. Get together with 3 or 4 classmates and plan a time when you can sit quietly and listen to a few records. Each person might bring in one favorite selection for the activity. After hearing a selection, each person uses sensory details to describe the mood he or she experienced because of the music.

5. Have a class taste party. Bring in a variety of fresh fruits and vegetables. Each class member can bring one sample. Use a form like the one below to list observations about each food you taste. Rate the food on a scale from 1 to 10, with 10 meaning a ''super delicious'' item.

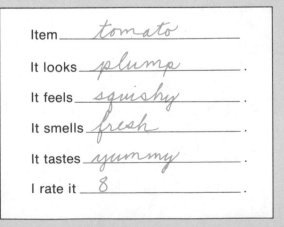

Item _tomato_

It looks _plump_ .

It feels _squishy_ .

It smells _fresh_ .

It tastes _yummy_ .

I rate it _8_ .

My Own Rhythm: An Approach to Haiku
by Ann Atwood

Ann Atwood presents a brief history of haiku and explains the differences among the three Japanese masters of this poetry form. The book contains the author's own haikus, along with her colorful photographs of nature.

How to Count like a Martian
by Glory St. John

Could you decode a message from Mars, using a Martian number system? This book will show you how. The book also shows and explains the Egyptian, Babylonian, Greek, Mayan, Chinese, and Hindu counting systems, along with those of the abacus and computer.

Shipwreck
by Vera Cumberlege

Jim, a boy who helps a lifeboat crew rescue ships off the coast of his small village, is upset about the new motorboat that will replace the old lifeboat. After a severe storm nearly destroys the old boat and its crew, Jim understands the value of the new boat.

Unit Three

A rock in the sun is a fine place for a sleeping snake!
This is the snake's environment.

The Time
We Climbed
Snake Mountain

Seeing good places
      for my hands
I grab the warm parts of the cliff
        and I feel the mountain as I climb.
Somewhere   around here
      yellow spotted snake is sleeping   on his rock
      in the sun.

So
   please, I tell them
      watch out,
don't step on the spotted yellow snake
      he lives here.
The mountain is his.

Leslie Silko

Words can also appear in a certain environment or context.
Often, we can figure out the meaning of an unfamiliar word
by looking at the other words that surround it. At other
times, we can use a dictionary to learn word meanings. In
this unit you will learn how to use context and a
dictionary to determine the meanings of words.

Word Meanings

We learn the meanings of words from many sources, and one of the most important is our own experiences.

Thinking It Through

The picture below shows some of the ways people learn the meanings of words. One of these ways is learning from a firsthand experience. For example, understanding what the word *sour* means by tasting the juice of a lemon is learning from a firsthand experience.

Hurt.

It's a kaleidoscope.

Planets

Satellites

Orbit

DRAGONS

- Which of the characters appear to be learning word meanings from their own firsthand experiences?
- Which appear to be learning word meanings from a book? by looking at something?
- What other ways of learning word meanings are shown?

    Think of ways in which you have learned the meanings of words.

Working It Through

A. Get together with four of your classmates and take a poll to find out how each of you thinks he or she learned the meanings of the words below.

1. Make a chart like the one shown.
2. Under the heading *Sources* list ways people can learn word meanings. Include sources you think of along with those presented in Thinking It Through.
3. Have each person make a mark under *Sources* to show how each word meaning was most likely learned.

bicycle
horse
modern
homework
sandwich
blue
decision
castle
happy
melancholy
measles
circle
yawn
Halloween

Words	Sources				
	Experience	TV	Reference Book	School	Magazine
bicycle					
horse					
modern					
homework					
sandwich					

B. Make up your own word list to use for a poll like the one described above.

Trying It Out

For each of the words listed below write an explanation of what you would do to teach a young child the meaning of the word. If possible, make arrangements to try out your ideas in a primary classroom.

1. fierce
2. special
3. rapid
4. dragon
5. jogging
6. cozy

Using a Dictionary

The dictionary is an important storehouse of word meaning. It also provides information about the pronunciation, spelling, and use of words.

Thinking It Through

Study the part of a dictionary page below to see the kinds of information provided.

Notice that each part of an entry gives specific information about the entry word.

a hat	i it	oi oil	ch child	(a in about
ā age	ī ice	ou out	ng long	e in taken
ä far	o hot	u cup	sh she	ə = i in pencil
e let	ō open	ù put	th thin	o in lemon
ē equal	ô order	ü rule	ŦH then	u in circus
ėr term			zh measure	

pronunciation key

entry

in clem ent (in klem′ənt), **1** rough or stormy. **2** severe; harsh: *The dictator was an inclement ruler. adj.* —**in clem′ ent ly,** *adv.*

entry word

in clined (in klīnd′), **1** favorable or willing; tending: *I am inclined to agree with you.* **2** sloping; slanting. *adj.*

pronunciation of entry word

in con se quen tial (in′kon sə kwen′-shəl), not important; trifling. *adj.* —**in con′se quen′ tial ly,** *adv.*

in cor rupt i ble (in′kə rup′tə bəl), **1** not to be corrupted; honest: *An incorruptible judge cannot be bribed.* **2** not capable of decay; lasting forever: *Diamonds are incorruptible. adj.* —**in′cor rupt′i bly,** *adv.*

definitions

in cred u lous (in krej′ə ləs), **1** not ready to believe; doubting: *Most people nowadays are incredulous about ghosts and witches.* **2** showing a lack of belief: *He listened to the neighbor's story with an incredulous smile. adj.* —**in cred′u lous ly,** *adv.*

illustrative sentence

in cum bent (in kum′bənt), **1** currently holding an office, position, etc.: *the incumbent governor.* **2** person holding an office, position, etc.: *The former incumbent had been very popular in the district.* **1** *adj.,* **2** *n.* —**in cum′bent ly,** *adv.*

part-of-speech labels

- Which part of the entry shows what the word means?

- Which part shows how to say the word?

- Which part shows how many syllables are in the word?

- Which part tells whether a word can be used as a noun, verb, or adjective and so on?

- Which part shows how to use the word correctly in a sentence?

Think about the times you have used a dictionary. Decide which part or parts of an entry have been most helpful to you.

Working It Through

A. Use the entries in Thinking It Through to learn the pronunciation of the underlined words in the following sentences. Then read the set of sentences as if you were a reporter making a TV broadcast about the event pictured.

1. It was feared that few people would attend the rally because of <u>inclement</u> weather.
2. However, the weather proved to be <u>inconsequential</u> because many people wanted to hear Dr. Subero speak.
3. Dr. Subero is a special assistant to our <u>incumbent</u> governor.
4. She also has a reputation for being an <u>incorruptible</u> part of the local government.
5. The crowd listened <u>incredulously</u> as Dr. Subero described problems that exist in our community.
6. But the facts she presented made everyone <u>inclined</u> to believe her.

B. Rewrite the sentences, using definitions in place of the underlined words.

Trying It Out

Use each phrase below in a sentence. Then choose 2 of them to illustrate. Your pictures should make the meanings of the underlined words clear.

1. an <u>inclement</u> day
2. an <u>incumbent</u> queen
3. an <u>inconsequential</u> snack
4. an <u>inclement</u> president
5. an <u>incorruptible</u> gem
6. an <u>inclined</u> path
7. an <u>incorruptible</u> senator
8. an <u>incredulous</u> look

Dictionary Definitions

You can use a dictionary to learn the appropriate meaning of a word used in different situations.

Thinking It Through

In each example sentence below the word *stock* has a different meaning. Each meaning is determined by the context of the sentence. The other words used with *stock* in each sentence make up the context.

stock (stok), **1** things for use or for sale; supply used as it is needed: *This store keeps a large stock of toys.* **2** livestock: *The farm was sold with all its stock.* **3** furnish with stock; supply: *Our camp is well stocked with everything we need for a short stay.* **4** lay in a supply: *stock up for the winter.* **5** keep regularly for use or for sale: *A toy store stocks toys.* **6** shares in a company. **7** part used as a support or handle; part to which other parts are attached: *the wooden stock of a rifle.* **8** raw material: *Rags are used as a stock for making paper.* **9** water in which meat or fish has been cooked, used as a base for soups, sauces, etc. **10 the stocks,** an old instrument of punishment consisting of a heavy wooden frame with holes to put a person's feet and sometimes hands through. 1,2,6-10 *n.* 3-5 *v.*

• Soon we'll have to stock up firewood for the winter.

This soup was made with chicken stock.

My uncle owns stock in a small toy company.

As you can see, the dictionary entry for *stock* includes several definitions. The definitions show how the word can have different meanings in different contexts.

● What does *stock* mean in each of the example sentences?
● Which definition in the entry is meant in each sentence?
● Which meanings of *stock* are shown in the picture below?

Working It Through

A. Use the dictionary entry for *cut* to determine what the word means in each phrase below. Write each phrase along with the number of the definition to which it refers. Then use each phrase in a sentence.

1. a *cut* on his knee
2. *cut* costs
3. *cut* through the alley
4. before they *cut* a record
5. *cut* the motor
6. *cut* her first set of teeth
7. a bad *cut* of meat
8. when you *cut* your hair

cut (kut), **1** divide, separate, open, or remove with a knife or any tool that has a sharp edge: *We cut a branch from the tree.* **2** pierce or wound with something sharp: *She cut her finger on the broken glass.* **3** opening made by something sharp: *bandage a cut.* **4** piece cut off or cut out: *A leg of lamb is a tasty cut of meat.* **5** make a cut, opening, channel, etc.: *This knife cuts well.* **6** make a recording on: *cut a record, cut tape.* **7** have (teeth) grow through the gums. **8** reduce; decrease: *We must cut our expenses to save money.* **9** shorten by removing a part or parts: *cut a speech, cut the hedge, cut one's hair.* **10** go by a shortcut: *She cut across the field to save time.* **11** stop: *cut an engine. The director said, "Cut!"* 1, 2, 5-11 *v.* **cut, cut ting;** 3,4 *n.*

B. Write 6 sentences, using *play* in different contexts. Then give your sentences to a classmate and ask him or her to tell which definition of *play* is meant in each.

play (plā), **1** something done to amuse oneself; fun; sport; recreation: *The children are happy at play.* **2** have fun; do something in sport: *He played a joke on his sister.* **3** take part in (a game): *Children play tag and ball.* **4** take part in a game against: *Our team played the sixth-grade team.* **5** a turn, move, or act in a game: *It is your play next.* **6** put into action in a game: *Play your ten of hearts.* **7** a story written for or presented as a dramatic performance; drama: *"Peter Pan" is a charming play.* **8** act in a specified way: *play sick, play fair, play the fool.* **9** make believe; pretend in fun: *Let's play the hammock is a boat.* **10** make music; produce (music) on an instrument. **11** cause to produce recorded or broadcast sound: *play a record, play the radio.* 1,5,7 *n.* 2-4,6,8-11 *v.*

C. Tell which meaning of *cut* or *play* is meant in each sentence.

1. Elmer wants to *cut* the bushes.
2. The *play* was sensational.
3. At the recital I am going to *play* my flute.
4. The singer *cut* his first album.
5. When it was my *play*, I lost my turn.

Trying It Out

1. Use *stock, cut,* and *play* in different contexts to describe events or situations you might be involved in. For example, you might tell how you watched a *play*, or *cut* through the park on your way to school.
2. Write 3 or more sentences for each word.

Lesson 4   Using Context Clues

You can discover the meaning of many words by examining the sentences or paragraph in which the words appear.

Thinking It Through

Look at the picture on the right.

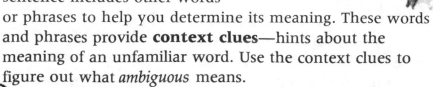

- What does the word *ambiguous* mean?
- Are there any clues in the boy's sentence to help you figure out what the word means?

Everyone thinks my answer was ambiguous.

The word *ambiguous* also appears in the sentences below, but each sentence includes other words or phrases to help you determine its meaning. These words and phrases provide **context clues**—hints about the meaning of an unfamiliar word. Use the context clues to figure out what *ambiguous* means.

His answer might have been ambiguous, but mine was definitely clear.

His answer was ambiguous, so he could mean one of several things.

His answer was ambiguous, and mine was just as unclear.

In the first example an **antonym,** or word that means the opposite of *ambiguous,* is given as a context clue.

- Which example gives a **synonym,** or a word that means the same as *ambiguous?*
- In which does a definition of the word serve as a context clue?

Although different kinds of context clues are used, each helps you understand the meaning of *ambiguous.*

Working It Through

A. Use the context clues in the following sentences to figure out the meaning of the underlined words. Then write each word and what you think its meaning is.

1. When I saw the champ's <u>somber</u> expression, I knew the problem was serious.
2. Although he could keep the trophies he had won, he would have to <u>forfeit</u> his title.
3. A group of the champ's fans tried to comfort him, but he was <u>inconsolable</u>.
4. "I'm not trying to be stubborn," he said as he <u>obstinately</u> refused to discuss the matter.
5. His statement that he would never take part in sports again was so <u>ludicrous</u> that even he had to laugh.
6. Being skilled in so many areas has made the champ one of the most <u>versatile</u> athletes in the country.

B. Context clues have been given for 3 of the underlined words in the man's sentences.

1. Decide what the 3 words are.
2. Write each word and what you think it means.
3. Use the 3 words in sentences of your own.

It <u>infuriates</u> me to have to deal with <u>ostentatious</u> people. They only want to show off, and I get angry just watching them. Actually, I don't <u>tolerate pretentiousness</u> of any kind. I simply cannot put up with it.

Trying It Out

1. Find an article in a newspaper or magazine, or a passage from one of your textbooks.
2. Skim the selection to identify any unfamiliar words. Then read it carefully to see what context clues are given to explain the meanings of those words.
3. Write the unfamiliar words along with the meanings you understood from the context clues.

Giving Context Clues

Sometimes a writer needs to provide context clues to help others determine the meaning of words he or she uses.

Thinking It Through

Sometimes a word you choose to express an idea or image is one that may be unfamiliar to your readers. Rather than choose a less effective word, you can provide context clues. Imagine the scene described in the following paragraph.

> The girl sprinted across the finish line and turned her gleeful face to the crowd. She was triumphant! Had her perseverance paid off? As she slumped into the arms of her coach and tears of exultation streamed from her eyes, she knew the answer.

A reader who does not know the underlined words might not be able to picture the scene. The writer can help such a reader by adding context clues.

● Notice the context clues that have been added to the first sentence of the paragraph.

> Leaving swirls of dust behind her, the girl sprinted like a flash across the finish line and turned her gleeful face to the crowd.

The word *sprinted* means *ran at full speed. Leaving swirls of dust behind her* and *like a flash* are phrases that suggest the meaning of *sprinted*.

● What other context clues could be given for *sprinted?*

Working It Through

A. Follow the steps below to rewrite the paragraph in Thinking It Through.

  1. Read the definitions of the underlined words.

  2. Add context clues to the paragraph for each.

gleeful — joyous
triumphant — successful
perseverance — never giving up
slumped — dropped heavily
exultation — great rejoicing

B. Think about how you would feel after losing a race you wanted very badly to win.

1. Using some of the words listed under these directions, write a paragraph to describe your feelings.

2. Provide context clues to explain the words you feel your readers will not know.

   miserable
   frustrated
   scorned
   unhappy
   despondent
   bleak

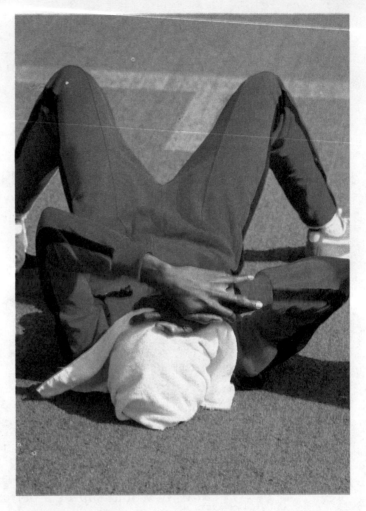

Trying It Out

1. Imagine that the words below name objects or actions in a language known only to you.

   swern   dolp   hefal
   ozexa   glafs   daorb

2. Use the words to describe a game or other activity you especially enjoy.

3. Since no one but you will know the meaning of the words, include context clues to explain each.

4. Ask a classmate to read your description and to tell you what he or she thinks each of the words means.

73

Using a Thesaurus

A thesaurus can be helpful in choosing more effective words
to use in your writing.

Thinking It Through

Look carefully at the following parts of an entry from a
thesaurus. The **entry word** is printed in heavy black type.
The other words listed are **synonyms** for the entry word.
Explanations are given to show the differences, or shades,
in meaning.

sneak	(v) *Sneak* means go or move in a secret or sly way.	lurk skulk	*Lurk* and *skulk* can mean move in a secret way or try to keep out of sight.
slink	*Slink* means sneak away in order not to attract attention.	slip	*Slip* can mean move quickly and quietly. You might *slip* in or *slip* out of a room without being noticed.
prowl	*Prowl* means sneak about looking for something.		

- Why would *slip* be a better word than *skulk* to describe
  how someone entered a campfire gathering?
- Why would *prowl* be better than *slink* to describe the
  bears that roamed the forest looking for food?
- What word would you use to tell about a stranger who
  hid in the shadows beyond the campsite?

Using a thesaurus can help you choose the most precise
word for expressing an idea.

Working It Through

A. Rewrite the following story starter, using synonyms
from the thesaurus entry in Thinking It Through for some
of the underlined words.

How stupid I had been to <u>sneak</u> away from the campsite! I had gone after one of the younger kids who had <u>sneaked</u> away from the group. I thought I saw her <u>sneaking</u> in the shadows of the nearby caves. She <u>sneaked</u> back into the group before I got to her, however, and *I* ended up getting lost. Even worse, I had a good chance of becoming some <u>sneaking</u> animal's breakfast!

Suddenly, . . .

B. Write an exciting ending for the story.

1. Choose synonyms for *find* to use in your ending. Some you might think about are *discover, detect, learn,* and *determine.*
2. Look at a thesaurus as needed to see the different shades of meaning in the synonyms you choose.

Trying It Out

Write a fanciful description of two or more of the people or things listed below, using as many synonyms as you can for the underlined word. Imagine that what you are describing is the largest of its kind, or the fastest, or the thinnest, and so on. Try to make your description as interesting as possible and, perhaps, even amusing.

1. a <u>large</u> head of lettuce
2. a <u>thin</u> super hero
3. a <u>sad</u> magician
4. a <u>fierce</u> insect
5. a <u>foolish</u> umpire
6. a <u>fast</u> elevator
7. a <u>funny</u> spaceship
8. a <u>weak</u> bridge
9. a <u>real</u> mess
10. a <u>silent</u> band

Take Another Look Use these questions to improve your description.

1. Did you use exact words to explain your ideas?
2. Did you provide context clues for words that may be unfamiliar to your readers?
3. Did you use complete sentences and punctuate each correctly?

Review • Context Clues

A. Read the following paragraphs. Then follow the directions below.

Tina rode her pinto over the green fields. Underfoot were lovely azure flowers. Suddenly her horse balked. Tina dismounted and walked forward. Then she saw the chasm in the earth ahead.

Tina rode her pinto, or spotted horse, over the green fields. Underfoot were lovely azure flowers that matched the color of the clear blue sky. Suddenly her horse balked and refused to go on. Tina dismounted so that she landed gently on the ground and walked forward. Then she saw the chasm, or deep crack, in the earth.

1. Tell which paragraph made it easier to determine the meanings of the underlined words.
2. Write each underlined word and what you think it means.
3. Tell which word or words provided context clues to help you determine the meanings of the words.

B. Choose 5 of the words below to use in a story about a person who tries to catch an elf. The elf has hidden a pot of gold that the person wants. Provide context clues so your readers will know the meanings of the words you choose.

avaricious — greedy	*deceive* — trick, lie	*agile* — lively
leprechaun — elf	*seize* — catch, grab	*fleetly* — quickly
impish — mischievous	*vigilant* — watchful	*fiasco* — failure

C. Think about the questions that follow.
1. Did you provide context clues for words that may be unfamiliar to your readers?
2. Did you use complete sentences?

76

Evaluation • Context Clues

A. Rewrite and improve the paragraph below for the following. Use the definitions to help you.

1. Context clues to explain the meaning of words the reader may not know
2. Complete sentences

soothsayer—fortune teller *dilapidated*—run down
renowned—famous *turban*—headdress
trudged—walked *bolted*—ran away

One day I read about a soothsayer who lived outside of town. To visit this renowned person. I trudged four miles to her house. The dilapidated house looked scary. I knocked on the front door. A woman in strange clothes. I think it was the turban that gave her such a weird look. I told her I must have the wrong house and bolted.

B. Choose one of the topics below.

Winter			Halloween		
toboggan	blizzard	ski	ghost	mask	bob (for apples)
skid	snowmobile	plow	haunted	witch	trick or treat
icicle	sleet	frost	costume	cider	jack-o'-lantern

1. Write a paragraph describing your topic. Imagine your readers do not know anything about the topic.
2. Include 5 of the words listed below the topic. Provide context clues to explain each word.

You will be evaluated on your use of the following:
context clues
complete sentences

Spotlight • Our International Language

Have you ever skied in Colorado? Do you practice yoga? Have you watched the Olympics or sailed on a yacht?

The underlined words have something in common. English has borrowed these words from other languages. The words, as well as the activities they stand for, have become familiar to us.

The words *ski* and *slalom*, a special kind of downhill skiing, are Norwegian. What do you know about Norway that gives a clue to the beginnings of these sports?

The *Olympics* have a special history. These athletic contests were held in ancient Greece every four years in honor of the god Zeus. The games got their name from the place where they were held, the plains of Olympia. Today the Olympic games are hosted by different countries and include athletes from all over the world.

The word *yacht* comes from the Dutch word *jaght*, which was shortened from *jaghtschip*, meaning "a chasing ship." Many other sailing terms, from *skipper* to *deck*, also come from Dutch.

Yoga is a word that has special religious meaning to Hindus in India. It is a Hindi word that means "yoke" or "union." The yoga system of quiet thinking and physical exercises is used by many people as a rest from the busy modern world.

The English language is full of words borrowed from other languages, including those listed below. Use a dictionary to find out from what countries and languages they come. Sometimes you can find this information in the dictionary definitions. At other times the sources for a word are listed after its meanings.

karate	decathlon	snorkel
judo	spelunker	rodeo

Spotlight • Homophones

Many jokes are funny because of the similarity of two
words, such as *hoarse* and *horse*. Words like these that
sound alike but are spelled differently and have different
meanings are called **homophones.**

- Can you think of homophones for these words?

piece	herd	fir
weak	scent	stake
guest	mist	rein

One of the easiest ways to know which homophone is
intended is to use the context around the word. The
context makes it clear which word, *peace* or *piece*, is
intended in this sentence.

> I hope there will never be another war and that we
> can all live in ＿＿ .

Use the sentence context in the paragraphs below to
choose the correct word from the sets of homophones you
made using the list of words above.

> My sister told us she was going to bring someone
> new home for dinner. How could I have ever ＿＿
> that our dinner ＿＿ would be a boy!

> How will I get home? I ＿＿ the last bus because I
> was late. I could barely see anything through the
> heavy ＿＿!

Lesson 7 **Common and Proper Nouns**

Nouns that name particular persons, places, or things are proper nouns. All other nouns are common nouns.

Thinking It Through

You will remember that a **noun** is a word that names a person, place, or thing. Nouns are often signaled by words such as *a*, *an*, and *the*. These words are called **noun markers.**

● Find the noun markers and nouns in the following sentence.

> Mr. Bennett rode on a cable car when he visited the city of San Francisco.

A noun that names a particular person, place, or thing is called a **proper noun.** All other nouns are called **common nouns.** Proper nouns are capitalized. Look at these nouns.

Aunt Agnes	Germany	Pittsburgh
Europe	continent	Empire State Building
Mr. Bennett	brother	Pennsylvania

● Which words are common nouns? proper nouns?
● Which proper nouns name people?
● Which proper noun shows a family relationship?
● Which proper noun names a city? a state?
● Which proper noun names a building?
● Which proper noun names a country? a continent?

The names of companies and organizations are capitalized. Bodies in the solar system, such as planets, are also capitalized. Look at these examples.

Southwest Electric Company	Camp Fire Girls
Pluto	Boy Scouts of America
Todd Motor Company	Mars

● Which proper nouns name planets?
● Which proper nouns name organizations and companies?

Working It Through

A. Copy the following groups of words. Capitalize the proper nouns. You should capitalize 20 words.

1. the planet saturn
2. james tool company
3. a city in florida
4. uncle ed
5. a country in europe
6. the author mark twain
7. rockefeller center
8. northern chemical company
9. american lung association
10. seattle, washington

B. Copy these sentences, capitalizing all the proper nouns. You should capitalize 13 words.

1. Last summer my teacher, miss robinson, went to europe.
2. She visited several countries.
3. In germany she took photographs of ancient castles.
4. In paris, france, she saw the eiffel tower and many museums
5. She also visited the cities of rome and venice in italy.
6. After traveling for three weeks, she was glad to come home to portland, oregon.

C. Copy the common nouns below. Then write a proper noun for each.

1. city
2. state
3. building
4. continent
5. organization
6. president
7. movie star
8. country
9. planet

Trying It Out

Write a paragraph about a state or a country you would like to visit.

1. Find information on the state or country in an encyclopedia.
2. Mention famous cities and buildings you want to see.
3. Be sure to capitalize all proper nouns.

81

Lesson 8 **Plural Nouns**

A regular plural is formed by adding *-s* or *-es* to a singular noun. Irregular plurals are formed in other ways.

Thinking It Through

Plurals formed by adding *-s* or *-es* to a singular noun are **regular plurals.** Plurals formed in other ways are **irregular plurals.** The chart below shows how to form plural nouns.

Plural Nouns	
Add *-s* to most nouns	building — buildings
Add *-es* to nouns ending in *x*, *ch, sh, ss*	fox—foxes ranch—ranches bush—bushes class—classes walrus—walruses
Change *y* to *i* and add *-es* unless a vowel precedes *y*	berry—berries monkey—monkeys
Nouns ending in *f* or *fe* Many change *f* to *v* and add *-es* Some add *-s*	knife—knives leaf—leaves wolf—wolves roof—roofs
Nouns ending in *o* Many add *-es* Some add *-s*	hero—heroes radio—radios piano—pianos
Nouns with changes in spelling	child—children goose—geese
Nouns that do not change	deer—deer trout—trout

If you are unsure about a plural, check the singular form in the dictionary. If the plural is irregular, the form will be shown right after the entry word or at the end of the entry. If no plural form is given, it is regular.

Working It Through

A. Read the story below. Write the plural of each numbered noun.

Danny certainly ruined our nature hike. First he scared a bunch of wild (**1.** goose) with his bellowing voice. Then he jumped into a small clearing and startled some (**2.** deer).

While the rest of us gathered (**3.** nut) and (**4.** berry), Danny plopped down on a tree stump. He complained about his sore, tired (**5.** foot).

The sudden crackle of dry (**6.** leaf) worried all of us a little. Danny said there was a pack of (**7.** wolf) in the (**8.** tree) behind us. A second later two (**9.** moose) came into the clearing. When they saw Danny, they scrambled back into the (**10.** bush).

B. Write the plural form of each noun below. Then choose 5 plurals and use each in a sentence.

1. building	**6.** trout	**11.** penny
2. piano	**7.** fox	**12.** witness
3. radio	**8.** spy	**13.** mouse
4. child	**9.** knife	**14.** ranch
5. dish	**10.** hero	**15.** roof

Trying It Out

1. Write a story about fishing or camping.

2. Use 5 plural nouns from the chart on page 82.

Take Another Look   Use these questions to improve your story.

1. Did you use a plural verb with a plural subject?

2. If you used the name of a river or a lake in your story, did you capitalize the name?

Lesson 9   Possessive Nouns

An apostrophe is used to signal that a noun is possessive.

Thinking It Through

The **possessive form** of a noun shows ownership or tells more about the noun. An apostrophe added to a noun is a signal that the noun is possessive.

To form the singular possessive of a noun, add an apostrophe and the letter *s* to the end of the noun. Look at these examples.

> The little girl's wagon was red.
> Mr. Smith's typewriter is broken.
> Charles's book is on the table.

In the first sentence the *'s* added to the singular noun *girl* shows that the word is possessive.

- Which word in the second sentence is a singular possessive?
- Which word in the third sentence is a singular possessive?
- What was added to each singular noun to make it possessive?

To form the plural possessive of a noun, first write the plural form. If it ends in *s*, add an apostrophe after the *s*. If the plural does not end in *s*, add *'s* to the end of the word. Look at these examples.

> The girls' softball game was
>   canceled because of the storm.
> It ruined the Smiths' garage.
> It flooded the children's gym.

- Which two plural possessives end with an apostrophe? Why?
- Which plural possessive ends with *'s?* Why?

Working It Through

A. Write the singular possessive, plural, and plural possessive forms of each noun below.

1. man
2. actress
3. hero
4. country
5. fox
6. child
7. friend
8. thief
9. lady

B. Rewrite each phrase below. Use the correct possessive form of each noun in parentheses.

1. the (babies) toys
2. the (monkeys) antics
3. (James) coat
4. the (woman) job
5. the (mice) tails
6. (Mr. Harris) house
7. my (sister) room
8. our (dog) bones

C. Rewrite the following sentences, adding apostrophes where necessary. You will add apostrophes to 5 nouns.

1. Last Saturday the O'Briens moved into the Glickmans old apartment.
2. We watched the movers unload the childrens bikes.
3. They carried all of the familys furniture carefully.
4. That night the O'Briens had dinner with us—Moms tuna casserole and Dads spinach salad.

Trying It Out

Write a story about a zoo or about a ranger in a state park. Use the singular possessive or plural possessive form of at least 5 of the following nouns.

1. Mrs. Simpson
2. Mr. Weiss
3. bear
4. snake
5. deer
6. wolf
7. child
8. zookeeper
9. camper

Take Another Look Did you use an apostrophe to show that a singular or plural noun is possessive? Did you put each apostrophe in the right place?

Confusion of Plurals and Possessives

An apostrophe is used to form the possessive of a noun. It is never used to form the plural of a noun.

Thinking It Through

Do you ever confuse plurals and possessives? You can tell the difference if you remember that an apostrophe is used to form a possessive. An apostrophe is never used to form a plural. Look at the following examples.

Sunday was Art James's birthday.
All the Jameses planned a party.
The Jameses' friends and relatives
  were invited.

Art James's is a singular possessive; *the Jameses* is a plural; and *the Jameses'* is a plural possessive. The possessives contain apostrophes, but the plural does not.

Now look at these sentences.

The witness testified in court.
The court reporter recorded the
  witness's testimony.
The defense called many witnesses
  to the stand.
The jury listened to all the
  witnesses' statements.

- Which sentence contains the singular form of the underlined noun?
- Which sentence contains the plural?
- Which sentence contains the singular possessive?
- Which sentence contains the plural possessive?

Working It Through

A. Choose 3 of the following nouns. For each noun write 3 sentences. Use the singular possessive form in the first sentence, the plural form in the second, and the plural possessive form in the third.

1. actor   **3.** jury   **5.** wolf   **7.** goose

2. moose   **4.** teacher   **6.** spy   **8.** monkey

B. Read this section from a report about the life of Leonardo da Vinci. Rewrite correctly the 9 words that have missing, misplaced, or unnecessary apostrophes.

> Leonardo da Vinci (1452-1519) was one of the greatest Renaissance painter's. He also studied anatomy and astronomy and drew plans' for machine's. Leonardos drawing's of inventions' and his observations on science are included in his notebooks.
>
> Many of Leonardos' inventions and idea's were ahead of their time. For example, his notebook's contain plans for a flying machine and a parachute.

Trying It Out

Write a description of your favorite hobby or of hobbies that members of your family enjoy.

1. Use the singular possessive, plural, or plural possessive form of at least 5 nouns.

2. Have a classmate read your paper and circle any words with missing, misplaced, or unnecessary apostrophes.

3. Rewrite correctly any circled words on your paper.

Lesson 11   Appositives

An appositive is a noun or phrase that follows a noun and identifies or explains it.

Thinking It Through

A noun or a phrase that follows a noun and gives more information about it is called an **appositive.** The following sentences contain appositives.

> Ralph's youngest sister, Kathy, is in the play.
> Jason, the boy next door, mows our lawn.

In the first sentence the noun *Kathy* is an appositive that tells who Ralph's sister is. In the second sentence the phrase *the boy next door* is an appositive that gives more information about the noun *Jason*.

When an appositive appears in the middle of a sentence, it is set off by two commas:

> Denver, my favorite city, is one mile above sea level.

- What is the appositive in the sentence above?
- What noun does it identify?

When an appositive appears at the end of a sentence, it is set off by only one comma:

> We visited my favorite city, Denver.

- What is the appositive in the sentence above?
- What noun does it identify?

Working It Through

A. Copy the following sentences. Circle the appositive in each sentence and underline the noun that it identifies or explains. If the appositive is a phrase, be sure to circle the whole phrase.

   1. Last night we ate dinner at my favorite restaurant, Luigi's.

2. The first course, a tossed salad, was served with hot rolls and butter.
3. Next we tried minestrone, a thick vegetable soup.
4. I was already full when the waiter brought the main dish, spaghetti.
5. I ordered spumone, an Italian ice cream, for dessert.

B. Rewrite the sentences below. Use two commas to set off an appositive in the middle of a sentence. Use one comma to set off an appositive at the end of a sentence. You should add 9 commas.

1. On Saturdays my friends and I usually go to the Biograph a movie theater.
2. My favorite movie *The Visitor from Taurus IV* is a science-fiction thriller.
3. Stephanie Davis the star plays a government agent.
4. Her job is to find and stop KLATU a robot from outer space.
5. KLATU is draining off all the world's energy and sending it to his home planet Taurus IV.
6. After outsmarting Dr. Ray an enemy agent Stephanie finds KLATU and reprograms him.

Trying It Out

Write a paragraph describing a movie or a TV program that you saw recently or make up another story about KLATU.

1. Use at least 3 appositives to identify or explain places or characters in the story.
2. Circle each appositive and underline the noun that it identifies or explains.

Using Appositives to Combine Sentences

Appositives can be used to combine two short, related ideas into one sentence.

Thinking It Through

Read the following sentences aloud and notice how choppy they sound.

> Duke is our pet dog. Duke is a fox terrier.

These ideas can be combined by making one of them an appositive and setting it off with commas. Notice how the ideas are combined into a single sentence.

> Duke, our pet dog, is a fox terrier.

- What is the appositive? What noun does it follow and help explain?
- Which one of the original sentences was changed to an appositive?

Now read these related sentences.

> Chipper is my pet parakeet. He can say twenty words.

- How would you reword these two ideas to form a single sentence with an appositive?

Working It Through

A. Rewrite each pair of sentences. Combine each pair into a single sentence with an appositive.

1. Today we had tryouts for our school play. Our school play is *The Detective*.
2. Ms. Atherton is our English teacher. Ms. Atherton is the director of the play.
3. Samantha Jones is a sixth-grader. Samantha wants to be an actress.
4. She will play the main character. The main character is Detective Higgins.

5. Her assistant is Officer Moore. Officer Moore will be played by Henry Bishop.
6. Josh Reynolds is playing the role of Mr. Lombard. Mr. Lombard is the villain of the play.

B. Rewrite each pair of sentences below. Combine each pair into a single sentence with an appositive. Be sure to set off the appositives with commas.

1. Hawaii is the fiftieth state. It is made up of a chain of islands.
2. Mesas are common in New Mexico. They are flat-topped hills.
3. Many tourists visit the Alamo. The Alamo is a famous historic landmark.
4. The Lowell Observatory is an astronomical laboratory. It is in Arizona.
5. Houston is the home of the Astrodome. Houston is the largest city in the Southwest.
6. Oil is Alaska's most important industry. Oil is also a very valuable resource.
7. Sears Tower is in Chicago. Sears Tower is one of the world's tallest buildings.

The Alamo

The Astrodome

Trying It Out

Write a story titled "The Case of the Missing Notebook."

1. Be sure to explain why the notebook is important.
2. Include at least 3 characters in your story.
3. Use an appositive to describe each character.
4. Set off the appositives with commas.

Review • Nouns

A. Write the following sentences. Underline all the nouns, both common and proper. Capitalize all proper nouns.

1. This year, labor day is on september third.
2. He went to dr. thomas j. walton, his dentist.
3. Our dog, scamp, flew to california on world airways.
4. The w. t. taylor building is on pine street.
5. The rhone river flows through lake geneva.
6. Write to jones, peterson, and company for information.

B. Complete the following sentences with the correct plural form of the noun in parentheses.

1. The ____ carried heavy loads. (donkey)
2. Put the kitchen ____ in this drawer. (knife)
3. In the spring the ____ are sheared. (sheep)
4. We have two ____ on Saturday. (class)
5. Rake all these ____ into a pile. (leaf)
6. Both rangers had ____. (radio)
7. The milk from both ____ is good. (dairy)
8. What a big flock of ____ that is! (goose)

C. Rewrite the following sentences, putting in the correct form of each possessive noun.

1. The books title sounded interesting to me.
2. The mens work in the mine was difficult.
3. James science experiment was well-done.
4. The oxens master encouraged them with praise.
5. The windshields glare almost blinded us.
6. He fixed the truckers lunches while the drivers rested.

For extra practice turn to page 363.

Take Another Look   Complete the sentence with the correct word in parentheses.

    Either Rodolfo or Emiko ____ the book.   (has, have)
Did you choose *has*?

For more practice turn to Handbook pages 346 and 347.

Evaluation • Nouns

A. Decide which of the following the underlined part of
each sentence is. Then write the letter of your answer.

a. a common noun   **b.** a proper noun   **c.** a noun marker

1. I asked <u>Mother</u> if I could go.
2. The <u>mountain</u> was far away.
3. Maria is in a Girl Scout <u>troop</u>.
4. <u>The</u> river flowed rapidly.
5. That woman is my <u>aunt</u>.
6. The <u>Lane Company</u> makes soap.
7. Chin is a <u>Boy Scout</u>.
8. Africa is a <u>continent</u>.
9. Brazil is <u>a</u> big country.
10. "The red planet" is <u>Mars</u>.
11. This is the <u>Scott Building</u>.
12. Their <u>farm</u> is in Illinois.

B. Write the letter of the word that correctly completes
the sentence.

1. Many truckers have CB ____.
   a. radioes   **b.** radios
2. We saw five ____ in Alaska.
   a. moose   **b.** mooses
3. She read a story about ____.
   a. fairys   **b.** fairies
4. Bob likes mashed ____.
   a. potatos   **b.** potatoes
5. The ____ were tall.
   a. chimnies   **b.** chimneys
6. This store sells ____.
   a. pianos   **b.** pianoes

C. Write the letter of the line that is correct in each
numbered item.

1. **a.** The dogs' tail wagged.
   b. The dogs's tail wagged.
   c. The dog's tail wagged.
   d. The dogs tail wagged.
2. **a.** Both boys eyes shone.
   b. Both boy's eyes shone.
   c. Both boys' eyes shone.
   d. Both boys's eyes shone.
3. **a.** We saw six sheeps' heads.
   b. We saw six sheep's heads.
   c. We saw six sheeps's heads.
   d. We saw six sheeps heads.
4. **a.** The elves's caps are red.
   b. The elves caps are red.
   c. The elfs' caps are red.
   d. The elves' caps are red.
5. **a.** Mavis's dad came to school.
   b. Mavises dad came to school.
   c. Mavis' dad came to school.
   d. Mavis'es dad came to school.
6. **a.** Ten geese's bills opened.
   b. Ten gooses bills opened.
   c. Ten geeses' bills opened.
   d. Ten goose's bills opened.

Spotlight • Activities to Choose

1. Make a family chart. Use proper and common nouns to make a chart that tells about your family. Include information such as full names of family members, names of cities and states in which they live, relationships of members to each other, and birthdates and marriage dates. You might also show the names of companies where some members work or schools some attend. A family chart decorated with pictures or designs should make a very special holiday or birthday gift.

2. Complete a story. Use appositives and your imagination to identify each underlined word in the story starter below. Make up an ending for the story.

There was a long line outside Bango's. Ferdie knew that something special must be taking place inside the store. Mitzi was near the front of the line. Carmen was directly behind her. They were both talking to Penny. All three of them looked very excited. Ferdie just had to find out what was going on.

3. Play a synonym game. This is a game for 6 to 8 players. Each player chooses a word that has several synonyms. (You might check a thesaurus for words to use.) Write each word on the left-hand side of an index card and its synonyms on the right. The first player says his or her word and then asks each of the others for a synonym. Every synonym given that is also listed on the card must be crossed off. The player gets 1 point for each synonym listed that is not named. After everyone has had a turn, the player with the most point wins.

4. Put context clues to work. Find a paragraph in one of your textbooks. It should be about something you feel is especially interesting. Rewrite the paragraph, giving context clues to explain words you feel a second-grader would not know. Then, if you can, read the paragraph to a second-grader to see how good your context clues are.

94

Daffynitions
by Charles Keller

Did you know that a *buccaneer* is "too much to pay for corn"? In this collection of *daffynitions*, over a hundred ordinary words are given comical definitions. Humorous illustrations add to the magic of the book.

The Story of the Dictionary
by Robert Kraske

What is the second most popular book in the English language? Who decides how a word will be pronounced? What different names do people in various parts of the country give to the same thing? These and other questions are answered in this book.

The Return of the Great Brain
by John D. Fitzgerald

T.D. is the 12-year-old Great Brain who uses his abilities in money-making schemes. His "wheel of fortune" invention bankrupts every child in town. Magic tricks are also a part of this story that takes place in Morman Utah at the turn of the century.

Unit Four

Can you recall the first time you were on roller skates?
Do you think the poet's description is true to life?

74th Street

Hey, this little kid gets roller skates.
She puts them on.
She stands up and almost
flops over backwards.
She sticks out a foot like
she's going somewhere and
falls down and
smacks her hand. She
grabs hold of a step to get up and
sticks out the other foot and
slides about six inches and
falls and
skins her knee.

And then, you know what?

She brushes off the dirt and the
blood and puts some
spit on it and then
sticks out the other foot

again

Myra Cohn Livingston

Words such as flops, smacks, grabs, slides, falls, and skins help
make the poem's description vivid and lively. One of the things
you will learn in this unit is that verbs are effective tools in
communicating, whether in poems or paragraphs. Once mastered,
like roller skates, they can get you where you want to go.

Lesson 1   Expressing One Idea

A paragraph develops one main idea. The topic sentence of a paragraph states that idea.

Thinking It Through

Notice that the main idea in each of the following paragraphs is underlined.

Mr. Klinger has one of the most unusual jobs I've ever heard of—he's a feather tester! He judges the quality of duck and goose feathers used to fill pillows. By squeezing the feathers and watching them drift in the air, he can tell whether they are good or not. In some ways, Mr. Klinger has quite a soft job.

Every October gray whales begin their incredible journey from the northern Pacific to waters off the coast of Mexico. They remain there until February and then swim north again. The round trip covers about 10,000 miles. Gray whales make one of the longest migrations of any group of animals.

Paragraphs tell about or develop one main idea. This main idea is called the **topic.** Many paragraphs, but not all, have a **topic sentence.** It is the sentence that best describes or states the main idea of the paragraph. The topic sentence most often appears first or at the end, but it can appear anywhere in the paragraph.

- What is the topic of each paragraph above?
- What is the topic sentence in each?
- Where do the topic sentences appear?

The other sentences in a paragraph support or explain the main idea. They give information that is important and related to the discussion of the topic.

Working It Through

A. Look at each set of sentences. Choose and write the sentence in each that would make the best topic sentence for a paragraph that contains all 3 sentences. Use

one set of sentences in a paragraph. Add 1 sentence of
your own.

Set 1: a. When he was four, Sam was bitten by a dog.

     b. Once, a dog chased Sam home from school.

     c. Although he likes animals, Sam is afraid of dogs.

Set 2: a. Wax figures of weird creatures line the walls.

     b. The Monster Museum is a frightening place.

     c. Creaking and moaning sounds fill the corridors.

Set 3: a. The glider was like a huge, silent sea gull.

     b. Its silvery wings glistened in the sun.

     c. The motorless machine touched down in a field
of flowers.

B. Look at the following pictures. Write a topic sentence
for a paragraph that could be written about each picture.
Then write a paragraph about one of the pictures. Your
paragraph should have 4 or more sentences.

1.   2.   3.

Trying It Out

Work with one of your classmates to do this activity, each
of you following the steps given.

1. List 4 topics that could be subjects for 4 paragraphs.
   Choose topics you feel your partner knows something
   about. They can be serious or amusing.

2. Give your topics to your partner and have him or her
   write a topic sentence for each.

3. Save what you write to use in an activity in Lesson 2.

Lesson 2 **Supporting Details**

Details in a paragraph should support the topic of the paragraph.

Thinking It Through

Details given in a paragraph should support the main idea of the paragraph. They should describe, explain, or in some other way provide interesting and useful information related to the topic. Details that do not stick to the subject of the paragraph should not be included.

Notice the details in the following paragraph.

> Everyone in the family had an excuse for being late for dinner. Mom had to stay late at the office. Kevin's hockey team had an extra long practice, and Maggie had to change a flat tire on her car before she could drive them both home. The twins, though, had the best excuse of all. They said they were just waiting until they got hungry.

- What is the topic of the paragraph?
- How are the details related to the topic?

Tell which of the following details also supports the main idea of the paragraph.

> Dad hated having to eat a cold dinner.
> Dad missed his regular bus and had to wait thirty minutes for another one.

Working It Through

A. Write each topic sentence below. Then write the related details that could be used in a paragraph about the topic.

   1. Jan works as a guide on a riverboat.
      a. She likes to water-ski in her spare time.
      b. She points out landmarks along the boat's route.
      c. Knowing how the boat operates is part of her job.

2. Benjamin Franklin was a man of many talents.
   a. He invented a heating stove and bifocals.
   b. He wrote many books and founded the first lending library.
   c. During his later years, he had to be carried from place to place in a sedan chair.

3. The new high school is one of the finest in our state.
   a. It has two Olympic-size swimming pools.
   b. Many feel it is too far from town.
   c. The student lounge has an area for studying and one for small group meetings.

B. Supply 2 additional supporting details for each topic given in Exercise A.

C. Complete the sentence, *The best sandwich in the world is* . . . . Use the completed statement as the topic sentence of a paragraph. Add supporting details that will provide the information below.

   1. what ingredients are in the sandwich
   2. how the sandwich looks
   3. how the sandwich tastes
   4. what you call the sandwich

Trying It Out

Write 4 supporting details for one of the topics and topic sentences you developed in Lesson 1 or another topic you choose. You may want to look in an encyclopedia to find interesting information about your topic to include in your paragraph.

Ordering Details by Time

You can arrange details in a paragraph to show the order in which things happen.

Thinking It Through

There are several ways to organize details in a paragraph. The way you choose often depends on your purpose for writing. For example, when you want to tell a story or recall something from the past, you can arrange details to show the sequence in which the events took place. Showing the order in which actions happen can also be important when you want to explain how to make or do something.

Find the topic sentence in the following paragraph, and then notice the arrangement of details.

Harriet Tubman and her band of runaway slaves traveled throughout the night. Shortly after ten they crossed the state line. Just before midnight they reached a river they would have to swim or wade across. It took over two hours to get everyone safely through the swirling waters. Finally, near dawn, they found a deserted barn in which they could safely hide and rest during the coming day.

- In what order did the events take place? What words and phrases help you know the order?
- What would happen to the sense of the paragraph if the details were arranged differently?

Words and phrases such as *shortly after*, *just before*, and *finally* help a reader follow the sequence described.

Working It Through

A. Use the details below in a paragraph that shows the order in which the events happened. Make up a topic sentence for your paragraph.

1. when 12, moved to Idaho and lived in a huge house
2. moved to Chicago at age 3, lived in an apartment
3. born in a small farmhouse in Iowa
4. at age 9, moved to Boston and lived in a townhouse
5. moved back to Chicago at age 15, lived in a new house

B. Carefully study the picture below. Then write a paragraph describing the sequence of events that must take place before the water in the balloon will splash over the clown.

BALLOON FILLED WITH WATER

START

Trying It Out

Write a paragraph about one of the topics listed below. Arrange the details to show the order in which things happened or should be done. Include words that will help your readers follow the order you are describing.

1. How to Make a Jack-o'-Lantern
2. The Worst Day of My Last Vacation
3. How to Be a Perfect Kid
4. My Best Day at School This Year
5. How to Get Rid of a Pest

Ordering Details by Importance

You can arrange details in a paragraph to show an order of importance.

Thinking It Through

Another way to organize details in a paragraph is to present them in the order of importance, beginning with either the most or least important detail. This order is useful when giving your opinion about something or when presenting an argument to persuade your readers to feel and think as you do about the topic.

See how details are arranged in the following paragraph.

> Dad, my birthday is next month and I think a new bike would be the perfect gift. The bike I have is over five years old. The handlebars are rusty and both tires have been patched twice. Lately, the brakes haven't been working well either. I'm afraid I'll have a serious accident if I have to keep using my old bike to deliver my papers.

- What is the topic of the paragraph?
- Which detail will most likely influence the father most?
- Is that detail first or last in the paragraph?
- How would you arrange the details if you were writing the paragraph?

Your answers to the following questions can help you arrange details by the order of their importance.

1. What are the best details to include in the paragraph? Which will make my point best?

2. Who will my audience be—a parent? my teacher or my class? a friend? Which details will be most meaningful to my audience?

3. Will my paragraph be more effective if I give the most convincing detail first or if I build up to it?

Working It Through

A. Write a paragraph by arranging the details below in an order that would present the best argument to your family for getting a bigger allowance. You may want to add or substitute 1 or 2 details of your own.

1. Money doesn't go as far as it used to.
2. My best friend gets a bigger allowance than I do.
3. Soon I'll be a year older and will need more money.
4. I want to begin a savings account.
5. I want to buy some things for myself.

B. Many feel that watching television is a waste of time while many others feel that watching it is educational.

1. Decide how you feel about the topic and then write a paragraph giving the reasons for your opinion.
2. Arrange the details in the order that you feel will present your point of view best.
3. Read your paragraph to a classmate. See whether he or she can tell if the most important detail is given first or last in the paragraph.

Trying It Out

Work with a classmate to do this activity. First, select one of the topics below and decide which side of the issue each of you will support. Then, each of you write a paragraph to support your different positions. Put your details in the order you feel will be most effective for making your point.

1. Birds make better pets than fish.
2. Baseball is more exciting than football.
3. Spring is a more pleasant time of the year than fall.
4. It's more fun to travel by plane than by train.

Beginnings and Endings

You can use beginning sentences of paragraphs to awaken interest in the topic. Ending sentences can summarize, emphasize, or draw a conclusion about what has been said.

Thinking It Through

Here are two points to help you write more effective paragraphs.

1. Begin with a sentence that gets the attention of the reader.
2. End with a sentence that in some way pulls together or wraps up what has been said.

As you read the following paragraphs, pay particular attention to the beginning and ending sentences.

Take *mo* as in *motor*, add *ped* as in *pedal*, and you have *moped*. But what is it? What you have is a small, lightweight machine that is a cross between a motorcycle and a bicycle, which in most cases it is not. Or you may think of it as an underpowered motorcycle with pedals added, which is not completely true either. A moped is a moped—a handy two- sometimes three-wheeled vehicle with its own design and its own purpose.

Lurking in the still, dark waters of the deep sea are some of the strangest creatures on our planet. Fishes with huge teeth and glowing lights cruise through a cold blackness that is studded with small blue lights like the galaxies of space. Bright red shrimp, oddly shaped squid, and transparent animals made of jelly also live at these depths. To those of us who live on the land, the deep ocean is an alien environment, almost as harsh as that of the moon or Mars.

- What words or phrases do you think the writer used in the beginning sentences to get the reader's attention?
- What do the ending sentences of the paragraphs do? For example, do they sum up the information? Do they draw a conclusion about what has been said?
- Which sentence in each paragraph makes the best topic sentence?

To get the reader's attention right away, use words and phrases in the beginning sentence that will make the topic sound interesting and exciting. When you feel it is necessary or would be effective, use an ending sentence that will help the reader better understand and react to what has been presented.

Working It Through

A. Rewrite each sentence below to make it a more effective beginning sentence for a paragraph. Try to make the sentence one that will make a reader want to finish the paragraph.

1. The world is getting too crowded with people.
2. Corn is easy to grow.
3. Halloween is a fun time of the year.

4. Many scientists believe that ghosts really exist.
5. It is important to be happy.
6. The spider is an interesting creature.

B. Write beginning sentences for paragraphs that develop each of the topics below. Then choose one of the topics and write a paragraph that includes 4 or more details.
   1. My Favorite Time of Day
   2. The Ideal Pet for Me
   3. A Rule Every School Should Have
   4. The Most Important Thing for Parents to Know

C. Write an effective ending for the paragraph below.

   If a spider could think and feel as we do, what thoughts might it have as it spins its silky web? Perhaps it would think of the unsuspecting insects that the silky threads might catch. Or, maybe it would spin and spin while wondering how high and wide the web could be. Then too, it might feel quite proud of its creation and think only of its beauty.

Trying It Out
   1. Look through newspapers, magazines, or your textbooks to find 5 paragraph examples. Newspaper editorials and social studies or science textbooks should be good sources.
   2. Write the paragraph that you feel has the most effective beginning or ending sentence, or both.
   3. Read your paragraph to a classmate. Then make it a part of a classroom collection of paragraphs.

Lesson 6 Improving the First Draft

Using a checklist for writing effective paragraphs can help you improve your paragraph. Proofreader's marks can help you make changes easily.

Thinking It Through

Miriam used the checklist below to help her decide whether a paragraph she wrote could be improved. As you read the checklist, think about what you have learned about writing effective paragraphs.

1. A paragraph develops one main idea. A topic sentence describes or states that main idea.
2. Supporting details should be related to the topic of the paragraph.
3. Details can be arranged according to time or importance. The order used often depends on the purpose of the paragraph.
4. The beginning sentence of a paragraph should awaken interest in the topic. The ending sentence can pull together or emphasize what has been said.

Miriam felt that she could improve her paragraph. She used proofreader's marks to show the changes she wanted to make. The picture shows the marks she used.

Proofreader's Marks

Make a capital letter.

Add a period.

Take out.

Put in one or more words.

Put in a comma.

one of the worst days I've ever spent

Yesterday was awful. First of all, I left my lunch on the bus. My best friend shared her lunch with me, though. During recess I lost my new watch while I was playing baseball. Just before math class I found out that I had done the wrong homework assignment. By the time I got home I was so angry that I told my little brother to get lost and he did and I had to spend almost two hours searching the neighborhood to find him. as if I never should have gotten up I went to bed feeling terrible.

- What changes show that Miriam used the checklist to help her improve her paragraph?
- Which proofreader's marks did Miriam use to show the changes?
- Why do you think Miriam changed her beginning and ending sentences?

Working It Through

A. Rewrite Miriam's paragraph, showing the changes indicated by the proofreader's marks.

B. Use the checklist in Thinking It Through along with other things you've learned about writing paragraphs to help you decide how to improve the paragraph that follows. Rewrite the paragraph, using proofreader's marks to show the changes you want to make. Then write the paragraph as it should be with your changes.

Dinosaurs were really something. Some were no bigger than chickens but others were the largest animals that ever lived. You can see huge dinosaur skeletons in museums. Some dinosaurs ate only plants. Others ate only meat. Some moved on four feet and others on two. Scientists have learned a lot about dinosaurs. They were all alike in one way. They all had small brains.

Trying It Out

1. Write a paragraph describing what you feel are your best qualities or those of a close friend. Or, choose another topic that is of special interest to you.
2. Reread your paragraph carefully, thinking of ways to improve it. Use proofreader's marks to show the changes you want to make.
3. Rewrite the paragraph, making the changes.

Take Another Look   Does your paragraph include a topic sentence? Are your details related to the topic? Are the details you chose the most effective you can use for the purpose of the paragraph?

Review • Paragraphs

A. Read each set of sentences and answer the questions.

Set 1: **a.** Our family reunion was wonderful!

b. Uncle Court came from Europe to be there.

c. My sister pretends to dislike family gatherings.

d. There were activities for young and old alike.

Set 2: **a.** I like my house much better.

b. At night eerie lights flicker in the house.

c. The deserted house on my street seems haunted.

d. Its shutters and doors creak and groan.

Set 3: **a.** Young pelicans eat from their parents' pouches.

b. Pelicans are interesting birds.

c. Condors are interesting birds too.

d. A pelican's unusual bill helps one identify it.

1. Which sentence in each set is the best topic sentence for a paragraph that includes most of the sentences?

2. What are the related details in each set? What information do the details give about the topic?

3. Which sentence in each set is not related to the topic?

B. Choose 1 topic below and write a paragraph that includes an interesting topic sentence and 3 or more related details.

1. an unusual pet

2. becoming a teenager

3. going away to camp

4. a favorite possession

5. the perfect house

6. daydreams

C. Think about the questions that follow.

1. How do the details you used support the main idea of your paragraph?

2. Do the details give interesting and useful information about the topic?

3. Is the paragraph made up of complete sentences?

4. Is it punctuated correctly?

Evaluation • Paragraphs

A. Improve and rewrite the paragraph below.
1. The paragraph should develop one main idea.
2. The topic sentence should describe or state the main idea and awaken interest in the topic.
3. All details should be related to the topic.
4. All necessary punctuation should be included.

I like my school's playground. It has several interesting pieces of equipment on it. My sister's school doesn't have any playground equipment for the students, but she's in high school. The jungle gym is made from old tires It's almost two stories high. There's a grassy area where kids can sit and talk or just be alone in peace. I wish I had a quiet grassy area around my house. One section of the playground is set aside for ball games, and there's a track for racing. One day soon I'm going to run around that track ten times without stopping.

B. Write a paragraph about one of the topics that follow. Be sure to include a topic sentence and 3 or more related details.

1. your favorite holiday
2. an interesting job
3. an ideal meal
4. a shopping trip
5. a famous sports figure
6. your favorite outfit
7. an unusual person
8. an awful experience

Your paragraph will be evaluated on the development of one main idea, an effective topic sentence, related details, and the following:

    complete sentences
    correct punctuation

SNURF or SKAND?

You can combine a little snow and sun fun by using a surfboard in the snow and go *snurfing* and taking your skiis to the beach to *skand!*

By combining parts of *snow* and *surf,* the new word *snurf* can be made. By putting *ski* and *sand* together, a new word, *skand,* is created.

Words made by combining parts of others are called blends, or portmanteau (pôrt man'to), words. The word *portmanteau* comes from the name of a kind of suitcase that has two equal halves. Likewise, a portmanteau word has two meanings packed into one word.

A writer who is famous for his portmanteau words is Lewis Carroll, who wrote *Alice's Adventures in Wonderland.* Carroll invented the *snark,* an imaginary creature which is a combination of snake and shark. In the introduction to his poem, "The Hunting of the Snark," he explains about portmanteau words:

> For instance, take the two words "fuming" and "furious." Make up your mind that you will say both words, but leave it unsettled which you will say first. Now open your mouth and speak. If your thoughts incline ever so little towards "fuming," you will say "fuming-furious"; if they turn, by even a hair's breadth, towards "furious," you will say "furious-fuming"; but if you have that rarest of gifts, a perfectly balanced mind, you will say "frumious."

What words did a "perfectly balanced mind" combine to create the following: *motel, brunch, chortle, smog?*

114

Spotlight • Sports Terms

The game was a real cliff-hanger!

In the bottom of the ninth, with the score tied 3 to 3, the slugger strode to the plate, her gaze riveted to the right-field fence. The hurler, tense on the mound, glared steel-eyed at the batter. Then came the wind-up.

A pop-up behind the catcher . . .

Strike one!

Again, the wind-up and throw . . .

A screwball, nearly dusting the batter . . .

Ball one!

To anyone unfamiliar with baseball, the description above probably doesn't make much sense. In baseball, as in many sports, there is a special language used to describe the action.

Usually, colorful language is created to describe events clearly. Fans then know what is meant, whether they are listening to the radio, watching television, or reading the sports report in a newspaper or magazine.

Here are some shorter descriptions. What words help you identify the specific sport being described?

They are coming down the final green. With his ball in the rough, coming around the leg in the fairway will be nearly impossible for the former PGA champion.

After the first set it looks like a tight match. Blackman has a tough service, catching the corners with his backhand.

The compulsory figures are over. Now we will watch the 5-minute freestyle competition. Watch for the double axel that should start the routine.

Pay attention to the vocabularies of sports. A word in one sport may mean something very different in another. *Love, ace, in the hole* — see if you can keep score!

Lesson 7 Action and Linking Verbs

Some verbs express action. Others link the subject to a word or words in the predicate.

Thinking It Through

The most important word in the predicate of a sentence is the **verb.** In each sentence below, the verb tells what action is taking place. Such verbs are called **action verbs.**

The runners <u>cross</u> the finish line.
The crowds <u>shout</u> with joy.

Linking Verbs		
present	past	future
am	was	will be
is	were	
are		

Verbs like those shown in the chart do not express action. They are called **linking verbs.** A linking verb joins, or links, the subject to a word or words in the predicate, usually ones that describe or name the subject.

The runners <u>are</u> fast.
The tallest one <u>is</u> the captain.

- In the first sentence, what word describes the runners?
- In the second sentence, what word names the tallest runner?

The verbs *seem* and *appear* can also be linking verbs, as in the following examples.

The runners <u>seem</u> excited.
The captain <u>appears</u> triumphant.

- What words describe the runners and the captain?

Working It Through

A. Use the action verbs below in 6 sentences describing activities that could take place on your school playground.

1. jump	**3.** climb	**5.** chase
2. meet	**4.** walk	**6.** run

B. Write the following sentences. Draw a line under each action verb and a circle around each linking verb.

1. Allison takes karate lessons.
2. She practices at least an hour every day.
3. She will be in her first exhibition in two weeks.
4. She seems quite confident.
5. The entire neighborhood plans to attend.
6. Allison's brother was in several exhibitions last year.
7. He won his first-degree black belt.
8. He was only thirteen at the time.

C. Complete each sentence with one of the linking verbs in Thinking It Through.

1. Leo said, "I _____ three years older than my sister."
2. "Even so, she _____ four inches taller than I."
3. "She and her friend Carole _____ the tallest kids in their class."
4. "Last year I _____ the shortest kid in my class."
5. "Dad thinks I _____ short even when I grow up."
6. "So I'm reading about great men of the past who _____ short."

Trying It Out

Imagine yourself as you would like to be ten years from now.

1. Think about what you would like to be doing then. Consider things you would like to have already done and things you might be planning for the future.
2. Write 5 or more sentences telling about yourself as you would like to be.
3. Use verbs such as *seem* and *appear* along with other linking verbs listed in Thinking It Through. Use a different verb in each sentence.

Lesson 8   Tenses of Verbs

A verb shows what a subject does and tells when something happens.

Thinking It Through

The tense of a verb tells whether something happens in the present, the past, or the future. Both action and linking verbs show tense.

Notice the tense of each verb in the examples below.

The clowns <u>are</u> very talented.
Delighted audiences <u>cheer</u> their act.
During one show a clown <u>was</u> on a tightrope.
He <u>tripped</u> on purpose over his own feet.
He <u>will be</u> the show's main attraction next year.
He <u>will begin</u> each show with his special act.

- Which verbs show that something is happening now, or show the **present tense?**
- Which verbs show that something already happened, or show the **past tense?** What ending has been added to these verbs?
- Which verbs show that something is going to happen, or show the **future tense?** What word is used to show that a verb is in the future tense?

Working It Through

A. Write the sentences below and underline the verb in each. Write *present*, *past*, or *future* beside each sentence to show the tense of the verb.

1. The Robinson family plans a visit to the old Robinson homestead in Virginia.
2. They will visit the beautiful Luray Caverns.
3. Dr. Robinson tells the children about the colorful stones hanging like icicles in the caves.
4. Gaynelle read about the limestone formations in one of her textbooks.

5. Many of the Robinsons moved away years ago.

6. During their visit the children will meet some of their cousins for the first time.

B. Write a statement to answer each question below. In each answer use a verb that is in the same tense as the verb in the question. Underline each verb.

1. Who is your favorite actor?

2. Who was your favorite actor two years ago?

3. Who is the best cook in your family?

4. Who cooked dinner yesterday in your home?

5. How old is your best friend?

6. What will be a good gift for your friend's next birthday?

C. Use verbs to tell about yourself.

1. Write 3 sentences telling 3 different things you did yesterday. Use verbs in the past tense.

2. Write 2 sentences about yourself as you are now. For example, you might describe how you look or how you feel. Use verbs in the present tense.

3. Write 3 sentences telling 3 things you will do after school today. Use verbs in the future tense.

4. Underline the verb in each sentence.

Trying It Out

1. Rewrite the following story starter, changing each underlined word to the past tense.

2. Write an ending for the story, using verbs in the future tense.

A very strange thing happens to me on my way to school. I bump into a little kid sitting in a huge wagon with a big, shaggy dog. They block the entire sidewalk. Twice I ask him nicely to move. He just looks at me. So I walk around him. Then he follows me, wagon and all. He yells at me, "Hey, you, wait for me!" Even worse, this happens every day for a week.

Well, enough is enough. I have a plan. . . .

Auxiliary Verbs

Some verbs become helping, or auxiliary, verbs when they are used with another verb in a sentence.

Thinking It Through

A verb is often made up of more than one word. The verb that tells what is happening is the **main verb.** The other verb or verbs with the main verb are called **helping verbs** or **auxiliary verbs.** The main verb and one or more auxiliary verbs together make up the **verb phrase.**

Auxiliary Verbs
Do: do, does, did
Be: am, are, is, was, were, be, being, been
Have: have, has, had
Can: can, could
Must
May: may, might

The chart shows some common auxiliary verbs. Forms of the verbs *do, be,* and *have* are the most common. Forms of *can, must,* and *may* are also used as auxiliary verbs.

Notice the verbs in these examples.

I <u>was called</u> home from school today.
Dad <u>had phoned</u> from Arizona.
He <u>has been offered</u> a job there.

In the first sentence *called* is the main verb and *was* is the auxiliary verb. The verb phrase is *was called.*

- What words act as main verbs in the other sentences?
- What words act as auxiliary verbs?

In a statement the auxiliary verb usually comes right before the main verb. In a question the auxiliary verb usually comes first and is separated from the main verb by the subject.

Notice the verbs in the following examples.

<u>Did</u> you <u>spend</u> your vacation in Arizona?
<u>Does</u> your grandmother <u>live</u> there?

- What is the main verb in each question? What are the auxiliary verbs?
- Where does each subject appear?

Working It Through

A. Write the following sentences. Draw two lines under each main verb and one line under each auxiliary verb.

1. The guitar is considered one of the most popular musical instruments.
2. Most guitars are made of wood.
3. The instrument was developed in Egypt over 5,000 years ago.
4. Electric guitars were introduced in the 1900s.
5. They can produce a variety of sounds.

B. Rewrite each of these statements as questions. Begin each with the auxiliary verb.

1. Jay has played with a music group for over two years.
2. He can play several instruments.
3. The group has traveled all over the state.
4. Jay must practice several hours a day.
5. The group has become very popular.

C. Use an auxiliary verb to make a verb phrase in each statement below.

1. Frances _____ give a party next Saturday.
2. She _____ invited several friends from school.
3. Everyone _____ dress as a storybook character.
4. Jimmy _____ come as Rumpelstiltskin.
5. He _____ think of clever things to do.

Trying It Out

1. Use the picture to help you imagine a lively afternoon at a dance or similar setting.
2. Use forms of the verbs below and auxiliary verbs to write 8 sentences describing what you might see and do.

dance	laugh
choose	rock
twirl	hum
enjoy	listen

121

Principal Parts of Verbs

The principal parts of a verb are the present, past, and past participle forms.

Thinking It Through

The principal parts of a verb are its three main forms. These forms are **present, past,** and **past participle.** The past participle form of a verb is the past form that is used with an auxiliary verb.

In regular verbs the past and past participle are formed by adding *-ed* to the present form. In irregular verbs all three forms may be different.

The chart shows the principal parts of several verbs. Tell which are regular and which are irregular.

Present	Past	Past Participle
clean	cleaned	(has/have) cleaned
guide	guided	(has/have) guided
move	moved	(has/have) moved
want	wanted	(has/have) wanted
watch	watched	(has/have) watched
become	became	(has/have) become
do	did	(has/have) done
go	went	(has/have) gone
see	saw	(has/have) seen
send	sent	(has/have) sent
tell	told	(has/have) told

Tell which form of the verb has been used in each sentence that follows.

Yesterday I <u>sent</u> a letter to my cousin.
I <u>have sent</u> her two letters this month.
I always <u>send</u> her funny drawings in my letters.

Working It Through

A. Write the following paragraph.
1. Draw a straight line under each verb in its past form and a wavy line under each in its past participle form.
2. Guess what animal the paragraph describes.

The animal had become hungry. It had moved soundlessly across the hollow log in search of food. Now its forked tongue worked its way in and out. Like radar, it touched surfaces and sent messages to the animal's brain. These messages told about the feel and smell of things all around the animal. Similar messages had guided the animal to food all of its life.

B. Complete each pair of sentences with the past or past participle form of the verb shown.
1. Charles and Carla have ____ to Hawaii.
   Pamela ____ there last winter. (go)
2. Kim ____ her homework after dinner.
   Her brother had ____ his earlier. (do)
3. Rosa ____ a member of our club.
   She has ____ a close friend of mine. (become)
4. I ____ Roberto at the party.
   I had not ____ him for weeks. (see)

C. Use each verb or verb phrase below in a sentence.
1. had told	3. cleaned	5. have wanted
2. watched	4. has sent	6. has gone

Trying It Out

During a lunch, recess, or free period, make a list of verbs you hear people use as they speak.
1. Identify each verb as regular or irregular.
2. Compare your list with your classmates' lists. See whether regular or irregular verbs seem to be used more frequently.
3. Use the past participle form of 5 of the verbs in sentences.

Two Groups of Irregular Verbs

Some irregular verbs follow a pattern.

Thinking It Through

The past and past participle forms of irregular verbs vary. Often you have to learn their individual forms in order to use them correctly. Sometimes you can figure out a verb's form by recognizing a pattern.

Look at the verb forms in the group below.

Present	Past	Past Participle
swim	swam	(has/have) swum
ring	rang	(has/have) rung
drink	drank	(has/have) drunk
begin	began	(has/have) begun

Notice that the *i* becomes *a* in the past form of each verb in the list above.

● What happens in the past participle form of each?

Now note the pattern of the verbs in this group.

Present	Past	Past Participle
blow	blew	(has/have) blown
grow	grew	(has/have) grown
throw	threw	(has/have) thrown
know	knew	(has/have) known

● What happens in the past form of each verb? What happens in the past participle form?

Working It Through

A. Write 3 sentences for each picture at the top of the next page.

    1. For each set of sentences choose one of the verbs listed in Thinking It Through.

    2. Use a different form of the verb in each sentence.

B. Rewrite the following sentences, supplying the correct form of each verb in parentheses.

1. Rico (begin) his day at the library.
2. He (know) that he would be able to get the necessary information there.
3. After reading for over an hour, his interest in the subject had (grow) even more.
4. At noon he (drink) some milk and ate a sandwich.
5. By two o'clock he had (begin) to find some of the answers he needed.
6. He got so involved he didn't realize that the closing bell had (ring).
7. When he stepped outside, a strong gust of wind (blow) his notes in every direction.
8. Rico (throw) his hands in the air and said, "Well, it'll be back to the books again tomorrow."

Trying It Out

Rico may have been at the library getting information to prove or disprove a fact.

1. Use each verb listed in Thinking It Through in a sentence that states a fact. Your sentences can be about you or about anyone or anything you know.
2. Use only the past and past participle forms of the verbs in your sentences.

Take Another Look   Did you use the correct past or past participle form of each irregular verb? Did you use a helping verb with each past participle?

Compound Predicates

A compound predicate is made up of two or more verbs or verb phrases joined by words such as *or, and,* or *but.*

Thinking It Through

You already know that a sentence having two or more subjects joined by *and* has a compound subject.

Ms. Lang *had a plan.*   Ms. Lang and her class *had*
Her class *had a plan.*   *a plan.*

A sentence may also have two or more verbs or verb phrases joined by conjunctions such as *and, but,* and *or.* The verb is then called a **compound predicate.**

They designed a robot.   *They* designed and built
They built a robot.   a robot.

Notice the compound predicates in these sentences.

The robot speaks and sings in a human like voice.
It tells riddles and works math problems, too.

● What is the compound predicate in the first sentence?
What is the subject?
● What is the compound predicate in the second sentence?
What is the subject?

Sometimes sentences have the same subject but different predicates as in the following sentences.

The robot moves its head.   *The robot* moves its head
The robot shakes its arms.   and shakes its arms.

● What are the two predicates in the sentence at the right?
● What subject do both predicates tell about?

Working It Through

A. Write only the sentences below that have a compound predicate. You should find 5 sentences.

1. Billie and Frank joined the Young Teens Interest Club.
2. The club meets on Tuesdays and has over forty members.
3. Meetings are always informative and fun.
4. Frank usually practices bowling or takes macramé.
5. Billie gives English lessons to a girl from Peru and learns a little Spanish at the same time.
6. Frank's cousin told him about the club but did not join it herself.
7. Billie's brother and sister are interested in the club and like the variety of activities.
8. Her brother, a musician, thinks the club's jazz group is terrific.

B. Combine each set of sentences to make 1 sentence that contains a compound predicate.

1. Adam got a bike for his birthday. He took a test drive right away.
2. He will take part in the bike rodeo. He won't do any difficult stunts.
3. Kelly took part in the rodeo last summer. She won first place in the distance race.
4. Kelly's mom is a newscaster for Channel 37. She covers the rodeo every year.

Trying It Out

Imagine that a robot has been built especially for you.

1. Write 5 or more sentences telling what your robot can do.
2. Use compound predicates in each sentence.

Review • Verbs

A. Complete each sentence with the verb in the tense indicated in parentheses.

1. Leonora _____ skiing at Green Lake.   (go, past)
2. Sachiko _____ over to study with me.   (come, future)
3. My brother _____ in the choir.   (sing, present)
4. Don and Pedro _____ tired.   (are, past)
5. Our dog _____ almost anything.   (eat, future)
6. She _____ thirteen in June.   (is, future)
7. Rosa _____ my favorite cousin.   (is, present)

B. Complete each sentence with the verb in the verb form indicated in parentheses.

1. Two squirrels _____ in the tree.   (play, past)
2. They _____ each other.   (chase, past participle)
3. The sparrows _____ birdseed.   (want, present)
4. We _____ two maple trees.   (plant, past participle)
5. The cats _____ on the door.   (scratch, present)
6. We _____ the door to let them in.   (open, past)

C. Complete the following sentences with the verb and verb form indicated in parentheses.

1. They _____ to Arizona.   (drive, past participle)
2. The plants _____ rapidly.   (grow, past)
3. They _____ their work after school.   (do, present)
4. The proud dad _____ everyone.   (tell, past)
5. We _____ signs of spring.   (see, past participle)
6. We _____ to camp last summer.   (go, past)
7. They _____ her a package.   (send, past participle)

For extra practice turn to pages 365 and 366.

Take Another Look   Write the sentence. Underline the four proper nouns.

     Aiko lives in Tokyo, Japan, in Asia.

Did you underline *Aiko, Tokyo, Japan,* and *Asia*?

For more practice turn to page 338 in the Handbook.

Evaluation • Verbs

A. Write the letter of the response that correctly completes the sentence.

1. Pedro ____ tomorrow.
   a. will go   **b.** went
2. She ____ tired now.
   a. seems   **b.** seemed
3. The rain ____ last night.
   a. will come   **b.** came
4. Kiku ____ here yesterday.
   a. will be   **b.** was
5. They ____ going now.
   a. are   **b.** was

6. Just ____ everything and come.
   a. will drop   **b.** drop
7. Felipe ____ here tomorrow.
   a. will eat   **b.** ate
8. I ____ there soon.
   a. will be   **b.** am
9. She ____ it next week.
   a. will study   **b.** studied
10. Last week they ____ home.
    a. will be   **b.** were

B. For each sentence, write the letter of the response that tells whether the underlined word is the principal part of the verb indicated in parentheses after the sentence.

1. Sam <u>cleaned</u> out the garage. (past)   **a.** Yes   **b.** No
2. We <u>have climbed</u> it. (past participle)   **a.** Yes   **b.** No
3. They <u>believe</u> you. (present)   **a.** Yes   **b.** No
4. Elena <u>pounded</u> the clay. (past participle)   **a.** Yes   **b.** No
5. Fumi <u>has painted</u> a dish. (past)   **a.** Yes   **b.** No
6. The dog <u>barked</u> all night. (past participle)   **a.** Yes   **b.** No
7. They <u>have washed</u> the car. (past)   **a.** Yes   **b.** No
8. We <u>turn</u> here. (present)   **a.** Yes   **b.** No
9. It <u>has become</u> a butterfly. (past)   **a.** Yes   **b.** No
10. Evan <u>wrote</u> a letter. (past)   **a.** Yes   **b.** No
11. Jen <u>hasn't flown</u> before. (past)   **a.** Yes   **b.** No
12. They <u>know</u> the answer. (present)   **a.** Yes   **b.** No
13. We <u>drove</u> to Chicago. (past participle)   **a.** Yes   **b.** No
14. Norio <u>has seen</u> it. (past participle)   **a.** Yes   **b.** No
15. Who <u>did</u> this work? (present)   **a.** Yes   **b.** No
16. The smoke <u>rose</u> slowly. (past participle)   **a.** Yes   **b.** No
17. Who <u>has gone</u> to gym? (past participle)   **a.** Yes   **b.** No
18. The puddle <u>has dried</u> up. (past)   **a.** Yes   **b.** No

Spotlight • Activities to Choose

1. Write about days past. Talk to an elderly member of your family or an elderly neighbor. Ask how his or her life as a child was different from life for children today. Then write a paragraph to describe one interesting thing you learned. Share your paragraph and other things you found out with your classmates.

2. Record action verbs. Get together with a group of your classmates and select a TV show you all can plan to watch. As you watch, list verbs naming actions that take place as a part of the show. Use each verb in a sentence that describes the show. Compare your sentences with those of others in the group.

3. Describe a mystery person. On a large sheet of paper write the title *Guess Who* and 4 or more interesting and important details about someone most of your classmates know. He or she can be a well-known person in your school or community, or even a famous personality. Display your sentences. Invite your classmates to arrange the details in a paragraph that also includes their guess about who the person is. Attach the paragraphs that correctly identify the person to your sentences.

4. Make a verb chart. Begin a class list of irregular verbs on a sheet of chart paper. For each verb, show the principal parts and an example sentence in which the past participle form of the verb is used. Display the chart and add to it as you find or think of more verbs. Refer to the chart to help you use irregular verbs correctly in your writing.

5. Solve a verb puzzle. Copy the group of letters below exactly as they appear. Then find the 7 linking verbs hidden in the puzzle. The verbs are spelled across and down. One has been found for you. Try making a similar action-verb puzzle for a friend to solve.

w	u	i	s	v	a	u
a	p	p	e	a	r	s
s	v	w	e	r	e	e
r	o	a	m	u	v	e
w	i	l	l	b	e	n

Ji-Nongo-Nongo Means Riddles
by Verna Aardema

This collection of African riddles deals with subjects ranging from animals of Africa to qualities such as courage and strength. Some of the riddles are humorous, but all of them tell a truth about life.

Searching for Shona
by Margaret J. Anderson

At the start of World War II, two young girls decide to trade places. Shy, wealthy Marjorie Malcolm-Scott becomes the adventurous orphan Shona McInnes, and Shona, in turn, adopts the life of Marjorie. Eventually, each girl realizes that she must seek her own identity.

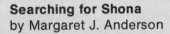

The Midnight Fox
by Betsy Byars

Being neither an outdoor person nor an animal lover, Tom dreads spending the summer on his aunt's farm. His feelings about animals change when he meets a graceful, black fox and her cub. Called on to save these animals, Tom acts heroically. In doing so, he begins to understand himself.

Unit Five

Excavations are hollows made by digging. How can a
workman with a spade push thousands of years away?

from Pompeii
New Excavations

A workman with a spade in half a day
Can push two thousand lagging years away.
See, how the tragic villas, one by one,
Like drowsy lizards creep into the sun.

Leonora Speyer

Have you ever thought of research as digging? Instead of a
shovel, what are some of the tools you might use in doing
research? In this unit, you will learn that it is not necessary
to store a lifetime of facts in your head as long as you have
them at your fingertips.

Lesson 1 Choosing a Topic for a Report

When you choose a topic for a report, select one that is interesting but narrow enough for a short report.

Thinking It Through

Carla's teacher usually assigned topics for class reports, but for this report the pupils were asked to choose their own topics. They were given these guidelines:

1. Choose a topic that is interesting.
2. Limit the topic if it is too broad for a short report.
3. Make sure you can find enough information.

First Carla listed general subjects that interested her. She was curious about earthquakes and wanted to write a report about them.

Next Carla went to the library to check the encyclopedia for an article on earthquakes. As she glanced over the article, she realized that the topic was too broad. Then she saw a chart titled "Major Earthquakes." San Francisco was the only U.S. city listed. In 1906 a major earthquake had killed 700 people there.

Carla felt this was a good topic, but she still had to find enough information about it. The librarian showed her how to check the card catalog. Carla was able to find several books listed under **Earthquakes** and **San Francisco Earthquake.**

● Do you think that the San Francisco earthquake is a good topic? Why or why not?

Working It Through

A. All of the subjects below are too broad to be covered thoroughly in a short report. For each general subject, list 3 specific topics that you think would make interesting reports.

1. Animals
2. Space Travel
3. Inventions
4. Volcanoes

5. Weather
6. Sports
7. Electricity
8. Pollution

B. Read each numbered topic and the key words that follow. For each topic write the letters of the key words that you might use to look up information in an encyclopedia or a card catalog.

1. The Loch Ness Monster
   a. Loch Ness Monster
   b. monsters
   c. Bermuda Triangle
2. Facts About Comets and Meteorites
   a. comets
   b. facts
   c. meteorites

3. Mt. Vesuvius as a Volcano
   a. Mt. Everest
   b. volcanoes
   c. Mt. Vesuvius
4. How Clouds Are Formed
   a. clouds
   b. rainbows
   c. weather

C. Choose 2 of the numbered topics from Exercise B. Look up the key words in an encyclopedia and in the card catalog to see if there is enough information for a report on each topic. Make a list of the books you find for each topic.

Trying It Out

Using the guidelines given in Thinking It Through, choose your own topic for a short report.

1. Be sure to choose a topic that interests you. In the following lessons you will learn how to research your own topic, take notes, and prepare an outline.
2. Follow Carla's steps if you need help in narrowing down your topic and finding information.

Using an Encyclopedia Index

An encyclopedia index tells you which articles contain
information on your topic.

Thinking It Through
Carla looked up *San Francisco* and *San Francisco
earthquake* in the encyclopedia index and found the
information below.

index
heading → **San Francisco** [California] **S:86**
           with pictures and maps   volume
index ────── California **C:33** *with picture;*   page number
entry   (People) **C:40** *with picture*
subheading   Earthquake (table) **E:19**   reference to
         San Francisco earthquake [1906]   illustration
           California (Early Statehood)
             C:51
           San Francisco (Earthquake
             and Fire) **S:88**

Index headings are an alphabetical list of general
subjects found in the encyclopedia. Sometimes a heading is
also the name of a specific article. **Index entries** are
always titles of specific articles.

● What articles are listed under *San Francisco earthquake?*

Many articles are divided into sections. These are listed
as **subheadings** in parentheses after the entries.

● What is the subheading after each index entry for *San
Francisco earthquake?*

The letter of the **volume** and the **page number** on
which an article begins are usually listed after the
subheadings.

● What volume has information about California's early
statehood? On what page does the information begin?

References to illustrations show that an article has
pictures, maps, or diagrams.

● Which articles have pictures?

Working It Through

A. Use the index entries in Thinking It Through to answer the following questions.

1. What index entries are listed under *San Francisco?*
2. What volume has information about the people of California? On what page does the information begin?

B. Use these encyclopedia index entries about pyramids to answer the questions below.

Pyramids [architecture] **P:810**
    with pictures
    Architecture (Beginnings) **A:574**
      with picture
    Egypt, Ancient (The Arts) **E:96;**
      picture on **E:92**
    Mexico *picture on* **M:374**
    Seven Wonders of the World
      (The Pyramids of Egypt) **S:253;**
    picture on **S:254**
Pyramids, Age of the
    Egypt, Ancient (The Old
      Kingdom) **E:97**

1. How many index entries are listed under *Pyramids?* under *Age of the Pyramids?*
2. In which volume does the article *Pyramids* appear? On what page does it begin?
3. Which volume contains the article "Seven Wonders of the World"?
4. Which index entries contain subheadings?
5. Which articles contain pictures?

Trying It Out

1. Use an encyclopedia index to look up the topic you chose in Lesson 1.
2. Write down the name of each article listed under your topic, the volume in which the article appears, and the page number on which it begins.
3. Read each article and list important facts you discover about your topic.

Lesson 3 Using a Book Index

Use the index at the back of a book to find specific
information on your topic.

Thinking It Through

Carla found some information about the earthquake in the
encyclopedia. She also discovered that a fire had followed
the earthquake, destroying most of San Francisco.

To find more details, Carla used the books listed under
San Francisco earthquake in the card catalog. She found
this under *Fire* in the index at the back of one book:

entry — Fire, 35-141
subentry — damage, 142-143, 150-153
dynamiting, *see* Firebreaks — cross-reference
fighting the fire, 49, 65, 105-125
Ham-and-Eggs Fire, 39, 87, 125
Market Street, 35, 78, 99
cross- water supply, 37, 48, 65, 139
reference — *See also* Alarm system

Index **entries** are an alphabetical list of the important
subjects in a book. **Subentries,** which give specific
information about an entry, are listed under the entry.
- How many subentries are listed under *Fire?*

The numbers after each entry or subentry tell which
pages give information about the subject.
- Which pages describe the Ham-and-Eggs Fire?

A **cross-reference** tells you to look at another entry for
the information you need. Notice the subentry *dynamiting.*
The *see* cross-reference tells you to look up the entry
Firebreaks to find information about dynamiting. Now look
at the last subentry. The *see also* cross-reference tells you
to look at the entry *Alarm system* if you need more
information than that given in the subentries under *Fire.*

Working It Through

A. Use the index entry on page 138 to answer the questions.
1. What is the entry word?
2. What are the cross-references for *fire?*
3. What pages tell about the fire on Market Street? about fighting the fire?

B. Use these index entries from a book about volcanoes to answer the question below.

Volcanoes
    causes of, 2–5
    dormant, 26–29, 40
    extinct, 26
    location of, *see* Volcanic belts
    See also Lava
Volcanologists
    definition of, 50
    instruments, 49, 51, 53

1. How many subentries are listed under the entry *Volcanoes?* under *Volcanologists?*
2. Which page has an explanation of extinct volcanoes?
3. Which other entry has information telling where volcanoes occur?
4. If you needed more information than that given under *Volcanoes,* which other entry would you look at?
5. Which page would you check if you wanted to find the definition of a volcanologist?

Trying It Out

Carla learned about the fire that followed the San Francisco earthquake when she checked the encyclopedia. Look back at the facts you listed about your own topic when you looked it up in the encyclopedia.
1. Check these facts in the index of books on your topic.
2. Keep a list of the facts and the pages in each book that contain more detailed information.

Lesson 4 Taking Notes

When you research a topic, take notes so that you can remember important information you have read.

Thinking It Through

Carla used several books about earthquakes in her research. The following is an excerpt from a book she read about the San Francisco earthquake and fire.

Almost before the earthquake gave its last gasp, flames broke from the ruins. All over the city, snapped electric lines sent blue sizzles into rubble. Gas from broken pipes blazed. Sparks from heated chimneys and burning fuel ignited roofs or household furnishings. Kerosene from overturned lamps flared up.

Galloping horses soon pulled fire engines to spots of worst threat. Fires had to be reported by messenger, for all telephone lines were down. Firemen simply moved from one fire to the next.

The men of Engine 38 were the first to make a dreadful discovery. They raced to a fire in a lodging house near the harbor. They screwed a hose into a hydrant and turned on the water. There came a trickle of muddy moisture. And then—nothing! There was no water in the mains. The earthquake had broken the pipes that led from reservoirs outside the city. There was water in the bay, and it could be pumped to fires near the harbor. There was water in old cisterns, dug in the early days. There was even usable moisture in the sewers. But these emergency sources would be only feeble aid in quenching the fast-spreading flames. Already several big fires were out of control.

Carla knew that she would not be able to remember all the main points in the excerpt. Her teacher suggested that she write notes on index cards. She could refer to these cards later.

First Carla wrote the **name of the book,** the **author,** the **date of publication,** and the **pages** on which she found information. She also wrote the **topic** of the excerpt. Then she took notes in her own words.

Carla shortened each **main idea** to a phrase and numbered it. Below each main idea she listed the **supporting details** in phrases or short sentences.

Here are the notes that Carla took:

The San Francisco Earthquake and Fire — name of book
by Helen Markley Miller, 1970, pp. 17, 19-20 — pages
author   Fires Follow Earthquake
                     topic   date of publication

1. Causes of fires — main idea
   Snapped electric lines
   Gas from broken pipes
   Sparks from chimneys   supporting details
   Burning fuel
   Kerosene from lamps
2. Problems fighting fires
   Messengers reported fires since telephone lines
      were down.
   Firemen discovered that earthquake had broken
      water mains.
   Emergency sources included water in bay, water
      in cisterns, and moisture in sewers.
   Emergency sources were not enough.

- What is the topic of the excerpt? What are the main ideas that Carla found? What are the supporting details?

Working It Through

Read the excerpt below. Then do the activity that follows.

By 1:00 P.M., the downtown fires were on all sides of the Palace Hotel, and there was real worry among the employees now as they rushed here and there with firemen, soaking down rooms and flooding the roof in an effort to drown the blazes set by falling sparks. Most of the guests had been evacuated and the rest were leaving now. Everyone was choking and gagging in the smoke clogging every corridor and room. The water in the basement and roof cisterns was running low.

Out in the street, firemen and policemen and soldiers kept looking anxiously at the roof. For most of the time, what they were trying to see was hidden in smoke, but every once in a while they could see it—the hotel's flag flying from its slender mast. Somehow, in their minds, it had become linked with the building's survival; so long as it flew and was visible, if only now and again, the Palace was not yet engulfed in flames. From hilltops and slopes all over the area north of Market, thousands of eyes were strained for a glimpse of the flag.

Then there were hoarse cries running along New Montgomery out to Market. Fire was in the rear of the hotel. Now it was in the corridors, now in the rooms, now in the kitchens. The last of the firemen and employees dashed from the building. Above their heads, windows shattered and filthy black smoke poured out over Market and New Montgomery, followed almost instantly by swirling flames. The fire spread over the roof, and the smoke there grew black with burning tar paper. The firefighters fell back from a solid wall of heat.

It was just after three o'clock in the afternoon. For an instant, a cleft appeared in the mountains of smoke. There was a cry from everyone who happened to be looking at the roof at that moment. The flag was gone.

Look at the unorganized notes below. Decide which details belong with each numbered main idea. Then rewrite the notes, following the note form that Carla used. List the details in the order in which they are mentioned in the excerpt.

Disaster 1906 by Edward F. Dolan Jr., 1967, pp. 91-92

      The Palace Hotel Fire
1. Early fire in the hotel
2. People outside the hotel
3. Spreading fire inside hotel
    Fire spread over roof.
    Everyone looked for flag.
    Guests evacuated.
    Windows shattered.
    Smoke poured out over Market and New Montgomery.
    Water ran low.
    Smoke clogged corridors and rooms.
    Employees and firemen fought fires.
    Flag linked with building's survival.
    Flag gone.
    Firemen and employees ran out of burning hotel.
    Firefighters fell back.

Trying It Out

1. Use your books from Lesson 3 to research your topic.
2. Take notes on index cards. Follow the form Carla used.

Lesson 5 Organizing Notes

When you finish your research, arrange your notes in the order in which you want to present them.

Thinking It Through

Carla had filled several index cards by the time she was done with her research. Before she could work on her report, she had to arrange the notes in logical order.

As Carla read through the topics written on her note cards, she realized that the events could be presented in the order in which they happened. The earthquake hit first. Then the fire started and continued for three days. Carla put the topics in this order:

> Earthquake Hits City
> Fires Follow Earthquake
> General Funston Calls In Troops
> Mayor Schmitz Forms Committee of Safety
> Major Fires Merge and Spread
> Palace Hotel Burns
> Firefighters Halt Fire

Carla's notes were arranged by time. A report about a person's life might also be organized by time.
- What other kinds of information do you think could be organized according to time?

Arranging details by importance is another way to organize. Notes for a report titled "The Causes of Air Pollution" would start with the major causes and then go on to mention some less important causes.

Information can be arranged by problem and solution. Notes for "How to Solve the Energy Crisis" would start with an explanation of the energy crisis (the problem) and continue with ways to solve the problem.
- What other kinds of topics do you think could be organized by importance? by problem and solution?

Working It Through

A. Study the following list of topics from note cards on "The History of San Francisco." Then rearrange the topics in the order in which they happened.

United Nations Charter Drawn Up
 Here in 1945
Two Bridges Built During 1930s
Under American Rule After 1846

Part of Mexico During 1820s
Bay Area Rapid Transit System
 Opened in 1972
1906 Earthquake and Fire

B. The following is a list of some of Thomas Edison's inventions. Rearrange the list, beginning with what you think is the most important invention.

Improved the Telegraph
Invented Machinery to Make
 Better, Cheaper Cement
Invented the Electric Light
Improved the Typewriter
Improved the Telephone
Invented the Phonograph
Invented a Motion-Picture Machine

C. Read the following list of topics. For each topic, decide whether a report should be organized according to time, importance, or problem and solution.
   1. How to Stop Car Thefts
   2. How to Solve the World's Food Shortage
   3. The Biography of Helen Keller
   4. Ways to Use Atomic Energy Peacefully

Trying It Out

Read through your own notes, making a list of the topics you have written on the note cards.
   1. Decide on the order in which you want to present your topics.
   2. Arrange your note cards in the same order and number them for quick reference.

Making an Outline

Organize your notes in an outline to show important points.

Thinking It Through

After Carla had put her notes in order, she made this outline showing the important points in her report:

The San Francisco Earthquake ———— title

I. Earthquake hits ———— main topic
  A. Rumble turns to roar ———— subtopic
  B. Earth shudders and moves in waves
  C. Pipes break and utility lines snap
  D. Buildings collapse

II. Fires follow
  A. Fires start in downtown district
  B. Firefighters cannot control fires
    1. Alarm system destroyed ———— detail
    2. Pipes to water supply broken
  C. Fires merge and spread

III. City fights back
  A. Troops are called in
  B. Mayor forms Committee of Safety
  C. Citizens help fight fire
  D. Firefighters use dynamite
  E. Fire under control after three days

The **title** appears on the first line of the outline. The first word and each important word in the title begin with capital letters.

● What is the title of Carla's report?

Each **main topic** is numbered with a Roman numeral followed by a period.

● How many main topics does Carla's outline contain? What are they?

A **subtopic** is an important point that explains or tells something about a main topic. Subtopics are indented under the main topics they explain. They are lettered in alphabetical order with capital letters followed by periods.

- How many subtopics are listed under the main topic *City fights back?*
- How many subtopics are listed under the main topic *Earthquake hits?*
- How many subtopics are listed under the main topic *Fires follow?*

A **detail** is a point that explains or tells something about a subtopic. Details are indented under the subtopics they explain. They are numbered in order with Arabic numerals followed by periods.

- How many details are listed in the outline?
- What subtopic are they under?
- What main topic does this subtopic explain?

Notice that the main topics, subtopics, and details begin with capital letters but do not end with periods.

A. Read the outline below. Then answer the questions that follow.

Babe Ruth (1895–1948)

I. Childhood
    A. Became interested in baseball at school
    B. Was star pitcher and batter of his team

II. Early career
    A. Signed by Baltimore Orioles in 1914
    B. Became known as "The Babe"
    C. Sold to Boston Red Sox
        1. Pitched and won over 20 games a year
        2. Played outfield

III. Yankees player
    A. Joined Yankees in 1920
    B. Hit more than 50 homers in four different seasons
    C. Set a record in 1927, hitting 60 home runs in a 154-game season

IV. Later years
    A. Ended playing career with Boston Braves in 1935
    B. Elected to National Baseball Hall of Fame in 1936

1. What is the title of this outline?
2. How many main topics does the outline have? What are the main topics?
3. How are the main topics numbered?
4. How many subtopics does the outline have?
5. How are subtopics indicated?
6. Which subtopic has additional details? What are they?
7. How are the details indicated?

B. Rewrite the following outline, using the correct form. Use Roman numerals, capital letters, numbers, and punctuation marks correctly.

the buried city of Pompeii

city built at foot of Mt. Vesuvius
   volcano in A.D. 63 damaged city
   people made repairs

Vesuvius erupted again in A.D. 79
   stones, ashes, and cinders fell
   air filled with poisonous gas
   city buried under stone and ash

Pompeii buried for about 1,700 years
   soil formed over stone and ash
   weeds and plants grew in soil

remains of city discovered in 1700s
   farmer found wall buried in field
   workers excavated city
   city preserved by stone and ash
      remains of 2,000 victims
      houses
      public square
      temples

Trying It Out
Make an outline from your notes.

1. Show important points as topics and subtopics.
2. Include some additional details.

Take Another Look Did you use Roman numerals, capital letters, numbers, and punctuation marks correctly?

A. Read the following outline of a report on plants. Then answer the questions that follow it.

Plants
  I. Plants that can make their own food
      A. Plants that have seeds
          1. Plants with cones that contain seeds
          2. Plants with flowers that make seeds
      B. Plants that do not have seeds
 II. Plants that cannot make their own food
      A. Bacteria
      B. Molds
III. Plants that are partners
      A. Lichens, plants with two partners
          1. Food-making algae
          2. Helpful fungi
      B. Peas and bacteria, plant partners
          1. Bacteria, nitrogen suppliers
          2. Peas, food makers

1. What is the title of the outline?
2. What are the main topics? How are they indicated?
3. What are the subtopics under the first main topic?
4. How are the subtopics indicated?
5. What are the details under the subtopic *Plants that have seeds?* How are details indicated?

B. Make an outline for a report about whales, or some other topic you are interested in and know something about.

C. Reread the outline you made.
  1. Did you use a title? main topics? subtopics? details?
  2. Did you number or letter the parts correctly?

Evaluation • Outlines

A. Rewrite the following outline, using the correct form. Use Roman numerals, capital letters, numbers, and punctuation marks correctly.

1. The outline should have a title.
2. There should be main topics and subtopics.
3. Some of the subtopics should have details under them.
4. The parts of the outline should be numbered or lettered correctly.

homes of beavers
    built of mud and branches in ponds
    excavated in banks

food of beavers
    leaves, twigs, bark, roots of trees and shrubs
    roots, tender sprouts of water lilies

young of beavers
    born in April or May
        covered with fur at birth
        eyes open at birth
    two to four in litter
    live with parents about two years

B. Make an outline for a report on some country you are interested in. Include some of the following topics:
location
official language or languages
important cities
chief products—agricultural and manufactured
sports
scenic areas

Your outline will be evaluated on the following:
    correct use of parts of an outline
    correct numbering or lettering of parts

Spotlight • Western Words

Pioneers heading west over the *prairie* . . .
A *roundup* of *mustangs* into the *corral* . . .
Steaming plates of *johnnycakes* and *succotash* . . .

These scenes and some of the words used to describe them are uniquely American. When early settlers and explorers came here they found a new life—new peoples, new foods, new plants, and new animals. They needed words to tell about these new things. So they made up their own words or borrowed from other languages, especially Spanish, French, and Native American languages.

Certain words came about as shortened forms from Native American words. *Squash* (from Narragansett Indian *askutasquash*) and *hickory* (from Algonquian language *pawcohiccora*) are two such words.

Some new words were made by combining two other words. Here are a few examples: *applesauce*, *pancake*, *cowboy*, *bullfrog*, *clambake*, and *cornstalk*. Can you think of others?

One unpleasant surprise in the New World was the *rattlesnake*. Do you know why that compound was chosen for the snake? A special kind of rattlesnake is the *sidewinder*. That name is another American creation. How do you think the sidewinder got its name?

Some colorful phrases have come from the American cowboy. One such cowboy, admitting he liked to talk, said he never was ''hog-tied when it comes to makin' chin music.'' Another cowboy described a person as being ''hungrier 'n a woodpecker with a headache.''

Spotlight · Synonyms

One of the great advantages of the English language is its variety. If you try hard enough, you can often think of half a dozen different ways to say the same thing.

Synonyms make this possible. As an example, *half a dozen* is a synonym for *six*. Synonyms are words that mean the same thing—generally. If you study a group of synonyms, you will find slight differences in meaning that make it important to choose carefully when you wish to get a particular idea across to your reader or listener.

Imagine that you were a newspaper correspondent at the scene of the San Francisco Earthquake and Fire. In order to keep your reports from repeating the same phrase, you would probably use some synonyms to refer to the event.

Study the explanations of the synonyms below. Then write a brief news dispatch, using several of these synonyms for *misfortune* and *fire*.

blaze   A *blaze* is an intense fire but not as intense as a *conflagration*. It puts out bright light and heat and may or may not be destructive.

calamity   A *calamity* is similar to a *catastrophe* but is not always so severe. It can describe public misfortunes but more often refers to bad fortune for a person or family.

catastrophe   A *catastrophe* is a misfortune that usually results in heavy casualties. It may be personal or public.

conflagration   A *conflagration* is an intense and rapid fire that causes widespread destruction. Usually, a *conflagration* is a fire that started accidentally or from natural causes.

disaster   A *disaster* is a terrible misfortune that hits suddenly and unexpectedly.

holocaust   A *holocaust* means great or wholesale destruction, especially by fire, and usually signals that lives were lost.

inferno   An *inferno* is a very intense fire, usually one which causes human suffering, but may result in escape rather than loss of life.

Lesson 7   Adjectives

Adjectives modify nouns by telling which one, what kind, or how many.

Thinking It Through

A **modifier** is a word that adds to or changes the meaning of another word. **Adjectives** are modifiers.

Notice the adjectives underlined in these sentences:

Are you going to wear <u>this</u> shirt with <u>those</u> jeans?
A <u>heavy</u> fog blurred the <u>full</u> moon.
<u>Several</u> chapters were written by <u>two</u> authors.

The adjectives in the first sentence tell *which one.* The adjective *this* modifies the noun *shirt,* and *those* modifies *jeans.* The adjectives *heavy* and *full* tell *what kind.*

- What noun does *heavy* modify?
- What noun does *full* modify?
- Which adjectives tell *how many?* What nouns do they modify?

The adjectives *this, that, these,* and *those* sometimes cause problems. Do not say or write *this here* or *that there. This* and its plural form *these* already point out something "right here." *That* and its plural form *those* already point out something "over there."

Working It Through

A. Add at least 1 adjective to the underlined word in each sentence below. The words after each sentence will help you.

1. <u>Socks</u> will keep you warm while skating.   (which ones)
2. Afterwards, you can sit by the <u>fire</u>.   (what kind)
3. I'll make you a cup of <u>chocolate</u>.   (what kind)
4. Mom wants to tell you a <u>story</u> about the first time she went skating.   (what kind)
5. It was <u>years</u> ago.   (how many)

6. It was a <u>day</u> in November.   (what kind)
7. "Don't skate on <u>ice</u>," a friend warned.   (which one)
8. But Mom didn't listen to his <u>advice.</u>   (what kind)
9. She put on her <u>skates.</u>   (what kind)
10. Then she skimmed over the <u>lake.</u>   (what kind)
11. She suddenly found herself in <u>feet</u> of water.   (how many)
12. Luckily, the fire department quickly got her out of the <u>water.</u>   (what kind)

B. Rewrite the following conversation, using *this*, *that*, *these*, and *those* in the blanks.

"How did (1) _____ shirt fit, sir?"

"(2) _____ shirt fit better than (3) _____ green one," Ralph replied. "But I'd like to try on one of (4) _____ blue ones."

"(5) _____ shirts, sir?" asked the sales clerk.

"No," Ralph said. "(6) _____ corduroy shirts there."

C. Read the following sentences. Then divide a sheet of paper into two columns. Write the adjective in each sentence in the first column and the noun it modifies in the second.

1. Watch out for that turn ahead!
2. Does this road go to Dallas?
3. I ate five apples at the picnic.
4. Do you like purple curtains?
5. Those flowers are magnolias.
6. Some people need wheelchairs.
7. Have you seen these pictures?
8. The loud thunder frightened me.

Trying It Out

Write a paragraph to describe one of the 3 pairs of topics below. Use adjectives that tell which one, what kind, and how many.

1. the clothes you are wearing now and the clothes in your closet at home
2. the classmate sitting beside you and the classmate on the other side of the room
3. the field trip you took to a factory or newspaper and a field trip you took to a museum

Using Adjectives to Compare

Almost all adjectives have a positive, comparative, and superlative form.

Thinking It Through

The first or basic form of an adjective is called the **positive.** The second form is called the **comparative.** It is used to compare two people or things. The third form, the **superlative,** is used to compare more than two people or things.

Positive	Comparative	Superlative
large	larger	largest
lovely	lovelier	loveliest
lovely	more lovely	most lovely
delicious	more delicious	most delicious

- What ending is added to *large* to form the comparative? the superlative?
- What word is added to *delicious* to form the comparative? the superlative?

To form the comparative, add the ending *-er* to the positive form or use the word *more*. To form the superlative, add the ending *-est* to the positive or use the word *most*.

When you are comparing people or things, do not use both the *-er* ending and the word *more*. Do not use both the *-est* ending and the word *most*. For example, do not say or write *more lovelier* or *most largest*.

Working It Through

A. Copy the following chart, filling in the correct forms of the adjectives. Then write a sentence using one of the forms from each word group. You should write 10 sentences.

Positive	Comparative	Superlative
1. wise		
2.		most frightened
3.	stormier	
4. different		
5.	fewer	
6.		most peaceful
7. tiny		
8.	more wonderful	
9.		funniest
10. exciting		

B. Rewrite the following paragraphs, using the correct form of each adjective in parentheses.

Whales and people are both mammals, but they are different in several ways. The bones of whales are (1. spongy) than the bones of people, and their jaws are (2. weak).

Whales' lungs are (3. large) and (4. powerful) than those of people. Whales can go for (5. long) periods without breathing—up to forty minutes or so.

Because whales have highly developed brains, they are among the (6. intelligent) of all animals. The blue whale is thought to be the (7. large) animal to have ever lived, growing to some 30 meters long. Other kinds of whales are much (8. small). The (9. small) of all whales only grows to about five meters in length.

Trying It Out

1. Write a sentence to compare each of the following: 2 hobbies, 2 sports, 2 books, 2 comedians, 2 buildings.

2. Choose one of the topics below. Write one paragraph that compares the items suggested.

   a. the 4 seasons

   b. your favorite 3 holidays

   c. your favorite 3 vacations

Using Irregular Adjectives to Compare

The comparative and superlative forms of some adjectives are formed in irregular ways.

Thinking It Through

Most adjectives are regular. They change form according to the rules explained in Lesson 8.

The comparative and superlative of some adjectives do not follow the usual rules.

Positive	Comparative	Superlative
good	better	best
bad	worse	worst
much	more	most
little	less	least
far	farther	farthest

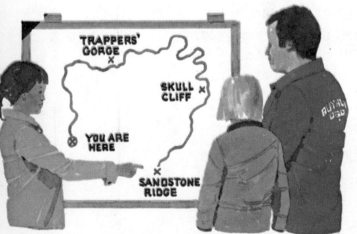

Do not add *-er* or *-est* to these words or use the words *more* or *most* with them. For example, do not say or write *worser, leastest, more better,* or *most worst.*

Working It Through

A. Look at the picture at the left to determine which form of *far* to use in the blanks in the following conversation.

"Trappers' Gorge is ____ all right!" Cassie said. "But Skull Cliff is ____."

"Let's try for the ____ point, Sandstone Ridge," Luisa suggested.

B. Rewrite the sentences on the following page. For each sentence choose the correct adjective in parentheses.

1. Pete's Place is too (far, farther) to drive to.
2. It's (far, farther) than Mama's Pizzeria.
3. Besides, her pizza tastes (better, best) than Pete's.
4. Two helpings are (much, more) than I can eat!
5. Is that a (good, best) salad?
6. The (better, best) salad of all was the spinach.
7. Lois ate very (little, less) pizza.
8. In fact, she ate (less, least) pizza than I did.

C. Rewrite the following sentences, supplying the correct form of the adjective at the end of each sentence.
1. It was a _____ day for hiking.   (bad)
2. By noon, the weather was _____ than before.   (bad)
3. The National Weather Service called it the _____ snowstorm in fifteen years.   (bad)
4. Shoveling the snow is too _____ work.   (much)
5. The _____ amount of money I ever earned was $2.00 for clearing the snow from a driveway.   (little)
6. The _____ snow that ever fell here in an hour was six centimeters.   (much)

D. Rewrite these sentences, using the correct comparative and superlative forms of the adjectives.
1. *Grog* was the worsest movie I ever saw.
2. It was worser than *Moth Man*.
3. Is that glass the biggest of the two?
4. Betsy's bike goes the most fastest of all.
5. The littler you exercise, the more worse you'll feel.
6. The fartherer you jog, the more better it is for you.
7. Do you think she is the more better singer?
8. That was the most ugliest costume I ever saw!

Trying It Out

Imagine that you and one of your parents are at a bike shop and that a sales clerk is showing you various models. Write a conversation that might occur. Try to use as many forms of these adjectives as you can: *good, little, comfortable, safe, fast,* and *durable.*

159

Lesson 10 Using Phrases to Describe

Prepositional phrases can modify nouns.

Thinking It Through
Match these two sentences with a picture at the left.

> The trees by the small lake are birches.
> The trees around that house are birches.

● Which group of words in each sentence helped you pick the correct picture?

The word groups *by the small lake* and *around that house* are **prepositional phrases.** A prepositional phrase begins with a preposition, such as *by*, *around*, or *with*, and ends with a noun or pronoun. There may also be modifiers and noun markers between the preposition and the noun.
● What are the prepositions in the two phrases above?
● What noun does each prepositional phrase end with?
● What modifiers and noun markers are in each phrase?

Prepositional phrases act as adjectives when they modify nouns by telling something about the nouns.

Look at the following sentences. The prepositional phrase in each is underlined once and the noun it modifies is underlined twice.

> The <u>water</u> <u>in that lake</u> is very polluted.
> <u>Trees</u> <u>with white bark</u> are birches.

Notice that in the first sentence, the prepositional phrase tells *which* water: the water *in that lake*.
● What does the prepositional phrase in the second sentence tell?

Besides *by*, *around*, *with*, and *in*, other commonly used prepositions include these: *above*, *at*, *between*, *for*, *from*, *near*, *of*, *on*, *over*, *through*, *to*, *up*.

Working It Through

A. Write the following sentences, underlining each prepositional phrase once and the noun each modifies twice. You should find 13 phrases.

1. Some trees in California are the largest trees in the world.
2. The oldest tree in the United States is 3,500 years old.
3. A redwood may reach a height of 110 meters.
4. Some cactuses are really trees with spines.
5. An apple tree at full growth can absorb 360 liters of water each day.
6. Leaves use energy from the sun.
7. Certain vessels in a tree carry water.
8. Minerals in the soil are important too.
9. Five percent of a tree's weight is minerals.
10. Trees with very thick bark can withstand the heat of severe forest fires.

B. Rewrite each sentence below 3 times, using a different preposition in the blanks each time. Be ready to explain the changes in meaning that result.

1. The plants ____ the house are mums.
2. The path ____ the canyon was rocky and narrow.
3. Both signs ____ the bridge were unreadable.

Trying It Out

Rewrite the following paragraph, adding prepositional phrases to modify the 8 underlined nouns.

The boy took his dog for a walk. It was a cold day. Napoleon wasn't the bravest dog. Erik had a difficult time getting him past the first snowdrift. Napoleon tugged and pulled at the chain. Erik didn't know what to do. Suddenly, Napoleon spied a rabbit. He chased it over the snow. Napoleon reached it just as it darted down its hole. Well, thought Erik, if I only had a rabbit every time I take old Napoleon for a walk!

161

Combining Sentences

You can sometimes combine two sentences by using a prepositional phrase.

Thinking It Through

Read the pair of sentences below. Notice how the idea in the second sentence is used in the third sentence.

That boy goes to my school.
He is wearing a green hat.

> That boy <u>with the green hat</u> goes to my school.

The underlined group of words in the third sentence is a prepositional phrase. The idea of the second sentence was made into a prepositional phrase modifying *boy*.

Now look at these sentences:

She is wearing a jacket.
The jacket has a plaid pattern.

> She is wearing a jacket with a plaid pattern.

- What is the prepositional phrase in the third sentence?
- What noun does it modify?

Read this pair of sentences:

Ben enjoys looking at the stars.
He uses his new telescope.

- Which sentence can be more easily made into a prepositional phrase?
- Use a prepositional phrase to make the idea of the second sentence part of the first sentence.

Sentences with prepositional phrases that describe the same person or thing can also often be combined:

A woman in a print dress is speaking.
A woman in a red scarf is speaking.

> A woman in a print dress and red scarf is speaking.

Notice that when both phrases begin with the same preposition, you do not need to repeat the preposition.

Working It Through

A. Combine the prepositional phrase in the second sentence of each pair with the prepositional phrase in the first.

1. The conservation of oil is important. The conservation of coal is important.
2. The strings on these guitars are steel. The strings on these banjos are steel.
3. The light on the singer is blue. The light on the drummer is blue.
4. Some roads to Spokane are under construction. Some roads to Walla Walla are under construction.
5. The bridges over the river need repairs. The bridges over the freight yard need repairs.

B. Use a prepositional phrase to put the idea of the second sentence in each pair into the first sentence.

Example: My boots are black.   My boots are black with silver
               They have silver buckles.   buckles.

1. The restaurant opened last week. It has singing waiters.
2. That boy is my brother. He is wearing sneakers.
3. My sister likes meat loaf. She likes gravy on it.
4. We went to the beach. It was our vacation.
5. They walked fifteen kilometers. The weather was extremely cold.
6. Wash that window! Use this bucket of water.
7. I like to read newspapers. They must have lots of sports coverage.

Trying It Out

1. Choose 5 famous people that you would like to describe or tell about in some way.
2. Write 2 sentences about each, using a separate sheet of paper for each person. Write sentences that can be combined by using prepositional phrases.
3. Give the pairs of sentences to a classmate. Ask him or her to combine the sentences by putting one of the ideas into a prepositional phrase.

Proper Adjectives

Adjectives formed from proper nouns are proper adjectives.
Proper adjectives are always capitalized.

Thinking It Through

A noun that names a particular person, place, or thing is a
proper noun. An adjective formed from a proper noun is
called a **proper adjective.**

Proper Noun	Proper Adjective
North America	North American
China	Chinese
Hawaii	Hawaiian
Europe	European

Look at these phrases:

African continent	Chinese restaurant
Hawaiian pineapple	European rivers

- What is the proper adjective in each phrase?
- What noun does each adjective modify?

Proper nouns can also be used as adjectives.

Proper Nouns	Proper Nouns as Adjectives
Memorial Day	Memorial Day picnic
the White House	the White House lawn
California	California coastline

- What is the proper noun used as an adjective in each
  phrase?
- What noun does each modify?

Proper adjectives and proper nouns used as adjectives are
always capitalized. Notice that common nouns, such as
picnic and *lawn*, modified by proper nouns are not
capitalized.

Working It Through

A. Rewrite the following sentences, capitalizing the proper adjectives, the proper nouns, and the proper nouns used as adjectives. You will need to add 15 capital letters

1. For lunch, laurie ate texas chili and polish sausage.
2. In honolulu, the smiths went to a hawaiian folk dance.
3. What are the three colors of the french flag?
4. My english friend showed us slides of the irish countryside.
5. Our friday music class went to see a german opera.
6. Last february, chris sent fifty valentine's day cards.

B. Write a sentence using each of the following. Be sure to capitalize all proper adjectives and proper nouns used as adjectives. Underline the noun each modifies.

1. american flag
2. cuban food
3. shetland pony
4. idaho potatoes
5. asiatic bears
6. israeli music
7. canadian football
8. australian accent

C. Write the proper adjectives formed from the following proper nouns.

1. Italy
2. Greece
3. Sweden
4. Egypt
5. Mexico
6. Vietnam
7. Poland
8. Puerto Rico

Trying It Out

1. Write a story about a field trip to the zoo. Use as many of the items below as you can, adding the names of other animals if you wish. Consult an encyclopedia to find out more about particular animals.
2. Be sure to capitalize all proper adjectives, proper nouns, and proper nouns used as adjectives.

african and indian elephants
siamese cats
central american bats

safari restaurant
virginia deer
north american porcupine

Take Another Look   Are the details in your story arranged in a sensible order? Did you use words such as *first, next,* and *then* to guide your readers?

Review • Adjectives

A. Complete each sentence with the correct comparative or superlative form of the adjective in parentheses.
1. This is the ____ of the two coats.   (expensive)
2. This tree has the ____ diameter of all.   (great)
3. This is the ____ of the three dogs.   (small)
4. Our garden has ____ weeds than yours.   (much)
5. Of the two streets, this one is the ____.   (bad)
6. Elena hiked the ____ of anyone.   (far)

B. Write the following sentences. Underline the prepositional phrase that acts as an adjective in each. Then circle the noun the phrase modifies.
1. The shadows on the snow look blue.
2. The Hawaiian chief wore a cape of feathers.
3. The detective studied the ground under the window.
4. This is a book about animal tracks.
5. The ice on the lake was thicker last week.
6. We reached the narrow ledge between two rocks.
7. The path through the woods will take you there.

C. Rewrite the following sentences, capitalizing all proper adjectives.
1. The chinese people welcomed the visitors.
2. The fourth of july celebration was noisy.
3. We enjoyed driving through the english countryside.
4. The mexican craftsmen created beautiful things.
5. She met the south american journalist.

For extra practice turn to page 368.

Take Another Look   Complete the sentence with the verb in the verb form indicated in parentheses.

Shigeo ____ camping with his dad.   (go, past participle)
Did you use *has gone*?
For more practice turn to pages 344–345 in the Handbook.

Evaluation • Adjectives

A. Some of the following sentences contain errors. Write the number of each sentence in which an error appears.

1. Nick is happier today than he was yesterday.
2. This is the worse thing that ever happened to me.
3. This here is the best cake I've ever tasted.
4. Of the two animals, the snow leopard is the wildest.
5. She is the most patient person I know.
6. Tina's picture is the better of the three.
7. Jo is more healthier than her brother.
8. Today his cold is worse than mine.
9. You have given her the best surprise of all.
10. Of the two trails, I like this one best.
11. Our cat is the smartest pet we've ever had
12. Which of those two rock walls is the steepest?

B. For each sentence, write the letter of the underlined part that acts as an adjective.

1. The boy with the dog is Hugo.
      a   b   c
2. Chiang is a member of our club.
     a   b   c
3. The boy in rags became rich.
     a   b   c
4. The hut by the lake is ours.
     a   b   c
5. The men of the East were wise.
     a   b   c
6. Our trip to Alaska was a thrill.
     a   b   c
7. Salmon in the river swim fast.
         a   b c
8. Celia is a painter of scenery.
     a   b   c

C. For each sentence, write the letter of the underlined part that is a proper adjective.

1. In Hilo we had Hawaiian food.
      a   b   c
2. The Irish parade was fun.
      a   b   c
3. Egyptian farms are small.
     a   b   c
4. We saw fish in Alaskan rivers.
     a   b   c
5. Chinese tourists came to Iowa.
     a   b   c
6. We like Mexican food.
     a   b   c

Spotlight • Activities to Choose

1. Play a comparison game. This is a game for 4 to 6 players. First, make a set of word cards for each of the following adjectives: *huge, fierce, small, beautiful, mysterious, swift, strange.* Show the positive, comparative, and superlative forms of each. Then make a set of cards naming the following categories: *Animals, Famous People, Storybook Characters, Machines.* Put the adjective cards in one bag and the category cards in another. The first player pulls one card from each set. He or she must use each form of the adjective to compare 3 people, animals, or things that fit the category For example, if a player pulls the cards *small* and *Animals*, he or she could compare a puppy, a frog, and a mouse. Each comparison must be stated in a sentence. Players get 5 points for each correct comparison. The game continues until all players have 4 turns. The player with the most points wins.

2. Make a poster. Use what you learned about preparing a report to make a poster that will help others. You might list steps to follow or use drawings to illustrate the steps. Display your poster in your classroom or school library.

3. Tell about good and bad times. Imagine the best and worst experiences you could possibly have. Then write a set of 3 sentences to describe each. Use *good, better,* and *best* in one set of sentences, and *bad, worse,* and *worst* in the other. Get together with others who do this activity and share your sentences.

4. Produce a class news broadcast. Work with a group of your classmates to do this activity. Select 3 or 4 topics to report about. Choose ones you feel will be of special interest to the class. Gather the information and then take notes that will help you make oral reports about the topics. Make up your own format for your broadcast or use one like that of an actual radio or TV news show. Plan for a show that lasts no more than 25 minutes.

168

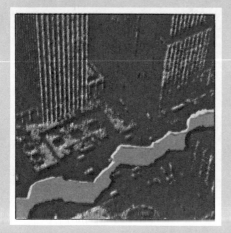

Why the Earth Quakes
by Julian May

Just what causes an earthquake? You'll find out in this clearly written book with outstanding drawings. Earthquakes, once thought to be caused by the earth's shrinkage, are now believed to be the result of liquid currents near the earth's core.

The Shadow of Vesuvius
by Eilis Dillon

Timon, a young Greek slave, escapes from the city of Pompeii as the volcano Vesuvius erupts. Timon's exciting adventures are a part of this book that also gives a good deal of historical background.

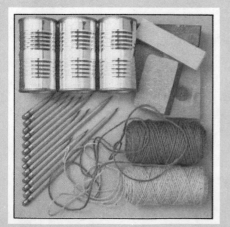

Games and Puzzles You Can Make Yourself
by Harvey Weiss

This book describes games and puzzles you can make from easy-to-find materials such as pencils, string, empty tin cans, and scraps of wood. The instructions are simple and can be changed easily to suit your own ideas.

Unit Six

Would you know what this "broad mouth" was if the poem had no title? Why do you think some of the words are arranged in a jumble?

Letterslot

Once each day this broad mouth spews

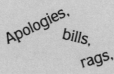

Apologies,
bills,
rags,
and news.

John Updike

Those who thought the telephone would completely replace the letter as a way of communication were wrong. We still depend on letters to express thanks and apologies and to send news. Whether you are writing a business or a friendly letter, you should express your ideas clearly. You must also pay attention to details such as spelling, grammar, and punctuation. This unit will help you write a better letter.

Lesson 1   **Listening for Opinions**

When you take part in a discussion, listen for the opinions that others express.

Thinking It Through

When you tell what you think or feel about something, you are giving an opinion. Different people often have different opinions about the same subject. One way to share opinions is by taking part in a discussion.

Here are some guidelines to help you listen for opinions during a discussion:

1. Be sure you understand what the discussion topic is.
2. Pay close attention to the discussion.
3. Try to identify each speaker's opinion.
4. Pick out the reasons given to support each speaker's opinion.
5. Compare each opinion to other opinions that have been given.
6. Think about whether you agree or disagree with each opinion given.

- What problems might you have if you let your mind wander?
- Why do you think it is important to identify each opinion and the reasons given to support it?
- How can taking part in a discussion help you form your own opinion?

Working It Through

A. The discussion on the next page is about a new shopping center that may be built on park land. Read the discussion carefully. Note each speaker's opinion and the reason that supports the opinion. Then copy and complete the chart.

172

"I think the shopping center is a great idea!"
exclaimed Nancy. "Our town is growing so quickly
that we need more stores."

"I agree," said Ted. "If we had a shopping center
here in town, we wouldn't have to go so far to shop."

"My dad says that we'd also be giving more business
to local store owners," added Ernesto.

"We can't give up our park, though," Kathy argued.
"We'll never get tennis courts or a swimming pool if
the park is taken away."

"Not only that, but we won't have any place to
fish," Frank reminded them.

"Maybe the town council could consider another spot
for the shopping center," suggested Sue Lee. "Then we
could have both the shopping center and the park."

	OPINIONS	REASONS
1. Nancy		
2. Ted		
3. Ernesto		
4. Kathy		
5. Frank		
6. Sue Lee		

B. Choose 1 of the following topics. Write your opinion
about the topic and support your opinion with reasons.

1. Our school is the best in town.
2. Winter is the nicest season of the year.
3. A tropical fish aquarium is a good project for a science fair.
4. Swimming is the best sport.

Trying It Out

Find 3 or 4 classmates who chose the same topic you did in
Exercise B.

1. Have a discussion about the topic.
2. Use the guidelines in Thinking It Through to listen for
   opinions and reasons.
3. As a group, produce a chart similar to the one in
   Exercise A.

Speaking to Persuade

When you give a speech to persuade others of something, state your opinion clearly and support it with reasons.

Thinking It Through

One way to express your opinion is by taking part in a discussion. Another way is by giving a short speech in which you try to persuade others to agree with your opinion. When you give this type of speech, try to give several good reasons to support your opinion.

Use the following guidelines when you are speaking to persuade:

1. Speak clearly.
2. Look at the audience.
3. Stick to the topic.
4. State your opinion briefly and clearly.
5. Give reasons and details to support your opinion.

- Why do you think it is important to speak clearly and to stick to the topic?
- Do you think that giving several good reasons for your opinion will help persuade the audience? Why or why not?

Working It Through

A. The following short speeches present two students' opinions on this topic: "Which kind of animal makes a better pet—a cat or a dog?"

As you read each speech, notice the sentence that gives the speaker's opinion. Try to pick out the reasons given to support the opinion. Then answer the questions that follow.

Toni's Speech

I feel that cats make better pets than dogs. Cats are very independent, so they're easy to care for. You don't have to give them baths or take them out for walks. Cats don't bite, and they don't bark at people. If they dislike someone, they simply walk away and find a place to nap until that person leaves.

Andy's Speech

I think dogs make better pets. They like to be around people, and they are very good companions. Dogs run to you when you call them, and they'll follow you anywhere. They're not snooty and independent as cats are. Dogs are loyal. They warn you of danger by barking loudly at noises or strangers.

1. What is Toni's opinion about the better pet? List the main reasons she gives to support her opinion.
2. What is Andy's opinion about the better pet? List the main reasons he gives to support his opinion.

B. Choose 1 of the topics listed below. Prepare a short speech in which you try to persuade the class to agree with your opinion about the topic.

1. the best holiday
2. the most interesting hobby
3. the nicest present
4. the most interesting book
5. the nicest restaurant in town
6. the best baseball team

Trying It Out

Work with a partner on this activity.

1. Choose a topic about which you and your partner have different opinions.
2. Each of you prepare a speech to persuade the class to agree with your opinion.
3. Support your opinion with reasons and details.
4. Use the guidelines given in Thinking It Through.

Writing a Letter to the Editor

When you write a letter to the editor, explain what you are reacting to. Give your opinion and support it with reasons.

Thinking It Through

People write to the editor of a newspaper or magazine as a way of reacting to a certain news event, a question, or a problem that affects the community. Students write letters to their school newspaper to express opinions about things that affect their school life.

The following is an example of a letter to the editor.

To the Editor:

On cold winter days it makes sense to have recess in the gym, but we should be able to choose the games we want to play. Right now we can play basketball on Monday, Wednesday, and Friday. On Tuesday and Thursday we have a choice of shuffleboard or Ping-Pong. If we don't want to play these games, we have one small corner of the gym to play in. There isn't enough space to have different games, so we end up walking or running into each other's games.

The gym is big enough to have several games going on at once. Why can't we have more choices of games? If this won't work, why not try sectioning off a larger area for pupils who don't want to play the assigned games? Then we will have plenty of room to organize different games.

Jeremy Clausson

Grade 6

- What problem is this writer reacting to?
- What is the writer's opinion?
- What reasons and facts does the writer give to support this opinion?
- How does the writer identify himself?

Working It Through

A. Include the following information in a letter to the editor. Follow the form used in the example.

1. The event you are reacting to:
   Yesterday after school a car almost hit your bike at the corner of Lawson and State.
2. Your opinion: A stoplight is needed at this corner.
3. Supporting facts and reasons:
   Heavy traffic makes it hard to turn at this corner. A curve up the road blocks the view. Other accidents have already occurred here. You are afraid someone may be seriously hurt soon.
4. Identification: Sign your name and write the grade you are in.

B. Write a letter to the editor in which you give an opinion about one of the following topics. Tell whether you agree or disagree with the statement. Support your opinion with facts and reasons.

1. Recess should be five minutes longer.
2. Your school should buy some new gym equipment.
3. Students should go to school all year around.
4. Your class shouldn't have to share textbooks with other classes.
5. School should start one-half hour later.

Trying It Out

Work with a partner to do this activity.

1. Choose a situation, event, or topic about which you have an opinion.
2. Write down the specific topic, your opinion, and any supporting facts and reasons.
3. Write a letter to the editor with your partner.

177

Lesson 4 Writing a Thank-You Note

When you write a thank-you note, you express gratitude for a gift or favor.

Thinking It Through

Writing a thank-you note is another way to express an opinion. A thank-you note shows appreciation for something that another person has done for you or for a gift you have received. You should try to write a thank-you note as soon as possible after receiving a gift.

Sometimes you may not really like the gift, or you may already have the same thing. In order to avoid being rude in such a situation, simply thank the person for his or her thoughtfulness.

The following is an example of a thank-you note.

heading

1729 Hillcrest Drive
Ralston, Wisconsin 53594
October 7, 19——

greeting —

Dear Grandmother,

body —

Thank you for the wonderful birthday party you gave me last Saturday. Mom, Dad, and even little Billy managed to keep your secret. I really was surprised to see my best friends and all the family when I walked into your living room! I appreciate all the planning and hard work that you did. It was a party—and a birthday—that I will never forget.

Love, —— closing

signature Jonathan

178

- What part of the letter shows the date on which the thank-you note was written?
- What words in the heading are capitalized? Where are commas used in the heading?
- What words in the greeting are capitalized? What follows the last word?
- What is Jonathan's opinion of the party?
- What is the closing? What type of punctuation follows the closing?

Working It Through

A. Use the following information to write a thank-you note. Make up specific details to add to the note. Be sure to follow the form for a thank-you note given in the example.

> **heading:** street
> city, state, Zip Code
> date
>
> **greeting:** Dear ____,
>
> **body:** Thank you for the ____ you gave me for ____.
>
> **closing:** Your friend,
>
> **signature:** Use your own name.

B. Write a thank-you note to a friend or a relative for one of the things listed below.

1. a record album by your favorite group
2. a sweater
3. a favor done for you
4. a book that you have been wanting to read

Trying It Out

Suppose that one of the following people visited your class on a day when you were discussing careers. Write a thank-you note to the person for giving a talk and for answering the class's questions.

1. a firefighter
2. an airline pilot
3. an architect
4. a ballet dancer
5. a nurse
6. a photographer
7. a newscaster
8. a violinist

Writing a Friendly Letter

When you write a friendly letter, you share opinions and experiences with friends who live far away.

Thinking It Through

Writing letters is one way to keep in touch with friends or relatives who live far away. In friendly letters you can share opinions, plans, and news about yourself.

Remember these guidelines as you write friendly letters:

1. Write as if you were talking to your friend.
2. Write about topics that will interest your friend.
3. Tell your friend about things that have happened lately.
4. Ask about your friend's interests and activities.

If you are answering a letter, use these guidelines too:

5. Respond to any questions your friend has asked.
6. Comment on activities or news your friend has mentioned.

Read the friendly letter on the next page.

- How many parts are there to a friendly letter? What are they?
- Which words are capitalized in the heading? greeting? closing?
- Where are commas used in the heading? greeting? closing?
- Which sentences show that Tina is answering a letter from Claire?
- How has Tina used the guidelines in writing her letter?

Now look at the envelope.

- Which address belongs to the sender of the letter?
- Which address belongs to the receiver of the letter?

675 Millbrook Road
St. Louis, Missouri 63178
October 10, 19—

Dear Claire,

Thank you for your letter. I especially enjoyed the story about your escaped hamster. Did you really find it gnawing a hole through the kitchen wall?

Our four baby gerbils are quite active now. We put them in an old aquarium with a screen covering so they can't get out. I wish you could see them. They look so funny when they stand on their hind legs, sniffing the air and rubbing their front paws together.

I wasn't chosen for the track team after all. I was pretty disappointed until I found out that no other 6th-graders were chosen either.

We're looking forward to seeing you the day after Thanksgiving. Let us know what time your train arrives.

Your friend,
Tina

Tina Borelli
675 Millbrook Road
St. Louis, Missouri 63178

Claire Daniels
735 Buchanan Street
Nashville, Tennessee 37208

Working It Through

A. Pretend that you are Claire.

    1. Write an answer to Tina's letter.

    2. Be sure to follow the guidelines given on page 180.

    3. Address an envelope to go with your letter.

B. Write a letter to a friend or relative. Include at least 2 of the following topics or 2 other topics you think would be of interest to the person.

    1. the new school you are attending

    2. your hobby

    3. your cat's kittens

    4. your new bike

    5. your job mowing lawns

    6. how your team won a close game in the finals

C. Choose one of the following people or another special person you would like to write to. Make a list of interesting topics you would write about in a letter to this person.

    1. a pen pal

    2. a friend who has moved out of town

    3. a former teacher

    4. a favorite uncle who lives in another state

    5. your parents (if you were writing from camp)

Trying It Out

Write a friendly letter using the information you listed in Exercise C above.

    1. Include the 5 parts of a friendly letter.

    2. Follow the guidelines given on page 180 to write the body of your letter.

    3. Address an envelope.

    4. Exchange letters and envelopes with a classmate and proofread each other's letters.

    5. Correct any mistakes in your letter. Recopy the letter, if necessary.

Take Another Look Did you capitalize the names of streets, cities, and states? Did you use commas wherever necessary? Did you position the addresses correctly on the envelope?

Lesson 6   Writing a Business Letter

When you write a business letter, be clear, brief, and polite.

Thinking It Through

People write business letters when they want to order something or ask for information. Since they are often sent to strangers, business letters are more formal and to the point than friendly letters.

The following are some examples of formal greetings and closings used in business letters:

Greetings	Closings
Dear Sir or Madam:	Sincerely yours,
Dear Ms. or Mr. ____:	Yours truly,
Ms. or Mr. ____:	Very truly yours,

- What type of punctuation is used after the greeting of a business letter? What punctuation is used after the greeting of a friendly letter?
- Would you ever use the closing *Your friend* in a business letter? Why or why not?

The following guidelines will help you write effective business letters.

1. Use a formal greeting and closing.
2. Explain clearly what you want.
3. Be brief and polite.
4. Include all the necessary information the reader needs.
5. Avoid giving additional, unnecessary information.
6. Sign and type your full name. Add your title if you are writing for a group.

Read the sample business letter on the next page.

- Name the parts in a business letter.
- Which part is not included in a friendly letter?
- What information in the letter makes up the return address on the envelope?
- What part of the letter becomes the mailing address on the envelope?

Some people indent paragraphs in a business letter and others do not. When paragraphs are not indented, an extra line of space is allowed between paragraphs.

- How does Marie show a new paragraph in her letter?

Working It Through

A. Rewrite and improve the business letter below. Follow the form given in the sample. Make the letter clear and brief. Use correct punctuation and capitalization.

2954 river road
racine wisconsin 53403
march 15 19___

director
restored colonial village
portsmouth virginia 24531

dear director

   Our social-studies class is studying the Colonial Period. Sandy Preston told us that her family visited your Restored Colonial Village two years ago.

   Our class project is to build a scale model of the village. Do you have any free brochures that might help us learn how the village was built and what village life was like?

   Enclosed is a stamped, self-addressed envelope.

yours truly
Benita Romero
class secretary

B. Write a letter to The Magic Factory. Order a giant 60-page catalog of magic tricks, jokes, and novelties. The catalog was advertized in the December issue of *Magician's Magazine* and costs 50 cents. Make up addresses and additional information you will need for the letter.

Trying It Out

Read the ad section at the back of 1 or 2 magazines.

  1. Choose an interesting ad.
  2. Write a letter ordering an item advertized.
  3. Follow the guidelines in Thinking It Through.
  4. Address an envelope to go with your letter.

A. Below is an example of a business letter. Read it and answer the questions that follow.

625 West Galena Avenue
Freeport, Illinois 61032
March 16, 19___

Radio Station WNIB
12 East Delaware Place
Chicago, Illinois 60611

Dear Sir or Madam:

Please put my name on your subscription list to receive your monthly program guide. I am enclosing a check for $15.00 to cover the cost of a year's subscription.

Yours truly,

Emiko Ozawa

Emiko Ozawa

1. What information is in the heading of the letter?
2. What does the inside address contain? Is the inside address used in a friendly letter?
3. What greeting did Emiko use? What closing?
4. What is the main part of the letter called?
5. Which two parts would be used on the envelope?

B. Write a letter to World Travel Company. Request their free brochure on Alaska or some other place you'd like to visit. Or write to another company for some purpose of your own. Make up addresses.

C. Reread the letter you wrote.
   1. Did you use all of the parts of a business letter?
   2. Did you use correct punctuation and capitalization?
For more practice turn to page 376 in the Handbook.

Evaluation • Letter Writing

A. Rewrite and improve the business letter below.
1. The letter should have six parts.
2. The parts should be correctly placed.
3. The letter should be clear.
4. There should be no unnecessary details.
5. Punctuation and capitalization should be correct.

942 pine street
clinton iowa 52732
june 10 19___

the lane company
46 river street
butler new jersey 07405

dear sir or madam

Our sixth-grade health class is studying dental hygiene. We are all trying to turn over a new leaf and trying to take better care of our teeth for a change.

We read your ad in *Health Care Magazine*. You offered to send out free sample toothbrushing kits. Please send us 30 of these.

yours truly

Alex Johnson

B. Write a letter to The Hobby Shop. Ask for the free catalog of hobby kits or for something else about hobbies you are interested in. Make up addresses.

Your letter will be evaluated on the following:
use of the six parts of a business letter
clearness and lack of unnecessary details
correct punctuation and capitalization

What do you know about your name?
Does your name have a special meaning?

Many given names have interesting histories or meanings. Some have been used as names for thousands of years. Others are brand-new, created by parents who wanted a special name just for their child alone.

Arlette

If you are interested in finding out about your own name, check the authorities. One good authority is your parents. Ask them why they chose the name they did for you. Another source of information about names is a dictionary. Some libraries also have special dictionaries that are just about given names.

A dictionary section or special dictionary of names gives information like the following:

Amy *(Latin)* beloved.
Catherine *(Greek)* pure.
Christine *(Greek)* feminine form: a Christian.
Kirsten Scandinavian form of *Christine.*
Rosalind *(Spanish)* beautiful rose.

Erik

Clifton *(Old English)* place name: cliff town.
David *(Hebrew)* beloved.
John *(Hebrew)* God is gracious.
Robert *(Germanic)* glory + bright.
Shaun Irish form of *John.*

Kiku

Many times parents choose names not just because they have been used in the past or have a special meaning but because of someone special who had that name. Girls are sometimes named for famous women like Susan B. Anthony, Chris Evert, and Coretta Scott King. Many boys have been named for John Fitzgerald Kennedy and Martin Luther King.

Cesar

Find out about the names of your classmates. Why are they named as they are?

Spotlight • Antonyms

Expressions like "now or never" and "sink or swim" are special. They include pairs of antonyms—words that mean the opposite of one another.

What antonyms can you think of that mean the opposite of the words below?

clockwise	night	under
on	cold	backward
sadly	win	buyer

As you can see, many different kinds of words can have antonyms—nouns, verbs, adjectives, adverbs, and prepositions.

A thesaurus is a good place to look for antonyms. Many entry words have a list of opposites at the end of the entry. However, some words, like *history* and *ice cream*, don't have opposites.

Try to think of common expressions that include pairs of antonyms. Start by completing the following expressions.

From near and _____
Ladies and _____
A matter of life and _____
From top to _____
In sickness and in _____
From beginning to _____
Sooner or _____

Think of other expressions that include a pair of antonyms.

189

Adverbs

Adverbs can modify verbs by telling how, when, or where.

Thinking It Through

An **adverb** is a word that modifies a verb by telling how, when, or where something was done. The underlined words in the following sentences are adverbs.

The strangers arrived <u>late</u> in the evening.
They knocked <u>quietly</u> on the door.
They crept <u>upstairs</u> to the attic.

- Which word tells *when* the strangers arrived? What verb does it modify?
- Which word tells *how* they knocked on the door? With what two letters does that word end? What verb does it modify?
- Which word tells *where* they crept? What verb does it modify?

Sometimes people confuse adjectives and adverbs when they try to identify them in sentences. One way to keep them straight is to remember that an adjective modifies a noun and an adverb modifies a verb. Notice how the addition of adjectives changes these sentences.

The two suspicious strangers arrived late in the rainy evening.
They knocked quietly on the scarred, old door.
They crept upstairs to the dark, musty attic.

- What are the adjectives in the above sentences?
- What noun does each adjective modify?

Working It Through

A. Divide a sheet of paper into 3 columns. For each sentence, write the adverb in the first column, and the verb it modifies in the second column. In the third column, write whether the adverb tells how, when, or where.

1. Sue ran eagerly to the shore.
2. She dove first into the water.
3. I dove next.
4. Mom and Dad soon followed.
5. Dad immediately screamed, "It's freezing!"
6. Mom gradually walked in.
7. "Play carefully," Dad called.
8. "I will be nearby on the shore."
9. Mom later played catch with us.
10. Sue lay down for a nap after our swim.

B. Add an adverb to modify the verb in each sentence.

1. The sun shone (how).
2. We put the umbrella (where).
3. (When) we ate our lunch.
4. Dad opened the basket (when).
5. Mom (how) poured the juice.
6. We (how) gulped it in three swallows.
7. Some seagulls soared (where).
8. A dolphin leaped (how) above the water.

C. Write whether the underlined words in the following sentences are adjectives or adverbs. Then write the word each modifies. You should find 6 adjectives and 6 adverbs.

1. Reefs are made slowly by tiny animals.
2. The animals die and gradually build many layers.
3. These layers eventually make reefs.
4. Reefs often are destroyed by violent storms.
5. Some coral can be brightly polished.
6. Fan corals wave gracefully in gentle currents.

Trying It Out

Write the paragraph. Supply an adjective or adverb to modify the underlined words. Then write "Adj." or "Adv." over each word added. Write an ending for the story.

Paul, Carrie, and I approached the house. It was late at night. I went, followed by the others. We tiptoed up the stairs, but stopped as the wind banged a shutter against the window.

"Wh-what was that?" Paul said. "This place gives me the creeps!"

"It's only the wind, "I said. "I think."

Adverbs with Adjectives and Other Adverbs

Some adverbs can modify adjectives and other adverbs.

Thinking It Through

Some adverbs can be added to adjectives and other adverbs to tell *how much*.

A <u>very</u> frightened mare reared on its hind legs.
The trainer had to take hold of its reins <u>quite</u> quickly.
An <u>extremely</u> beautiful horse trotted around the track.

Notice that *very* tells how frightened the mare was. The adverb *very* modifies the adjective *frightened*. The adverb *quite* modifies another adverb *quickly*. The word *quite* tells how quickly the trainer grabbed hold of the reins.

● What word in the third sentence tells how beautiful the horse is?

● Is *beautiful* an adjective or an adverb?

Here is a list of some common adverbs that can modify adjectives or other adverbs.

slightly	extremely	nearly
very	really	too
quite	somewhat	rather
hardly	almost	so

Working It Through

A. Write the following sentences 3 times, using a different adverb from the list in Thinking It Through each time.

1. The kick from a horse can ____ injure a person.

2. Cowboys used quarter horses because they could start, stop, and turn ____ quickly.

3. Shetland ponies are ____ small, weighing about 140 kilograms.

4. Horses are said to be ____ intelligent animals.

5. Many move ____ gracefully.

B. Each sentence below can be completed with an adverb that modifies an adjective. Supply an adverb for each. Then write the adjective it modifies.

1. Horses have _____ large eyes.
2. Their _____ good eyesight helps them see in the dark.
3. Most of them have _____ powerful leg muscles.
4. Some ponies are _____ small for adults to ride on.
5. _____ heavy and _____ strong draft horses were once used to pull plows on farms.
6. Some _____ tall draft horses stand 200 centimeters.
7. The legs of baby horses seem _____ long for their _____ small bodies.
8. A horse's body temperature is _____ higher than a human's.

C. Each sentence below can be completed with an adverb that modifies another adverb. Supply an adverb for each. Then write the other adverb it modifies.

1. My horse, By-A-Nose, was trained _____ easily.
2. She trusts me _____ completely.
3. She will move _____ suddenly if she is startled.
4. By-A-Nose taps her foot _____ lightly if she wants water or attention.
5. I try to groom her _____ frequently.
6. I have the vet check her health _____ often.
7. She trots _____ slowly to make a good harness racer.
8. She is a _____ beautifully colored chestnut brown.

Trying It Out

Write a paragraph about a pet you have or one you would like to have. Use as many of the words from the following list as you can to describe it. Include several of the adverbs listed on page 192.

smart	playfully	beautifully
stupid	gently	softly
quick	roughly	small
slow	alertly	large

193

Lesson 9   Using Regular Adverbs to Compare

Many adverbs have three different forms.

Thinking It Through

Many adverbs have three different forms: the **positive,** the **comparative,** and the **superlative.**

Sybil

Positive	Comparative	Superlative
soon	sooner	soonest
early	earlier	earliest
often	more often	most often
quickly	more quickly	most quickly

- What ending is added to *soon* to form the comparative? the superlative?
- What word is used with *often* to form the comparative? the superlative?

To form the comparative of most adverbs, add the ending -*er* to the positive form or use the word *more*. The superlative is formed by adding the ending -*est* to the positive form or by using the word *most*.

Look at these sentences.

Theo

> Laura ran <u>faster</u> than Sybil.
> John arrived <u>earliest</u> of the three.
> Sharon <u>often</u> looks through her microscope.

- Which form of the adverb is used in each sentence?

Do not use both the -*er* ending and the word *more*. Do not use both the -*est* ending and the word *most*. For example, do not say or write *more higher* or *most hardest*.

Working It Through

Emilia

A. Look at the pictures at the left. Then use the correct form of <u>high</u> in the blanks in these sentences.

Sybil jumped __(1)__ all right, but Theo jumped even __(2)__. Of course, Emilia won since she jumped __(3)__ of all!

B. Write the following sentences, using the correct form of the adverbs in parentheses. After each, tell which form of the adverb you used—positive, comparative, or superlative.

1. Beth does things (slowly) than I do, but she does them (carefully) and (neatly) than I.
2. You write (childishly) than my baby brother.
3. This is the (carelessly) written paper I have ever read.
4. Print your name (neatly) at the top.
5. Next time, erase your mistakes (thoroughly).
6. This picture is (beautifully) drawn than the one you did before.
7. Those who were quiet during the exam will be dismissed (early) than those who were not.
8. Did you finish (soon) today than yesterday?
9. I learned French (easily) than German.
10. Does Jake or Rita speak (clearly)?

C. Write the following sentences, correcting the forms of the adverbs.

1. Can't you run more faster?
2. Of all the bands I've heard, this one plays the most loudest.
3. Sears Tower was built most recently than the Empire State Building.
4. You need to dress warmly in the winter than in the summer.
5. These books are stacked most neatly than those over there.
6. The movie started more earlier than we thought.
7. Doesn't Venus shine brightly than Mars?
8. Which of the three cars rides most smoothest?
9. Stan held his breath the most longest.
10. Does Frank speak more quicklier than Helen?

Trying It Out
Write a sentence which describes each of the following.

1. how 3 sports cars moved
2. how 2 animals act
3. when 2 friends arrived at your house
4. how 3 people sing
5. how 1 person woke up
6. when 3 flowers bloomed
7. how 2 girls swim
8. when 3 classmates answered a question in class

Lesson 10 Using Irregular Adverbs to Compare

The comparative and superlative forms of some adverbs are formed in irregular ways.

Thinking It Through

Most adverbs are regular. They change form to show comparisons according to the rules in Lesson 9.

The comparative and superlative forms of these adverbs do not follow the usual rules.

Positive	Comparative	Superlative
well	better	best
badly	worse	worst

- Use the correct form of *well* in this sentence:
  Did Lurleen perform _____ than Rick?

Do not add *-er* or *-est* to *well* or *badly* or use the words *more* or *most* with them. For example, do not say or write *more better* or *worstest.*

Using *good* or *well* correctly in a sentence can sometimes cause problems. Notice their use in the following.

　　Al is a good artist.　He paints well.

- What word does *good* modify? Is that word a noun or verb?
- What word does *well* modify? Is that word a noun or verb?

An adjective is a word that modifies a noun or pronoun. An adverb is a word that modifies a verb, an adjective, or another adverb. The adjective *good* should not be used where the adverb *well* is needed.

Working It Through

A. Write the sentences, using the correct adverb forms.
   1. Mickey plays the oboe _____.　(well)
   2. I don't play too _____.　(badly)

196

3. In fact, my music teacher says I play ____ than Kurt does.   (well)

4. Which of this rock group's four great albums sell the ____?   (well)

5. Debbie thought Mark sang ____ than Don.   (badly)

6. Of all who auditioned, he danced ____.   (badly)

7. You could swim ____ than Jean if you would take some lessons at the "Y."   (well)

8. Andy reads ____ than Arnetta.   (well)

9. She does ____ in math than he does.   (well)

10. Did Room 101, 102, or 103 run ____ in the sack race?   (badly)

11. Why do you think Pete plays first base the ____ of anyone else on the team?   (badly)

12. Sue pitches ____ than her younger sister.   (well)

B. Complete each set of sentences below by using *good* or *well* in the blanks.

1. Gordon is a ____ athlete. He swims and skates ____. He also takes ____ care of his health.

2. Why don't you wear your ____ suit? This tie will go quite ____ with your striped shirt.

3. Marla is ____ aware that she is a ____ student. She studies ____ and listens ____ in class.

4. That was a ____ game! All of you played very ____.

Trying It Out

Use each adverb below in a sentence. Use the form of the adverb indicated. **C** stands for comparative and **S** stands for superlative.

1. well (S)	**4.** carefully (C)	**7.** badly (S)
2. badly (C)	**5.** quietly (S)	**8.** often (C)
3. soon (C)	**6.** well (C)	**9.** brightly (S)

Take Another Look   Did you begin each sentence with a capital letter? Did you end each sentence with a period, question mark, or exclamation mark?

Phrases as Adverbs

Prepositional phrases can act as adverbs.

Thinking It Through

A prepositional phrase begins with a preposition, such as *with*, *on*, or *at*, and ends with a noun or pronoun. There may also be modifiers and noun markers between the preposition and the noun. Prepositional phrases act as adverbs when they modify verbs by telling *how* something was done, *when* it was done, or *where* it was done. A prepositional phrase usually follows the verb it modifies.

Look at these sentences.

> Kim worked with enthusiasm.
> Kim worked on Monday.
> Kim worked at her desk.

- Which prepositional phrase tells *when* Kim worked?
- Which tells *how* she worked?
- Which tells *where* she worked?

Some sentences may contain two or more prepositional phrases modifying the same verb.

> He ran down the street and around the corner.
> They hiked through the woods, over the mountain, and into the valley.

- What verb is modified in each sentence?

Working It Through

A. Follow the directions in parentheses to add a prepositional phrase to each sentence.

1. My first class starts.   (Tell when.)
2. When the bell rings, we line up.   (Tell where.)
3. No running or talking is allowed.   (Tell where.)
4. We walked.   (Tell how.)
5. Dawn threw a snowball.   (Tell where.)

6. Ms. Butu, the principal, spoke.   (Tell how.)

7. First period ends.   (Tell when.)

8. We then go to our next class.   (Tell how.)

B. Write the following sentences. Underline each prepositional phrase once and the verb it modifies twice. You should find 17 prepositional phrases and 15 verbs.

1. Our class went on a tour.

2. We left at 8:30 A.M.

3. The bus was stuck in traffic.

4. Finally, we arrived at the newspaper office.

5. We walked in single file through the entrance.

6. Presidents' pictures were hung on the walls.

7. The tour leader, Mr. Jacobsen, spoke with a German accent.

8. First, we went to the city room.

9. News stories are assigned from that office.

10. Some news is received over the telephone.

11. These stories are rewritten by several editors.

12. Mr. Jacobsen's voice was garbled by the noise.

13. The noise was coming from the press room.

14. There, giant machines run through the night and into the morning.

15. Our tour ended at noon.

C. Look again at the 17 prepositional phrases in Exercise B. Write what each tells—*how, when,* or *where.*

Trying It Out

Write a story about an outing or short trip you have taken. Use at least 6 of the verbs from the list below. Modify each verb you choose with a prepositional phrase that tells how, when, or where.

1. left	**5.** stopped	**9.** swam
2. drove	**6.** looked	**10.** hiked
3. rode	**7.** stayed	**11.** fished
4. ate	**8.** slept	**12.** skied

Using Negative Words

To make a statement mean "no" or "not," use only one negative word.

Thinking It Through

A **negative** word is a word that means "no" or "not." Each word below is a negative word.

neither, never, no, nobody, none, not, nothing, nowhere

A contraction that ends in *n't* is also a negative word:

aren't, can't, couldn't, didn't, don't, wasn't, weren't

● What does *n't* stand for at the end of a contraction?

Study the correct ways to say and write negatives.

Incorrect	Correct
There wasn't nobody in the booth.	There was nobody in the booth.
	There wasn't anybody in the booth.
I won't never try that game again.	I will never try that game again.
	I won't ever try that game again.

● How have the incorrect sentences been changed to make them correct?
● How many negative words are in each correct sentence?
● Say the following sentence correctly:

I didn't even win no prize!

A negative word means "no" or "not." Never use more than one negative word to make a statement negative.

Working It Through

A. Choose the correct word and write the following sentences.

1. I'm not (ever, never) going to get this done.
2. I haven't (any, no) time.
3. There isn't (anybody, nobody) to help me.

4. My parents do not want (any, none) of us to miss a homework assignment.

5. I (have, haven't) never been in a situation like this.

6. Many of my friends don't live (anywhere, nowhere) near me.

7. Isn't there (anything, nothing) I can do?

8. I (will, won't) ever avoid doing my homework again!

B. Rewrite each sentence below to make it have a negative meaning. You can either substitute a negative word for one of the words in the sentence or add a negative word.

1. The carnival comes here often.

2. Everyone in my family wants to go.

3. They think they will have fun.

4. Cindy likes all of the rides.

5. She always plays the games.

6. I have someone to go with me.

7. I could talk any of my friends into going.

8. Now there is something to do.

Trying It Out

Choose a partner. Close your book and listen as your partner reads aloud the part of a story in the first column. Be prepared to supply the correct word. Then read the rest of the story in the second column to your partner and have him or her choose the correct word.

Jan doesn't like to do (any, no) shopping, but if she didn't do it, she wouldn't get (any, no) allowance.

"I don't like to go (anywhere, nowhere) that's crowded," Jan told her mother when asked to go to the store. "Why not send Mark? He does (anything, nothing)."

"Mark's cleaning his room," her mother explained.

When Jan got to the store, there was (anyone, no one) behind the counter. She rang a bell and Mrs. Reinhart came.

"Six pork chops, please," Jan asked.

"Sorry. We (have, haven't) any pork chops today. How about some liver or stew meat?"

"I don't like (either, neither)," Jan said. "I guess I won't get (anything, nothing) today. Thanks."

Review • Adverbs

A. Write each sentence. Decide whether the underlined part is used as an adjective or an adverb, and circle the word it modifies. Then write *adjective* or *adverb* after the sentence.

1. We used <u>scientific</u> methods to discover the answer.
2. The trees <u>in the forest</u> were tall.
3. The deer jumped <u>over the log</u>.
4. The rain beat <u>steadily</u> on the window.
5. The girl's eyes blazed <u>with fury</u>.
6. The plants <u>by the step</u> came up early this year.

B. Complete each sentence with the correct comparative or superlative form of the adverb in parentheses.

1. Tuffy got here ____ than you did.   (soon)
2. These are the ____ spring flowers to bloom.   (early)
3. He calls me ____ than Carl does.   (often)
4. She skated much ____ today.   (well)
5. He hurt himself the ____ yet.   (bad)
6. This article is ____ written than the other.   (poorly)

C. Complete each sentence with *good* or *well*. Correct the sentence if it has more than one negative word.

1. He can't do a ____ job.
2. She can't see very ____.
3. Joe won't never sing ____.
4. We scarcely ever have this ____ pie.
5. Nobody told me no ____ news.

For extra practice turn to pages 370–371.

Take Another Look   Complete the sentence with the comparative or superlative form of *dry*.

　　Around here, August is the ____ month.   (dry)
　Did you use *driest*?

For more practice turn to pages 348–349 in the Handbook.

Evaluation • Adverbs

A. For each sentence, write the letter of the response that tells what the underlined part of the sentence is.

1. Jim called us <u>immediately</u>.
   a. adjective   **b.** adverb
2. It was a tree <u>without leaves</u>.
   a. adjective   **b.** adverb
3. Ann played <u>on the beach</u>.
   a. adjective   **b.** adverb
4. She left for work <u>early</u>.
   a. adjective   **b.** adverb

5. <u>Later</u> we knew that we were lost.
   a. adjective   **b.** adverb
6. A new flag waved <u>above the tent</u>.
   a. adjective   **b.** adverb
7. This is a book <u>about Canada</u>.
   a. adjective   **b.** adverb
8. This is our <u>third</u> time to move.
   a. adjective   **b.** adverb

B. For each sentence, write the letter of the underlined part of the sentence that is not correct.

1. <u>Of the two dogs</u>, <u>Red</u> <u>is</u> <u>the friendliest</u>.
       a   b   c   d
2. <u>Mt. McKinley</u> <u>is</u> <u>one of</u> the <u>most highest mountains</u>.
         a   b   c   d
3. <u>This tree</u> <u>grew</u> <u>the faster</u> <u>of all these six trees</u>.
       a   b   c   d
4. <u>We will try</u> <u>to start</u> <u>more</u> <u>earlier tomorrow</u>.
       a   b   c   d

C. For each sentence, write the letter of the response that completes the sentence correctly.

1. Juana is a ____ swimmer.
   a. good   **b.** well
2. Aiko didn't find ____ books.
   a. no   **b.** any
3. Tim writes very ____.
   a. good   **b.** well
4. He writes such ____ stories.
   a. good   **b.** well
5. Nobody ____ see in this fog.
   a. can   **b.** can't

6. You can paint as ____ as Al.
   a. good   **b.** well
7. There ____ no milk left.
   a. is   **b.** isn't
8. We can't tell ____ just yet.
   a. nobody   **b.** anybody
9. How ____ can he whistle?
   a. good   **b.** well
10. They don't know ____ about it.
    a. nothing   **b.** anything

Spotlight • Activities to Choose

1. State your complaint in a letter.
Get together with a group of your classmates and have a discussion about some of the problems that affect young people in your community. For example, there may be busy intersections that do not have any traffic signals. Or, there may be litter-filled empty lots that need to be cleared to make safe play areas. Select an issue to deal with and think of possible solutions to suggest. Then write a letter that will bring the problem and your suggestions to the attention of a local newspaper or community organization.

2. Create adverb riddles. Write riddles about people or animals for your classmates to guess. Each riddle must include at least 4 adverbs. The example may give you some ideas. Notice the underlined adverbs.

Slowly, carelessly, sometimes
  growling,
This gigantic creature was always
  prowling.
Its long tail swished lazily, to and fro.
This animal lived millions of years
  ago.

3. Write letters to bring cheer.
This can be an individual, small group, or class activity. Contact a nursing or convalescent home in your community. Ask for the names of a few residents who would especially enjoy receiving a friendly letter—perhaps an elderly person who has little or no family. Compose for one of the residents a cheerful letter that tells about yourself, your activities, your family, your school, and so on. Be sure to check your punctuation and spelling before you send the letter.

4. Play "Simon Says." This is a game for 8 or more players. Choose one player to be the leader. All the other players stand in a line facing the leader. The leader gives directions for the players to follow, and each direction must include an adverb. For example, the leader could say, "Simon says, wave your arms slowly," or, "Simon says, quickly sit on the floor." Each time the direction includes *Simon says*, everyone must perform the action. If the leader does not include the words *Simon says*, any player who performs the action is out of the game. The leader should give directions quickly and try to trick the other players. The winner is the player who remains in the game the longest.

Nothing Is Impossible: The Story of Beatrix Potter
by Dorothy Aldis

Beatrix Potter's childhood was isolated and sometimes lonely. Yet, it was not unhappy because she had the company of her pets. These pets later became the subjects of her books, one of which is the much-loved *The Tale of Peter Rabbit*. Parts of Potter's own journal and letters are included in the book.

Whirlwind Is a Ghost Dancing
by Natalia Belting

Imagine sun rays breaking through the rain clouds as being "Earth-Maker's eyelashes," or clouds as being smoke from the moon's pipe. In this book, many examples of Native American lore, or stories, are woven into poetry.

A Pocket Full of Seeds
by Marilyn Sachs

Nicole, a member of a French Jewish family, is forced to escape with her family from the Nazis. Helped by a teacher, Nicole hides in a school in France. Through the course of the story she tells, Nicole changes from a carefree eight-year-old to a mature thirteen-year-old.

Unit Seven

"Proud words" are words that can hurt. What warning does
the poet give to those who use "proud words"?

Primer Lesson

Look out how you use proud words.
When you let proud words go, it is
      not easy to call them back.
They wear long boots, hard boots; they
      walk off proud; they can't hear you
      calling—
Look out how you use proud words.

Carl Sandburg

This poem might be a general warning about using all words.
We should be aware of the power of different words—to
hurt, to soothe, and to excite. This unit tells about the
history of the English language and should help you get a
better understanding of words.

How Languages Are Related

English is one of a large group of modern languages that developed from an ancient language called Indo-European.

Thinking It Through

Almost 200 years ago, early **linguists**—that is, people who study languages—began making some important discoveries. For example, they found that the ways words are pronounced may change in a certain pattern over a long period of time. One pattern they found is that old Germanic words that began with **d** now begin with **t** or **th** in English. (*Drie* became *three.*)

Linguists then wanted to learn more about how languages are related. They began to search for words in different languages that look and sound somewhat alike and are close in meaning.

Look at these four words:

Mutter	*moeder*
mother	*mauthr*

- In what ways do they look and sound alike?
- How are they different?

The first three words are the modern German, Dutch, and English ways of saying the old Germanic word *mauthr*, meaning "mother."

By using clues like the different forms of *mother*, linguists have traced one group of related languages back to their Indo-European roots. The tree chart shows how some of these languages are related.

208

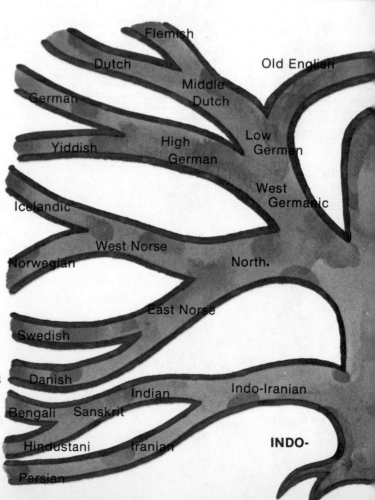

Flemish
Dutch
Old English
Middle Dutch
German
Low German
High German
Yiddish
West Germanic
Icelandic
West Norse
Norwegian
North.
East Norse
Swedish
Danish
Indian
Indo-Iranian
Bengali   Sanskrit
Hindustani   Iranian
INDO-
Persian

The roots of the tree chart show the Indo-European language of long, long ago. The first languages to come from Indo-European are shown on the main branches coming from the trunk. Two of these are Indo-Iranian and Celtic. Newer languages branch out from these. For example, Indian and Iranian both came from Indo-Iranian. Languages most closely related are shown as limbs on the same branch of the tree. Modern languages are shown at the end of each branch.

- Look at the large branch marked *Germanic*. Can you find the twigs from the West Germanic limb that are marked *English*, *Dutch*, and *German?* This means that these languages all came from one language (West Germanic) far back in time.

- What other modern languages are descended from Germanic and thus closely related to English?
- Can you guess why many modern languages, such as Japanese and Hawaiian, are not on this Indo-European language tree?

Working It Through

A. Use the tree of language chart to answer the questions.

1. The main languages that developed from Indo-European are the branches coming from the trunk of the tree. What are those 6 ancient languages?
2. The smaller branches stemming from each larger branch show some of the later languages that came from those 6 ancient ones. What languages developed from Celtic?

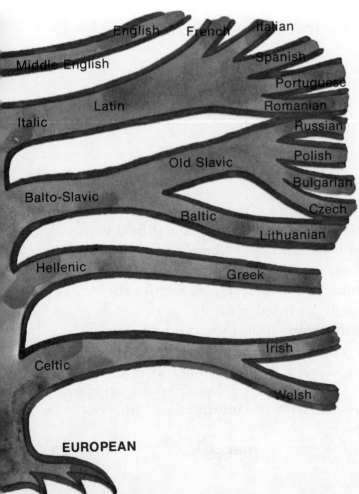

English French Italian
Middle English Spanish
Portuguese
Latin Romanian
Italic Russian
Polish
Old Slavic
Bulgarian
Balto-Slavic Czech
Baltic
Lithuanian
Hellenic Greek
Irish
Celtic
Welsh

EUROPEAN

3. What language did Italian and Spanish develop from?
4. What 2 languages developed from the East Norse branch of North Germanic?
5. Which language is most closely related to French?

Spanish   Dutch   Polish   Iranian

6. Which of the following is <u>not</u> a Germanic language?

English   Yiddish   Greek   Dutch

Canine

B. From the following list, choose the English word that belongs in each family of words below.

sing   foot
brother   group
night   school
soup   canine

1. *noctis, Nacht, nuktos*
2. *cane, chien, canis*
3. *broder, broeder, Bruder*
4. *soep, soppa, Suppe*
5. *synge, zingen, singen*
6. *skola, Schule, Skole*
7. *Fuss, fot, voet*
8. *gruppo, groupe, grupo*

Trying It Out

Linguists get most of their information by doing field work. Here is a way that you can do linguistic field work too.

1. Talk to members of your family and to neighbors to find out what other languages besides English they speak or have some knowledge of.
2. Take notes on any information they can give you about similarities between related languages.
3. List any words you learn that are similar to English words.
4. Pool your discoveries with the information gathered by 3 or 4 classmates.
5. Report what you learned to your class.

Lesson 2 **How English Developed**

English developed from an earlier Germanic language and was influenced by events in the ancient history of England.

Thinking It Through

All languages grow and change over time. The growth of the English language is closely related to events in England long ago.

Read the following paragraphs about the history of English.

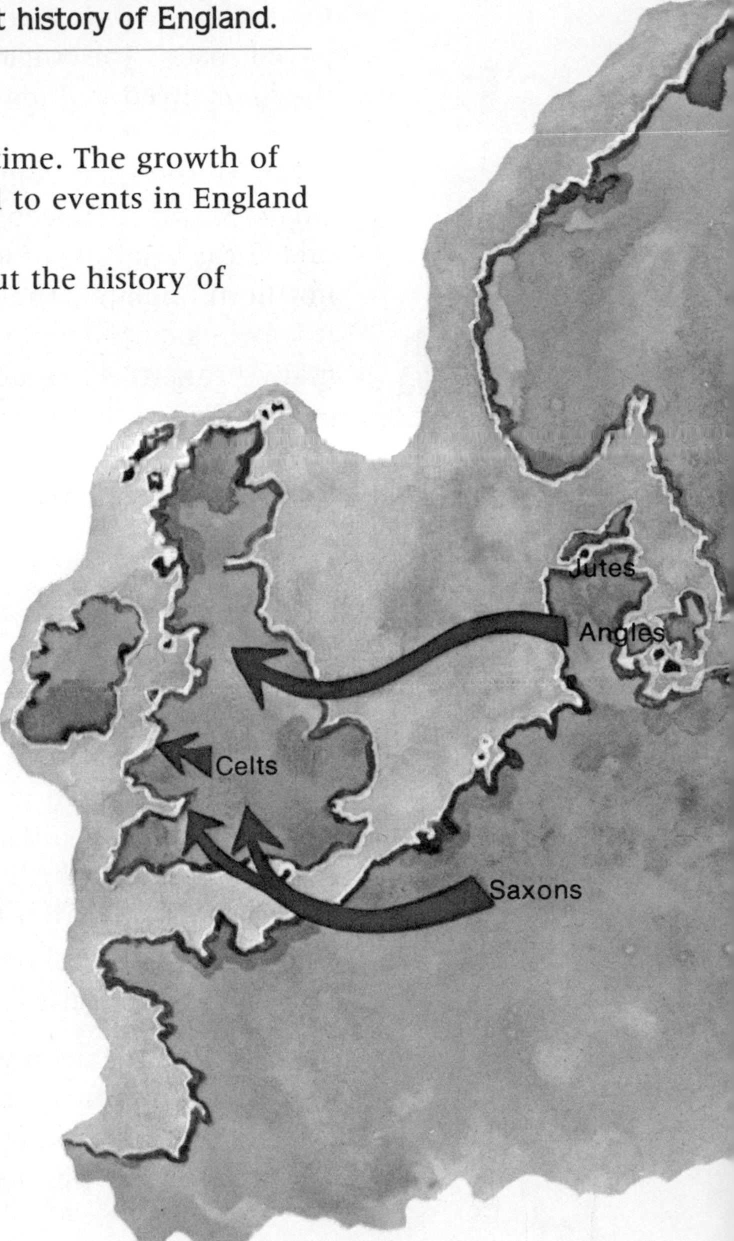

The English language we know today can be traced back to around 400 A.D. At that time, several West Germanic tribes, including two large tribes called the Angles and the Saxons, migrated to England. They drove many of the Celts who already lived there into the hilly back country. The area controlled by the Angles and Saxons became known as *Angle-isc Land*, or *England* in the modern form.

The similar languages of the West Germanic tribes blended together to become the main language of England: Anglo-Saxon, or Old English. Many of the short common words that English speakers use every day—words like *many, of, the, short,* and *word*—come from Old English. So do most irregular verbs.

A few words were borrowed from the Celts—not Celtic words, though. The Celts had been conquered by the

(Map labels: Jutes, Angles, Celts, Saxons)

211

Romans in earlier centuries. Many Celts had adopted the Latin language of the conquerors. When the new Anglo-Saxon invaders borrowed a few words from the Celts, those words were Latin ones like *strata*, meaning "a paved road." The Anglo-Saxons changed it to *strāet* when they borrowed it. Today we use the same word in a newer form: *street*.

Not all the short common words in English come from Anglo-Saxon. Between 700 and 1100 A.D., Viking pirates raided the English coast and began to settle parts of northern England. They spoke a North Germanic language. It was related to Old English but somewhat different. After many years, these settlers became part of the English people, and some of their words entered the English language. Some of the words Modern English has inherited from the Vikings are *egg*, *gate*, *take*, *gift*, *skirt*, and *sky*.

- What groups and events influenced English in ancient times?

Working It Through

A. The 4 underlined words in the paragraph below are the Old English forms of Latin words. Rewrite the paragraph, replacing the Old English words with their modern spellings. Choose from the following list:

biscuit, bishop	street, strait
cross, cruise	cattle, kettle

Once a <u>bisceop</u> was about to <u>cros</u> a <u>strāet</u> near the wharf. Suddenly, a truck turned the corner and a large pot fell off, spilling herring all over the clergyman's shoes. The bishop exclaimed, "This is a fine <u>cetel</u> of fish!"

B. Write each sentence, using the irregular verb from Old English. Remember that regular verbs form past tenses by adding *-ed*, but irregular verbs may change in other ways.

1. The Mild-Mannered Recorders are (led, directed) by my cousin Wilburt.
2. They (donated, gave) their time to play for the charity concert.
3. Our scout troop sponsored the concert and (operated, ran) the box office and refreshment stand.
4. The group had (put, placed) their speakers so that everyone could hear the music well.
5. Flashing lights (illuminated, lit) the stage.
6. A trio (sang, chanted) the lyrics.
7. David (beat, banged) on the drums during rehearsal, but he missed the concert.
8. At the end, excited fans (jumped, leapt) onto the stage.

Trying It Out

Most English words that start with **sk** and many that start with **sc** come from the Norse languages of the Vikings.

1. Make a list of all the words you can think of that begin with **sk** or **sc.**
2. See how many of them you can use to write a tongue twister worthy of a Viking. Try to use at least 6.

How English Has Changed

In the Middle Ages, English grammar became simpler, and many French words entered the English vocabulary.

Thinking It Through

In 1066 England and the English language faced an invasion much more serious than that of the Vikings. Duke William of Normandy came from France, killed the Anglo-Saxon leader Harold in battle, and had himself crowned king of England. He made his French soldiers the new lords and barons of the land. The conquered Anglo-Saxons almost became slaves.

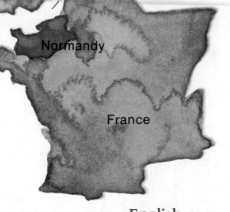

England
English Channel
Normandy
France

For several hundred years, Norman French (the French dialect spoken in Normandy) was the official language in England. But gradually, the Norman lords lost contact with France. Many nobles married Anglo-Saxon women. Bit by bit, the language the common people had used all along began to be used in business, in law, and even at the king's court.

English as spoken in the fourteenth century was different from Old English—so different that it is considered a separate language called Middle English. Its grammar was much simpler, and also thousands of French words had come into English. Many of the new words dealt with things that the ruling classes were interested in, like law, finance, fashion, and food. Words that had to do with simple life and work kept their English form, sometimes slightly changed or shortened.

Read the groups of words below.

Law: *attorney, inquest, trial, verdict*
Finance: *account, bond, mortgage, receipt*
Simple life and work: *bucket, cottage, hedge, field*

- Which words do you think were borrowed from French?
- Which words do you think are native English words?

Working It Through

A. After the Norman Conquest, the Anglo-Saxon peasants still raised most of the farm animals, but the Norman French nobles got to eat most of the meat.

1. Read the list of words below.
2. Arrange the 5 words for animals from Old English in one column and the 5 words for meats from French in another.
3. Then match the pairs that go together.

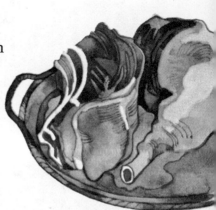

beef	calf	cow	deer	mutton
pig	pork	sheep	veal	venison

B. Many words show clues to their origin in the way they are spelled. Words from Old English often begin with **sh, wh, kn,** or **gh.** Words from French often have vowels spelled **eau,** or end with *-ine, -et, -ette,* or *-on.*

Write a sentence using the word from French in each pair.

1. ghost, phantom
2. prettiness, beauty
3. hoe, shovel
4. knit, crochet
5. white, blank
6. marine, sailor
7. redhead, brunette
8. onion, garlic

Trying It Out

Here is a riddle written in Middle English. Can you translate it into Modern English? Don't forget the punctuation.

A yonge goste askede his mother Whan seke oute monstres ye lyvyng roum Trewly she sayde in answere they wende ther whan they are deying.

Take Another Look Did you use quotation marks and other punctuation correctly? Did you use the correct Modern English spelling for all the words?

Lesson 4 Where Words Come From

Just as English and other languages have histories, each individual English word has its own history, too.

Thinking It Through

Most English words come down to us from the distant past. Many were borrowed from other languages. Often the pronunciation and spelling have changed over the years, and sometimes so has the meaning. Usually, if you see the old and new forms together, you can see similarities.

Tracking down the histories of words is called **etymology.** This term also means the history of a particular word.

Look at the dictionary etymology for *umbrella.*

etymology ——— **um brel la** (um brel'ə), a light, folding frame covered with cloth or plastic, used as a protection against rain or sun. *n., pl.* **um brel las.** [*Umbrella* comes from Italian *ombrella*, and can be traced back to Latin *umbra*, meaning "shade, shadow."]—**um- brel'la like'**, *adj.*

- From what language was the word *umbrella* borrowed?
- What was its form in Italian?
- What did the original Latin word mean?

Although most English words either come from Old English or are borrowed from other languages, there are other sources for words. Some words, such as *pasteurize* and *china,* come from the names of people and places. Other words, such as *zoom, whiz,* and *chug,* imitate the sounds of things and actions.

Working It Through

A. Use each imitative word below in a descriptive sentence about a thing or action that the sound of the word imitates.

1. boom	**4.** crunch	**7.** gurgle	**10.** slurp
2. buzz	**5.** flip	**8.** hiccup	**11.** squeak
3. cluck	**6.** gulp	**9.** jump	**12.** strum

B. Study the following list of words that come from the names of people or places.

1. academy	**5.** derrick	**9.** sandwich
2. afghan	**6.** limerick	**10.** saxophone
3. boycott	**7.** marathon	**11.** tarantula
4. chauvinism	**8.** mayonnaise	**12.** volt

Match each word with a person or place listed below.

a. Adolphe Sax

b. Alessandro Volta

c. Captain Charles Boycott

d. Derick, a hangman

e. the Earl of Sandwich

f. Nicolas Chauvin

g. Afghanistan

h. the Grove of Academe, Greece

i. Marathon, Greece

j. Limerick, Ireland

k. Taranto, Italy

l. Mahon, Minorca

C. Dictionary definitions and etymologies for the following words are given below. Write the word that matches each definition and etymology beside the correct number.

badminton   canasta   game   polo   tennis

__(1)__ pastime; amusement. a contest with certain rules. [__(1)__ comes from Old English *gamen*, meaning "joy."]

__(2)__ game played on a court, in which a ball is hit with a racket. [__(2)__ came into English about 600 years ago from French *tenetz*, meaning "hold!" and can be traced back to Latin *tenere*, meaning "to hold."]

__(3)__ game in which players use rackets to keep a shuttlecock moving back and forth over a high net.

[__(3)__ was named after an estate belonging to the Duke of Beaufort in England, where the game was first played.]

__(4)__ a card game played with two decks of cards. [__(4)__ is the Spanish word for "basket" and can be traced back to Latin *canistrum*. See CANISTER.]

__(5)__ game like hockey, played on horseback with long-handled mallets and a wooden ball. [__(5)__ may come from Tibetan *pulu*, meaning "a ball," used in playing the game.]

Trying It Out

Choose one of the words in Exercise B and find out more about it. Share the information you discover.

How Words Change

Words change in form and meaning over time.

Thinking It Through

Sometimes whole groups of English words have changed at once. For example, many words now spelled with an **i** were spelled with **y** in Middle English. The **y** was pronounced /ē/ as in *feet*, and so *hym* would have been said "heem," and *wyf* "weef." Today these two words have become *him* and *wife*.

In other cases a word may look much as it did in Middle English, but the meaning may be different.

Corn meant any important grain grown in an area, often wheat, barley, or rye.

Staff meant a long stick used for support.

● What do *corn* and *staff* mean in these sentences?

> We had corn and chicken for lunch at school.
> The senator thanked his staff for their support.

Corn is an example of a word that has become more specialized in meaning. In American English today it can only mean one grain plant and never wheat, barley, or rye.

Staff is an example of a word that has become more generalized in meaning. Once it meant only a long stick used for support. Now it can also mean a group of workers who support the efforts of a supervisor.

Working It Through

A. The 17 underlined words in the following paragraph have all changed in form in the same way as they developed from Old English to Modern English.

1. Figure out how the words have changed and tell how in one or two complete sentences.
2. Rewrite the paragraph, replacing the Old English words with their Modern English forms.

Summer won't be here tō sōna for me. When scōl is out, I'll hōc fish for my fōda at the brōc. At nōn I'll cōc it beside a quiet pōl while I read a gōd bōc. In the cōl of evening I'll sit on my camp stōl and lōcian at the mōna. That will put me in a gōd mōd.

B. Study the words below and their earlier meanings. Then give the modern definition for each word.

1. **flood**   a river (in any stage)
2. **barn**   a building just for storing barley
3. **starve**   to die (in any way)
4. **meat**   any kind of solid food
5. **deer**   any wild forest animal

C. Four of the words in Exercise B have a more specialized meaning now than they did in earlier times. Can you tell which one has a more general meaning?

Trying It Out

The following 15 words each have a very different meaning now than they did originally.

1. Choose one word and find out more about it, including its earlier meaning.
2. Work with classmates to present your findings on a bulletin board, wall hanging, or classroom banner.

caterpillar	glamour	mumps
cattle	groom	opera
chenille	humor	pen
clock	lady	quick
girl	lawn	write

What's Ahead for English

English words are still changing. Common changes are compounding, blending, clipping, and adding affixes.

Thinking It Through

English has not stopped changing. New words are still being created to fit new situations and will continue to be in the future. When two words are simply joined together to form a new word, the new one is a **compound word.** *Blacktop* and *printout* are compound words.

- What two words were joined to form *shortstop?*

When parts of two words are put together to form a new word, it is called **blending.** *Smog* blends *smoke* and *fog.*
- What word is a blend of *cheese* and *hamburger?*

When a short word is formed from part of a longer word, it is called **clipping.** *Bus* came from *omnibus.*
- What is the clipped form of *hippopotamus?*

Sometimes new words are formed by adding an **affix,** either a **prefix** at the beginning or a **suffix** at the end, to another word. The prefix *bi-* is added to the word *weekly* to form *biweekly.* The suffix *-like* is added to the word *dragon* to form *dragonlike.*
- What prefix was added to *pronounce* to form *mispronounce?*
- What suffix was added to *care* to form *careful?*

Working It Through

A. Write the term *affix, blend, clip,* or *compound* to tell how each of the following words was formed.

1. surfer
2. lab
3. defrost
4. killjoy
5. empower
6. brunch
7. leapfrog
8. cloverleaf
9. exam
10. twilight
11. basketball
12. math
13. bike
14. bakery
15. pinchpenny

B. At least 38 compound words contain *hand* as one part. How many can you think of? Try to list at least 10.

C. Listed below are 20 words that have come into English in the last twenty years. Number from 1 to 20. Then write the new words that should be substituted for the numbered clues in parentheses in the story.

Amtrak	condo	hatchback	rap
bikeway	deli	jumpsuit	subcompact
boatel	doubleknit	mayo	takeout
brown-bag	environmentalist	minibike	underwhelmed
chairperson	glasphalt	presoak	unflappable

Donella was usually (**1.** flap, able, un-), but 2029 was already a very busy year. As (**2.** chairman, person) of the (**3.** environmental, -ist) (**4.** rapport) group, she decided to call the meeting at her family's (**5.** condominium). That way Rob would have only a short walk from the (**6.** American, track) station, Su-Ling could come by (**7.** bike, mini-) on the (**8.** asphalt, glass) (**9.** bike, highway), and Juan could put his boat in the (**10.** boat, hotel).

Donella had expected the group to (**11.** bag, brown) it, but they wanted (**12.** out, take) sandwiches from the **13.** delicatessen). Donella's father picked them up in a (**14.** compact, sub-) (**15.** back, hatch).

After the meal, Rob pointed to Su-Ling's (**16.** double, knit) (**17.** jump, suit). "You'll have to (**18.** soak, pre-) that to get out the (**19.** mayonnaise) stains," he said. Su-Ling was (**20.** overwhelmed, under) by the idea.

Trying It Out

Being aware of how new words have been formed in recent years will give you clues to the kinds of new words you can expect to encounter throughout your life.

1. Write your own story about life in the future.
2. Use 4 of the modern words listed below.

Affixed Words	Blends	Clips	Compound Words
containerize	heliport	binocs	flashcube
nonstick	moped	disco	skateboard
supertanker	workaholic	rev	spinoff

221

Review • Understanding Words

A. The words in the left column are related in spelling and meaning to the words or forms of words in the right column. Match the words with the correct letters.

1. buzz	Developed from Old English Words
2. smog	**a.** from *cniht* meaning "boy"
3. gardenia	**b.** from *scead* meaning "shelter"
4. knight	Came into English from Other
5. tux	Languages
6. attic	**c.** from Latin *aequus* meaning "even"
7. mustang	**d.** from Spanish *mestengo* meaning
8. equal	"untamed"
9. shed	Imitative Word
	e. imitates the sound of a bee
	Word from the Name of a Person or
	Place
	f. Attica, Greece
	g. Dr. Alexander Garden
	Blend
	h. smoke + fog
	Clip
	i. tuxedo

B. Write the words which come from the words or forms of words below. Then use each word in a sentence.

1. Clip for *spectacle*.

2. Word for a food taken from the Italian word *ballone* meaning "ball"

3. Blend for *motor + hotel*

4. Word that imitates the sound that snakes make

5. Word for a bird from the place, the Canary Islands

6. Clip for the word *gymnasium*

C. Think about the following questions:
   1. Are the words you wrote related in spelling and meaning to the words or forms of words given?
   2. Did you use the words correctly in sentences?

Evaluation • Understanding Words

A. Complete the paragraph below.
1. Fill in the blanks with words that are in our language today.
2. Use words that are related in spelling and meaning to the words or forms of words described below the paragraph.

Last night my family had a _____ in the park. Mother started the fire, and I put the _____ on the grill. The meat _____ and a pleasant aroma filled the air. My younger sister was especially hungry. She had been jogging to prepare for a _____. She was _____ that we had cooked such a big meal. For dessert we had lime _____. Mother took _____ most of the evening.

1. Word from the American Spanish word *barbacoa* meaning a "frame of sticks"
2. Blend of *cheese* + *hamburger*
3. Imitative word for the sound meat makes when cooking or burning
4. Word from the place, Marathon, Greece
5. Word from the Old English word *glaed* meaning "bright"
6. Word from the Arabic word *sharbet* meaning "a drink"
7. Clip for *photographs*

B. Write the words that come from the words or forms of words below. Then use each word in a sentence.
1. Clip for *grandmother*.
2. Clip for *telephone*
3. Word for a poem, taken from the place, Limerick, Ireland
4. Blend for *twitch* + *fiddle*
5. Word from the Old Spanish and Portuguese word *briza* meaning "northeast wind"
6. Compound for a sea animal shaped like a star.

You will be evaluated on the following:
correct choice of words from our language today
correct use of words in sentences

"Papa, do you believe all the Shaker Law?"

"Most. I'm glad it's all writ down in the Book of Shaker."

"How do you know it's all writ down, Papa. You can't read."

"No, I cannot read. But our Law has been read to me. And because I could not read, I knew to listen with a full heart. It might be the last and only time I'd learn its meaning."

"I don't cotton to all those Shaker Laws. Especially one."

"Which one?"

"The one that says we can't go to the baseball game on Sunday. Jacob Henry and his father always go. Why can't we?"

from *A Day No Pigs Would Die*
by Robert Newton Peck

This discussion between Robert Peck and his father may sound a little different from the way you would talk with your parents. The Pecks used a **dialect** of English spoken by many Shaker people. There are many places in the United States where people speak in different ways than you do in your area. Words, expressions, pronunciations, and grammar may vary in dialects.

Have you ever listened to someone speak in a Southern dialect? You may hear what is called a "Southern drawl," or slowed way of pronouncing words. New Englanders tend to shorten words and speak in a clipped fashion. Westerners have their own way of talking, too, with a bit of a twang. Listen to people from different parts of the country and try to identify their dialects.

Keep your eyes open, too. As you read, look for examples of dialect. From the books of Mark Twain to those of E. L. Konigsburg and many other modern writers, you will find good examples of the rich variety of dialects of American English.

Spotlight • Prefixes and Suffixes

It is almost magic what we can do with words just by adding something to the beginning or end. Take the word *human,* for example. Just add *super-* to the beginning and what have you got? That's right, a SUPERHUMAN!

Or try another prefix, *sub-.* Add it to *human* and what do you have? A *subhuman* creature like . . .

or   or

Suffixes can be added to the end of the word that change the word, too. Take *-kind,* for example. Added to *human*, it changes the word to *humankind,* and the whole world of people is then included.

The short suffixes *-ity, -ly,* and *-ism* change the word even further. *Humanity, humanly,* and *humanism* are words that you will hear and see used often. Suffixes can even be added after other suffixes: a person who is very good about working to make life better for all is called a *humanitarian.* As you can see, many words can be made from one simple word like *human!*

Words can be changed to mean their opposites with the quick switch of a prefix or suffix. Perform your own magic on these words:

Change <u>outdoors</u> to its antonym _____ *(in-).*
Change <u>inhale</u> to its antonym _____ *(ex-).*
Change <u>pretest</u> to its antonym _____ *(post-).*
Change <u>bearded</u> to its antonym _____ *(-less).*
Change <u>colorless</u> to its antonym _____ *(-ful).*
Change <u>careful</u> to its antonym _____ *(-less).*

Direct Objects

A noun that follows an action verb and tells who or what was the object of the action is called a direct object. A direct object is in the predicate of the sentence.

Thinking It Through

Notice what the underlined words tell in each of the following sentences.

> The orchestra gave a <u>concert.</u>
> Ramona Perez played her <u>violin.</u>
> She had a <u>solo.</u>
> She saw <u>Mr. Perez</u> in the audience.

Each underlined word is a **direct object.** Each direct object is a noun that follows an action verb and tells who or what received the action of the verb.
- What did the orchestra give?
- What did Ramona play? What did she have?
- Whom did she see in the audience?

Now look at the example below.

> Mr. Perez gave flowers to Ramona after the concert.

- What is the verb in the sentence?
- What noun is the direct object of the verb? What does the direct object tell?

Working It Through

A. Complete each sentence with a direct object that answers the question under the sentence.
1. We met ____ at the zoo.
   (Whom did they meet?)
2. We saw a very strange ____ there.
   (What did they see?)
3. It had a ____ on its head.
   (What did it have on its head?)

4. We tossed ____ to the creature.
   (What did they toss to it?)
5. Then it threw ____ at us.
   (What did it throw?)
6. Dad took ____ to get a closer look.
   (Whom did he take?)

B. Write the following sentences. Underline the verb and circle the direct object in each sentence. Above each direct object write *who* or *what* to show what the direct object tells.

1. Martha read an interesting article.
2. It described John Evans, an 18-year-old millionaire.
3. He invented two electronic games.
4. He sold his games to a big toy company.
5. A newspaper woman interviewed Mr. Evans.
6. Martha also has an idea for a new game.

C. Write each sentence that follows. Draw one line under each simple subject, two lines under each verb, and a circle around the direct object of the verb.

1. Our family visited Death Valley.
2. We pitched our tent on a campground there.
3. Rangers guide tourists through the valley.
4. They describe the fascinating sites.
5. Prospectors found gold in the valley years ago.
6. We explored an old gold mine one day.
7. We spent one entire day in a ghost town.

Trying It Out

Write a sentence to tell about each of the things described below. Use the underlined verbs for your sentences. Include a direct object in each sentence.

1. a food you <u>eat</u> for breakfast
2. a book you've <u>read</u> more than once
3. a person you <u>like</u> very much
4. a place you <u>pass</u> on your way home from school
5. a game you <u>play</u>

227

Lesson 8 Predicate Nouns

A noun that follows a linking verb is called a predicate noun. A predicate noun is in the predicate of the sentence.

Thinking It Through

A noun that follows a linking verb and tells about or means the same thing as the subject of the sentence is called a **predicate noun.**

Notice the underlined words in the example sentences.

My grandmother was a <u>doctor.</u>
My mom is a <u>teacher.</u>

In the first sentence the word *doctor* is a predicate noun. It follows the linking verb *was* and tells about the subject of the sentence, *grandmother.* In the sentence, *grandmother* and *doctor* are the same person.

- What is the predicate noun in the second sentence? What linking verb does it follow?
- Whom does the predicate noun tell about?

Look carefully at the following list of commonly used linking verbs.

am   is   are   was   were   will   be

- Identify the subject, linking verb, and predicate noun in the next example.

I will be a magician someday.

Working It Through

A. Read the first sentence in each pair to get a clue that will help you complete the second sentence. Each word you supply should be a predicate noun.

   1. For years Uncle Calvin baked bread, cakes, and cookies.
   He was a _____ .

2. Recently, Maxine got her license to fly a jet.
  She is a ____.

3. Marilyn does ballet exercises three hours every day.
  She will be a ____.

4. Mr. Johnson is solving the drugstore robbery.
  He is a ____.

B. Write the sentences. Write **S** over each simple subject,
LV over each linking verb, and **PN** over each predicate noun.

  1. Michelle was the star of the last community play.
  2. She is a very good actress.
  3. Her father was a stuntman in Hollywood.
  4. Now he is a coach.
  5. Michelle's aunts were acrobats.
  6. Her grandfather was a radio announcer.
  7. Her younger brother will be the wolf in a play.
  8. Her little sister Doris was an elf in a play her
    kindergarten class presented.
  9. The entire family will be participants in the talent
    show taking place in a few weeks.

C. Write only the 7 sentences in which the underlined
word is a predicate noun. Write **S** over the simple subject,
LV over the linking verb, and **PN** over the predicate noun.

  1. We sold over 200 <u>books</u> at our school's book fair.
  2. The most popular selection was a <u>book</u> about space.
  3. Mitzo and his robot cat are the main <u>characters.</u>
  4. My dad was a <u>cashier</u> for the fair.
  5. He is an <u>accountant</u> for his own firm.
  6. He and my uncle are <u>partners</u> in business.
  7. Miguel's mom set up the <u>fair.</u>
  8. She is a terrific <u>organizer.</u>
  9. Next year our big project will be an <u>auction.</u>

Trying It Out

Make up 6 sets of sentences like those in Exercise A for
your classmates to complete. You can describe animals,
places, or occupations for the exercise.

Predicate Adjectives

An adjective that follows a linking verb is called a predicate adjective. A predicate adjective is in the predicate of the sentence.

Thinking It Through

An adjective that follows a linking verb and modifies the subject of the sentence is called a **predicate adjective.** Like other adjectives, a predicate adjective describes or in some way tells about the noun it modifies.

Look at the underlined words in the sentences below.

> The books were <u>heavy</u>.
> Patrick was <u>tired</u> after carrying them.

In the first sentence, *heavy* is the predicate adjective. It follows the linking verb *were* and modifies the subject of the sentence, *books. Heavy* describes the books.

- What is the predicate adjective in the second sentence? What linking verb does it follow?
- What noun does the predicate adjective modify?

In addition to forms of the verb *be, seem,* and *appear,* the verbs *look, feel,* and *become* can be linking verbs. Notice the examples that follow.

> Rama looks terrible.
> Her eyes have become red.

- What are the predicate adjectives in the sentences? What linking verbs do they follow?
- What words do the predicate adjectives modify?

Working It Through

A. Underline the simple subject in each sentence. Then complete the sentence with a predicate adjective.

1. The sky was _____ .
2. The day seemed _____ .

3. Betsy felt _____ .
4. The book she was reading soon became _____ .
5. She was _____ she had started it.
6. All in all, Betsy's day had been _____ .

B. Copy the following sentences. Write **S** over each simple subject, **LV** over each linking verb, **PA** over each predicate adjective, and **PN** over each predicate noun. You should find 6 predicate adjectives and 6 predicate nouns.

1. Joseph is a man who builds kites.
2. His kites are magnificent.
3. His best kite was a sculpture of a dragon.
4. The dragon appears fierce as it wiggles over trees.
5. Its body looks enormous.
6. Joseph's funniest kite has been a huge doghouse.
7. Kites have become very popular in Joseph's hometown.
8. The annual kite race is a big event.
9. Joseph is usually a judge.
10. The race was fantastic last year.
11. Joseph was once a skydiver.
12. He seems happiest out in the open.

Trying It Out

Follow the directions below to write 9 sentences.

1. Use the words *thoughtful*, *busy*, and *helpful* as predicate adjectives in 3 different sentences.
2. Use *doctor*, *teacher*, and *parents* as predicate nouns in 3 different sentences.
3. Use *party*, *home*, and *clothes* as direct objects in 3 different sentences.
4. Underline each predicate adjective, predicate noun, and direct object in your sentences.

Subject Pronouns

Some pronouns can be used as the subject of a sentence or as a predicate pronoun.

Subject Pronouns	
Singular	**Plural**
I	we
you	you
he	they
she	
it	

Thinking It Through

Pronouns are words that stand for nouns. The pronouns listed in the chart at the left can take the place of a noun as the subject of a sentence.

Notice the pronouns in the following sets of sentences.

1. Frances was late. **2.** John and Paco were late.
She missed the bus.   They missed the bus too.

- What pronoun is used in the first set of sentences? What noun does the pronoun stand for?
- What is the pronoun in the second set? What nouns does the pronoun stand for?
- How is each pronoun used?

The subject pronouns shown in the chart can also take the place of a predicate noun. When a pronoun follows a linking verb and means the same thing as the subject of the sentence, it is called a **predicate pronoun.**

Look at the pronouns in these examples.

1. The first player is Tom. **2.** The caller was Frances.
The first player is he.   The caller was she.

- What is the predicate pronoun in the first set of sentences? in the second set?
- What linking verbs do the predicate pronouns follow?
- What nouns do the predicate pronouns refer to?

Working It Through

A. Rewrite the sentences on the next page. Substitute a pronoun for each underlined word or group or words.

1. <u>Judith</u> took the dog for a walk.
2. The chefs for the banquet will be <u>Louis and Vincent.</u>
3. After the storm, <u>the sky</u> looked sunny.
4. The artist must have been <u>Irene.</u>
5. <u>Eduardo</u> was not at the party.
6. <u>Clarence and Elva</u> built a fireplace.
7. <u>Timothy</u> will not be quiet.

B. Write the sentences. Write **S** above each pronoun that is the simple subject of a sentence and **PP** above each that is a predicate pronoun.
1. I learned the poem in school last year.
2. The last person to arrive was he.
3. They have been very happy in the new house.
4. The person Jake talked with was I.
5. She has not been feeling well lately.
6. We must have lunch again soon.
7. The speaker representing the new school will be he.
8. The mysterious caller could have been you.

C. Choose the pronoun that completes each sentence correctly.
1. (He, I) likes to play chess.
2. The good friends were (he, they).
3. (They, She) is coming for a visit.
4. Meiko said, "(I, She) don't feel good today."
5. (We, He) were rivals in school.
6. The lifeguard was (they, he).
7. "(You, I) am going camping!" shouted Lisa.
8. (It, He) was a strange book that Jackson read.

Trying It Out
Use each pronoun below in a sentence. Use 3 as simple subjects and 3 as predicate pronouns.
1. you   3. they   5. it
2. we   4. I   6. he

Lesson 11 Object Pronouns

Some pronouns can take the place of nouns as direct objects or objects of prepositions.

Thinking It Through

Object Pronouns	
Singular	**Plural**
me	us
you	you
him	them
her	
it	

The chart in Lesson 10 lists pronouns that can take the place of nouns as subjects or as predicate pronouns. The chart at the left lists object pronouns. These can take the place of nouns as direct objects or objects of prepositions. The pronouns *you* and *it* have the same form both as subjects and objects.

Look at the pronouns in the following examples.

Jonathan saw him yesterday.
The dog chased us all the way home.
The coach will meet you and me tomorrow.

In the first sentence the pronoun *him* is the direct object of the action verb *saw*.

● What are the direct objects in the second and third sentences? What action verbs do they follow?

Now notice the pronouns in the next examples.

Phyllis will go with them.
Richard can sit between her and me.

In the first sentence the pronoun *them* is the object of the preposition *with*.

● What is the preposition in the second sentence? What are the objects of the preposition?

The following is a list of other common prepositions.

about   across   among   at   behind   beside   by   to   without

Working It Through

A. Complete each sentence with a pronoun that is a direct object.

1. I showed ____ my new bike.
2. He rode ____ around the block.
3. Tina invited ____ to her party.
4. Luis told ____ about the sale.
5. Jerry called ____ on the phone.

B. Write the sentences. Circle each pronoun that is a direct object. Underline each pronoun that is an object of a preposition.

1. We took him to the dance.
2. To me, the event was quite exciting.
3. Yoko left without us.
4. Later, we met him and her at the snack shop.
5. Rico sat between her and me.

C. Write sentences using the pronouns below. Use 2 pronouns as direct objects of verbs, 2 as objects of prepositions, and 2 as simple subjects or predicate pronouns.

1. me   3. us   5. her
2. she   4. them   6. we

Trying It Out

Use pronouns to complete the story starter below. Then write an ending for the story that includes at least 4 additional pronouns.

    All the guests had arrived. ____ sat quietly waiting for David to arrive. ____ was very late. Joan had called ____ at four o'clock. David told ____ that he would be at the house by six.

    "David won't disappoint ____," said Joan. "This surprise party for ____ will be a success."

    Suddenly there was a loud noise. ____ came from the front yard. Everyone looked around. The noise had frightened ____.

Using Possessive Pronouns

Some pronouns show ownership.

"This book is <u>mine</u>."

"The book is <u>his</u>."

Thinking It Through
Each of the underlined words in the illustration below is a **possessive pronoun.** A possessive pronoun tells who has something or to whom something belongs.

"I thought the book was <u>yours</u>."

"And I thought the book was <u>hers</u>."

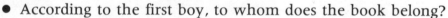

- According to the first boy, to whom does the book belong?
- To whom does the book belong according to the second person shown? the third? the fourth?

Words That Show Possession	
mine	my
yours	your
hers	her
ours	our
theirs	their
its	
his	

All of the words listed in the chart can show possession or ownership. Some, like the pronouns in the sentences in the picture, can stand alone. Some of the words modify nouns to show possession, as in these examples.

Rita found <u>her</u> pen.
The children opened their presents.

In the first sentence, the word *her* modifies the noun *pen.* It shows that the pen belongs to Rita.

- What word in the second sentence shows possession?
- What noun does the word modify?

Some word groups, including some possessive pronouns, are easily confused because they sound alike or look similar.
- Which word in each group below shows possession: our/are, their/they're/there, its/it's, your/you're?

Remember that *are* is a form of the verb *be*, *they're* is a contraction for *they are*, *it's* is a contraction for *it is*, and *you're* is a contraction for *you are*.

Working It Through

A. Rewrite each sentence. Replace each underlined word or group of words with a word from the chart in Thinking It Through.

1. Todd took <u>Todd's</u> savings to the bank.
2. I found the cup and glued <u>the cup's</u> handle back on.
3. The car the Bensons wrecked was <u>the Bensons'</u>.
4. Paula said, "This has been <u>Paula's</u> nicest birthday."
5. The twins asked, "When will we get <u>the twins'</u> turn?"
6. Maria thought the tennis racket was <u>Maria's</u>.

B. Choose the word that correctly completes each sentence.

1. Take your helmet, but leave (our, are) football here.
2. (Their, They're, There) leaving for Cleveland at noon.
3. The puppy hurt (it's, its) paw.
4. I like (you're, your) shoes better than mine.
5. The children made a gift for (their, they're, there) mother.
6. Is it true that (you're, your) moving to Pittsburgh?
7. Move the table over (their, they're, there).
8. (Our, Are) you going to the show this Saturday?

Trying It Out

Follow the directions below to write 8 sentences.

1. Use *his*, *hers*, and *mine* in 3 different sentences about yourself and 2 of your friends.
2. Use *our* and *their* in 2 different sentences about your family and the family of a friend.
3. Use *my*, *its*, and *her* in 3 different sentences about an interesting or exciting experience you have had.

Take Another Look Did you spell correctly any pronouns that might easily be confused with another word?

Review • Pronouns

A. Write each sentence. Beside each tell whether the underlined word is a direct object, predicate adjective, or predicate noun.

1. Our neighbor on the west side is a <u>barber</u>.
2. David bought <u>fruit</u> at the supermarket.
3. Elizabeth quietly aimed her <u>camera</u> at the deer.
4. The path through the woods seemed <u>narrow</u>.
5. The next season will be <u>spring</u>.
6. Ann appeared <u>tired</u> after her swim.
7. Dr. Alphonso took the patient's <u>temperature</u>.

B. Complete each sentence with the correct pronoun in parentheses.

1. You and ____ are dressed just alike.   (he, him)
2. The most surprised person was ____.   (she, her)
3. The horse pushed ____ with its nose.   (they, them)
4. Tammy chose Rudolfo and ____ to race.   (I, me)
5. The contest was between Tory and ____.   (she, her)
6. Mr. Williams wants Clara to go with ____.   (we, us)

C. Complete each sentence with the correct word in parentheses.

1. Can you find ____ cabin in this storm?   (our, are)
2. ____ coming to visit us.   (Their, They're, There)
3. The elephant held up ____ foot. (its, it's)
4. What time is ____ plane due? (their, they're, there)
5. ____ the one I want to see. (Your, You're)
6. Get that book over ____. (their, they're, there)

For extra practice turn to pages 372 and 373.

Take Another Look   Write the sentence and underline the prepositional phrase. Tell whether the phrase acts as an adverb or adjective. Circle the word it modifies.
    They left many instruments on the moon.
Did you underline *on the moon*, say *adverb*, and circle *left*? For more practice turn to Handbook pages 354–355.

Evaluation • Pronouns

A. Write the letter of the response that tells what the underlined part of each sentence is.

    a. direct object   **b.** predicate noun   **c.** predicate adjective

   1. David caught the curve <u>ball</u>.
   2. Spring flowers are <u>colorful</u>.
   3. Josh was not very <u>good</u>.
   4. Emiko will be a <u>dancer</u>.

   5. Laurie's foot seemed <u>swollen</u>.
   6. These people are circus <u>clowns</u>.
   7. Sam raised the <u>flag</u> every day.
   8. We measured the <u>rooms</u>.

B. Some of the following sentences contain mistakes. Write the number of each sentence in which a mistake occurs. Then write the letter of the word that is wrong in the sentence.

   1. Don't go without Sumi and them.
      a   b   c   d   e   f

   2. I said, "This is he speaking."
      a   b   c d   e   f

   3. They put Leon and he up front.
      a   b   c   d   e   f   g

   4. Him and Al played with magnets.
      a   b   c   d   e   f

   5. She ran between Jean and I.
      a   b   c   d   e   f

   6. The winners were her and Jack.
      a   b   c   d   e   f

   7. It was Tom and her at the door.
      a   b   c   d   e   f   g   h

   8. He gave Jo and I a puppy.
      a   b   c   d e   g

C. Some of the following sentences contain mistakes. Write the number of each sentence in which a mistake occurs. Then write the letter of the word that is wrong in the sentence.

   1. Please come to are concert.
      a   b   c   d   e

   2. It's almost time to start.
      a   b   c   d   e

   3. Tell us when their coming.
      a   b   c   d   e

   4. Your sure it was Anita?
      a   b   c d   e

   5. What are there names?
      a   b   c   d

   6. The dog wagged it's tail.
      a   b   c   d   e

   7. There was complete silence.
      a   b   c   d

   8. When is you're dad coming?
      a   b   c   d   e

   9. This is our school library.
      a   b   c   d   e

   10. Isn't they're garden lovely?
      a   b   c   d

Spotlight • Activities to Choose

1. Write a play. Work with 2 or 3 of your classmates to write a short play about an event that involves a Norman lord and lady and their Anglo-Saxon cook, maid, and gardener. Include words from French in the dialogue of the Norman characters and words from Old English in the dialogue of the Anglo-Saxon characters. Try to end your play with a joke or clever twist. Present the play for your class or another class in your school. <u>Words from French:</u> *trespass, culprit, jail, cost, constable, pay, debt, bracelet, dinner, pastry, dessert;* <u>Words from Old English:</u> *dough, knead, churn, bake, acre, knit, field, yarn, sew, sheep, heard, harvest.*

"My bracelet has been stolen! Who can the culprit be?"

2. Have fun with special words. Write 10 sentences in which direct objects, predicate nouns, predicate adjectives, or predicate pronouns can be supplied. Leave space in each sentence to write the missing word. Then, without revealing the sentences, ask a friend to give you the kind of words you need to complete them. For example, suppose one sentence read, *Elephants are very _____.* You would say to your friend, "Give me a word that can be a predicate adjective." Or, with the sentence, *You carried a _____ on your back,* you would ask for a word that could be a direct object. Complete your sentences with the words your friend supplies. Then read them aloud.

3. Analyze names. Make a list of the names of all the students in your class. Then go through the list to see whether any of the names are compounds (as *Lauralanne*), clips (as *Sam*), or blends (as *Marjoe*), or include an affix (as *Janie*).

4. Guess what they mean. Each of the following foreign words and phrases was borrowed from the English language: *Das Komik Buch, un pullover, futbol, atomobil, biftek, sukuruderiba.* Try to pronounce each. (When you do, you should be able to guess what each means.) Then use each in a sentence.

Answers: the comic book, a pullover, football, automobile, beefsteak, screwdriver.

240

The Guardians
by John Christopher

Set in England in 2052, this science-fiction story centers around the lives of two teen-agers, Rob Randall and Mike Gifford. The boys work for freedom in a land divided by two societies at war.

Cathedral: The Story of Its Construction
by David Macaulay

This richly illustrated book traces the step-by-step construction of a cathedral during the 13th century. The book presents the entire process—from laying the foundation to completing the towers.

The Code and Cipher Book
by Jane Sarnoff and Reynold Ruffins

If you want to learn how to turn a telephone into a code machine or how to make invisible inks, this is the book to read. Some of the secret messages are very old, some are modern; all are fun and challenging.

Unit Eight

Imagine that human life were discovered on Mars.
That would be news!

The Planet of Mars

On the planet of Mars
They have clothes just like ours,
And they have the same shoes and same laces,
And they have the same charms and same graces.
And they have the same heads and same faces
But not in the
Very same
Places.

Shel Silverstein

What might a newspaper headline say to announce such a discovery? What information might an article give to report the event? This unit will help you answer these questions.

Lesson 1 Finding What You Want to Read

Newspapers have indexes which help you find what you want to read.

Thinking It Through

Newspapers contain enormous amounts of information on a wide variety of subjects.

Look at these examples from different parts of a newspaper.

Because so much of this information is in different parts or sections of a newspaper, an index will help you find such items as comics, editorials, columns, and sports news. Study these two indexes.

A.

Amusements	36	Crossword	40
Bridge	35	Editorials	29
Business	64	Finance	65
Classifieds	74-88	Sports	89-98
Columnists	30-32	TV, Radio	34
Comics	40-41	Weather	88

B.

	Sec.	Pg.		Sec.	Pg.
Classifieds	4		Medicine	2	
Comics	3	2-3	Movies	3	5-6
Cooking	3	7-8	Sports	5	1-6
Editorials	2	2-5	TV, Radio	2	8
Horoscope	3	4	Weather	5	7

Notice that both indexes are arranged in alphabetical order. If you want to find out about the weather, you look under W in the index.

Index A lists just the page number after an entry. The pages in that newspaper are numbered in order.

- On what page would you find information on the weather?
- What would you find on page 64?

Index B lists both a section and a page number after each entry. This newspaper groups its news and features into related sections. Some newspapers identify sections by using letters instead of numbers.

Look at Index B again.

- What is the section and page number of the editorials? the sports?
- What would you find in Section 3, page 4?

Working It Through

A. Study the index printed on the next page. Then answer the following questions.

1. How are the sections identified?
2. How many sections are there in all?
3. Write the section and page number where you would find the entries listed below the index.

a. TV, Radio

b. Your Money's Worth

c. Classifieds

d. Agriculture News

e. Gourmet Today

f. Barbra Jones Says

g. Sports

h. Births, Weddings

i. Books

j. News Briefs

k. Obituaries

l. County Notes

B. Some of the entries you might find in a newspaper's index are listed below. Write the items, arranging them in alphabetical order. Use a columnist's last name to determine that item's position.

a. Crop Report

b. Ask Jerry White

c. Finances

d. Sports

e. Editorials

f. Letters

g. Fashion News

h. Marie Rodriguez

i. Weather

j. Crossword

k. Movies

l. Announcements

m. Ms. Quarterback

n. Health Report

o. National News

p. Hobbies

q. Berry Bergman

r. Washington Scene

s. Job Outlook

t. Gardening

Trying It Out

A pollster interviews people to determine their opinions and views on issues. Interview 5 people to find out each one's answers to the following questions. Compare your answers with those of your classmates.

1. How often do you read a newspaper?

2. Which newspaper do you read?

3. Do you read the entire paper or just certain parts?

4. If you read just certain parts, which ones?

5. Why do you read a newspaper?

Lesson 2   Headlines and News Stories

Headlines and news stories give you information about
something that has happened or something someone did or
said.

Thinking It Through

Look at the following cartoon.

● Does a headline such as "Principal Caught Stealing"
make you want to read the story?

A news story gives you the important facts in the first
sentence or paragraph which is called the **lead.** The lead
usually tells you the 5 Ws, or *who, what, when, why,* and
where:

> WHO said something, did something, or had
>   something done or happen to him or her?
> WHAT has WHO done? What has happened?
> WHEN did WHAT happen?
> WHY did something happen? Why was something
>   done or said?
> WHERE did it happen?

The remainder of the story gives you information in
order of importance, with the least important details at the
end. If you read only the headline and the lead, you will
still get the important information.

Read the news story on the following page. Notice how
the headline and the lead give you the important information.

Balloonists may have to ditch

WHO —
WHERE —
WHAT —
WHY —
WHEN —

ST JOHN'S Newfoundland (AP)—Two Britons trying to make the first crossing of the Atlantic in a balloon may be forced to ditch in the ocean because of a large split in their balloon, a project spokesman said Thursday.

Don Cameron and Christopher Davey took off from this Canadian city Wednesday and it was reported earlier Thursday they might reach the coast of France as early as Friday.

Working It Through

A. Find the answers to the 5 Ws in the following story.

Fawn milked her luck to the end
Epitaph for a flying cow

DAVENPORT, Iowa (AP)—Fawn The Flying Guernsey, the luckiest cow in Scott County, is dead at 25.

She died Saturday and was buried Monday in the orchard on the Chris Lohse farm north of Davenport.

"We just put her to rest in the orchard where she liked to graze," Mrs. Lohse said tearfully. "She had a very good life."

After two brushes with death, Fawn died of old age.

Twice—in 1962 and 1967—Fawn was swept off the ground by tornadoes and carried through the air. Both times she escaped unharmed. That was how she got to be the luckiest cow in Scott County.

Fawn was presumed lost after she disappeared in the first tornado on May 9, 1962. But a few days after the wind picked her up, she wandered back to the Lohse farm.

In 1967, during a freakish January tornado, Fawn was swooped into the air, blown across the road and once again escaped unharmed.

The event was witnessed by a busload of startled travelers who saw the cow fly by.

In her later years, she was a treasured family pet who spent her time grazing in the orchard with one eye on the sky.

"She knew her storms. Whenever a storm came, she always wanted to get out of the yard and into the barn," said Mrs. Lohse. "She could tell when one was coming."

248

B. Find the answers to the 5 Ws in each of the following two stories. Remember that stories do not always answer all the questions. Then, write a short headline for each story.

1.
The Israeli Scout Friendship Caravan, a group of 10 Boy and Girl Scouts from Israel, will present two programs of folk music and dance at the Museum of Science and Industry Aug. 3.

The 10:30 a.m. and 1:30 p.m. programs incorporate the songs and dances into a story telling about life in Israel. The performances will be held in the museum's auditorium.

2.
Mike Schmidt doubled to ignite a two-run third inning and added a two-run double in the sixth Tuesday night to lead Philadelphia to a 5-3 triumph over visiting San Diego. The victory combined with the Cubs' loss to the Astros put the first-place Phils four games in front of the Cubs.

Since moving to the leadoff spot in the Phillies' batting order, Schmidt has had eight hits, including two doubles and two home runs with seven RBI. He hasn't struck out.

Trying It Out

Write a headline and a story on one of the topics below, or choose one of your own. Include as many of the 5 Ws as you can in your lead paragraph.

a. a severe storm in your area

b. the birth of a brother or sister

c. a sports game or event you've seen

d. receiving a special award or honor

e. a class trip

f. an accident in your neighborhood

g. the birthday of a friend

h. a recent visitor to your classroom

Take Another Look Did you indent each paragraph in your story? Did you put the least important information at the end of your story? Did you write a headline that would make readers want to read your story?

Facts and Opinions in News Stories

News stories should present only facts, not the personal feelings and opinions of a reporter.

Thinking It Through

A **fact** is something that can be checked. You can check reference books to find out if a thing existed or an event happened. Your own experience also can prove whether something is a fact.

An **opinion** cannot be checked. Opinions are someone's personal thoughts and feelings about something. No reference book will tell you that an opinion is right or wrong.

Read these two examples.

A.

A bill was introduced by Sen. J. Doe in the Senate today to create two new 50,000-acre parks. Dawes Park would add three new campgrounds and two lakes to Fernwood Forest in the south. The Tulip Recreational Area will be a separate park, 45 miles from the capital.

B.

Another tax bill designed to waste the taxpayer's money was introduced in the Senate today. Sen. J. Doe wants two valuable 50,000 acre tracts to be parks, though the land would be better used for houses and factories. This bill is just another sneaky attempt by Congress to create 100,000 acres of additional noise and pollution.

Both stories present certain facts:

Sen. J. Doe presented a bill in the Senate today.

The bill would create two new parks.

Each park will contain 50,000 acres.

You could check written records or talk to senators and spectators to discover if these things occurred.

In addition to the facts, Example B also contains several opinions. You cannot check whether the new bill is "designed to waste the taxpayer's money." You cannot check whether the land "would be better used for houses and factories."

● What opinion is stated in the last sentence of Example B?

Working It Through

Read each of the following statements. If a statement can be checked, write *Fact*. If it cannot be checked, write *Opinion*. You should find 6 facts and 6 opinions.

1. Sleeping bags can be filled with synthetic fibers or with goose down.
2. Sleeping bags with goose down are the best.
3. They'll protect you from the cold to $-10°$ Centigrade.
4. Moosehorn Park has 300 campsites.
5. The good campsites are in Area G.
6. Nothing is better than cooking over a campfire.
7. Birchwood burns longer and brighter than pine.
8. Radios and TVs have no place in the campgrounds.
9. Radios and TVs cannot be played after 10 P.M.
10. Hiking is more fun than jogging.
11. Rainbow Falls is the best sight in the park.
12. Madman's Trail leads to the falls.

Trying It Out

The following story contains both facts and the personal opinions and feelings of the reporter. Rewrite it to eliminate the opinions.

COUGAR—The annual Pioneer Days Festival will be held August 3-4 this year at Bull Moose Park. Everyone should come because they'll have a great time!

Beginning Friday afternoon, our great town will host a pet parade, an event not to be missed. Pet dogs, cats, sheep, frogs, and a lizard will be dressed in circus outfits to march down Main Street. Prizes will be awarded.

Friday evening at 8, there will be a hootenanny of folk music for teens, and ghost stories around campfires for children. Don't bring kids under 10, since they might get scared.

Try not to miss the Soap Box Derby at 10 Saturday morning. It's really hilarious watching those homemade contraptions go 100 yards with just muscle power! Jackie Smith, who shouldn't have won last year, will be in the race.

Take Another Look

Does your story contain only facts? Have all personal opinions and feelings been eliminated? Did you use complete sentences?

Lesson 4　Opinions

A news story presents information. Editorials, columns, and letters to the editor present opinions.

Thinking It Through

Most newspapers have an editorial page. Editorials present the opinions of the editors and publishers. Columns and letters to the editor also present opinions. All three present opinions supported by facts which can be checked.

Read the following editorial and consider which sentences present facts and which present opinions.

[1]In 1975 our school day started at 8:30 in the morning. [2]This year it was decided that school should start at 8:10. [3]We believe that a later starting time is more convenient and considerate for both teachers and students. [4]A recent survey of teachers shows that 8 out of 10 preferred the later starting time. [5]We think most students would agree.

[6]The school board believes that a later tardy bell will only encourage students to be late for classes. [7]But the current attendance records show that tardiness has neither increased nor decreased with the new starting time. [8]We think the school board should reconsider its decision. [9]Everyone likes to sleep a little later in the morning.

In the first paragraph, sentences 1, 2, and 4 present facts. You could check if school started at 8:30 in 1975, if school starts at 8:10 now, and if 8 out of 10 teachers preferred the later starting time. Sentences 3 and 5 present opinions. Some people may agree that a later starting time is more convenient and considerate. Some may not. Some students may agree with the teachers while others may not.

- Which sentences in the second paragraph present facts?
- Which sentences in the second paragraph present opinions?
- Which facts in both paragraphs support opinions?

Working It Through

Read the following editorial carefully.

1. Make two columns, one labeled *Fact*, one labeled *Opinion*.
2. Write the sentences presenting facts under the column labeled *Fact.*
3. Write the sentences presenting opinions under the column labeled *Opinion.*

You should find 6 facts and 6 opinions.

Last week the state legislature voted to cut back educational funding by fifteen per cent. Yesterday, it was announced that because of those cutbacks, the school library would be forced to purchase fewer books. Our school's music programs will also be eliminated. We believe this is unfair.

Keeping the information available in the library up to date requires getting new books. You can't get good grades or learn anything without new books. The last reference books purchased by the library go back to 1960.

Music is an essential part of learning. Students have said they feel that music is as important to them as any other subject. The state should get rid of sports programs instead. Nobody likes to play football or jump over hurdles anyway.

To us, the legislature doesn't seem to care about students.

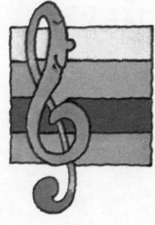

Trying It Out

1. Write a letter to the editor agreeing or disagreeing with the opinions presented in the editorial in either Thinking It Through or Working It Through.
2. State which opinions you agree or disagree with, and then present your reasons for feeling the way you do.

Take Another Look Did you follow the correct form for a letter to the editor as given on page 176? Did you present specific facts and reasons to support your opinions? Did you start a new paragraph each time you presented a new thought or idea?

Classified Ads

Classified ads can help you find a part-time job and buy or sell something.

Thinking It Through

Classified means "organized into classes or categories." The classified section of a newspaper contains advertisements for a variety of subjects organized under such categories as "job openings," "apartments for rent," and "items for sale." Information in this section is arranged alphabetically by subject and is listed in a separate index.

The ads are usually quite brief and written with many abbreviations. Read the ad below.

> **STUDENTS** needed for wknd. wk. Mow lawns, rake leaves. Sml. apt. bldg. $3.75/hr. Call 555-8246 after 5 P.M.

● Notice that the ad answers four of the 5 Ws:

WHO:	students
WHY:	to mow lawns, rake leaves
WHERE:	a small apartment building
WHEN:	weekends

Notice, too, that the pay is listed as well as when and where to call.

Remember that newspapers sell space for ads, but the advertisers write the words used. Learn to read carefully any ads you may be interested in. Don't be fooled by ads that may promise a lot of money for little work, or those which advertise an expensive item at a very low price.

Working It Through

A. Read the following advertisement. Identify the who, What, When, and Why.

> **INDY** 3-spd. bike for sale. Used once. Moving out of town. Must sell. Call Terry, 555-1000 after 3.

B. Imagine that your family wants to rent out your house or apartment. Write an ad, answering these questions:

1. WHAT is for rent—a house, apartment, trailer?
2. WHERE is it located?
3. WHY are you renting it—did your family buy a larger place or are you moving out of town?
4. WHO should be called? What is the telephone number?
5. WHEN can people call? When is the place available?

C. Write a help-wanted ad for a job you would like to have. You may use abbreviations.
1. Use only four lines.
2. Use only 35 letters for each line.
3. Put in as many of the 5 Ws as you can.

Trying It Out

1. Look through the help-wanted part of the classified ads in your newspaper to find a job you would enjoy. You may use instead the ad you wrote in Exercise C.
2. Write a letter to the employer to say that you are interested in the job.
3. Be sure to include WHO you are, WHERE you go to school or have worked before, WHAT job you want, WHY you want the job, and WHEN you could start.

Take Another Look   Did you include your address and date in the upper right-hand corner of your letter? Did you include the inside address? Did you include a closing and sign your letter legibly?

Your Own Newspaper

Your own bulletin-board newspaper can keep you informed of what's going on in your school and in your class.

Thinking It Through

Your class can keep informed of news, features, opinions, and things for sale by creating a bulletin-board newspaper. Groups of pupils can take responsibility for certain jobs.

School News Reporters. Report on what is happening in and around your school, including plays, a campaign to clean up the school grounds, and a new teacher.

Sports News Reporters. Report on sporting events in which your school and class participate.

Classroom News Reporters. Report on such items as a classmate's new puppy or baby brother or sister, a new student, a biology or science fair, or a class play.

Feature Writers. Write on hobbies, crafts, and other interests, such as installing a bicycle horn or making a pinhole camera. Features also include interviews with interesting people—a visiting artist or entertainer, a new principal, or someone who does something unusual for a living.

Columnists. Write, offering advice and information in a wide range of subjects, such as manners, photography, fashions, safety, movies, music, and books. Some columnists express opinions.

Advertising Department. Takes care of ads students might place to sell or give away bikes, pets, and clothing.

Each group should have individuals who do these jobs:

Assignment Editors. Find out what needs to be covered, assign reporters to do the stories, and give specific lengths and deadlines for the stories.

Reporters. Get an assignment, gather the information, interview sources, and write the stories.

Rewrite Editors. Rewrite a story so it is the correct length, and check to make sure the 5 Ws are in the lead of each story.

Other Editors. Write headlines or ads, proofread for spelling and punctuation, or recopy a story in their best handwriting.

Photographers or Illustrators. Provide pictures and drawings, such as maps and graphs, for certain stories which need them.

Working It Through

Study the list of groups in Thinking It Through.

1. Divide the class evenly into groups.
2. Each member of a group should choose one of the specific jobs.
3. No matter which job you have, keep your eyes and ears open and your notebook handy for news events you think should be in your newspaper.
4. Allow time for stories to be assigned, written, and recopied.

Trying It Out

Once groups are chosen, jobs are assigned, and stories and articles written, you will want to display your newspaper.

1. Divide a hallway, part of a wall, or a large bulletin board into sections labeled *School News*, *Sports News*, *Room _____ News*, *Columnists*, *Features*, and *Classifieds*.
2. Study newspapers to see how stories, photos, and illustrations, such as maps and graphs, are arranged.
3. Replace "stale" news with recent stories.

Review • Writing Opinions

A. Read the following paragraphs. Then follow the directions below.

The students at our school do not go on enough field trips. Last year each grade only took one field trip, and this year only one field trip per grade has been planned. In other years, classes have taken two or three field trips a year. The students at the other junior high schools in the area take more field trips than we do.

Field trips are worthwhile. There are many museums, science centers, and other interesting places to visit in this area. Many of these places have special tours just for students. Students learn many new things from field trips.

Students can easily earn money for field trips. They could earn money by having bake sales or car washes. Last year the French Club earned the money they needed to visit a French restaurant.

1. Tell what opinions are stated in the paragraphs.
2. Tell what facts are stated.
3. Tell whether you agree or disagree with the opinions. Give reasons to support your feelings.

B. Choose one of the statements below. Write two or more paragraphs telling whether you agree or disagree with the statement. Support your opinions with facts and reasons.
1. Our school is too strict.
2. Students should have to work around the school.
3. There are not enough school activities.

C. Think about the following questions.
1. Did you state your opinions clearly?
2. Did you give specific facts or reasons to support your opinions?

Evaluation • Writing Opinions

A. Read the paragraph below. Then follow these directions.

   1. Write the headings Facts and Opinions on a sheet of paper.

   2. Under Facts, write the sentences that present facts in the paragraph. Under Opinions, write those giving opinions.

   3. Describe your feelings about the topic. State reasons to support your feelings.

> A new state law was passed that requires all dog owners to keep their pets on leashes. It's a good law. Over 150 people were bitten last year by dogs allowed to run free. Most people are afraid of dogs, especially big ones. Dogs kept on leashes are better behaved. Dogs behave best when they are kept in and around their owners' homes.

B. Choose one of the statements below. Write two or more paragraphs telling whether you agree or disagree with the statement. Support your opinion with facts and reasons.

   1. There should be more jobs for children.

   2. People should read the newspaper every day.

   3. There should be stricter laws for littering.

   4. Parents should control what their children watch on TV.

You will be evaluated on how clearly you stated your opinions and the specific facts and reasons given to support them.

Have you ever . . .

"hissed your mystery class"
  instead of missed your history class?

"tasted the whole worm"
  instead of wasted the whole term?

These goofs, caused when someone mixes up the first parts of two words, can be fun, but also sometimes embarrassing. Such mistakes are called **spoonerisms,** after a man who became famous for coming up with many of them. Reverend W. A. Spooner, the Warden of New College, Oxford, England, seemed to have a real habit of mixing up words in this way. One of his well-remembered mix-ups came when he was trying to usher a woman into church. He came out with "May I sew you to a sheet?" What did he mean to say?

Here are a few more spoonerisms for you to unravel:

"A well-boiled icicle"

"A twenty-one sun galoot"

"The defeat was a blushing crow."

Have you heard any funny spoonerisms?

The word *spoonerism* was made from W. A. Spooner's name. Many other words also come from the names of people. For example, *maverick* comes from the name of Samuel Maverick, a Texas cattleman who didn't brand his calves but let them wander unmarked. The word now is used to mean either an unmarked animal or more informally to mean a person who won't join a regular political party.

Use a dictionary to find out about the people whose names were used to make these words.

bloomers	diesel
bobby	sideburns
braille	watt

Spotlight • Word Games

One way you can work on improving your vocabulary is by playing the word games you find in newspapers and magazines. Crossword puzzles are an all-time favorite, but here are some examples of other kinds of word games.

Rhyme Time

Each answer is a rhyming pair of words. The number in parentheses tells how many syllables each word has.

1. A rabbit that tells jokes (2)

2. A present that arrived quickly (1)

3. Recently bought piece of footwear (1)

4. A quacking waterfowl that landed in glue (1)

5. A seabird who is not very bright (1)

6. Library thief (1)

7. Fun with pirates' loot (2)

Word Scramble

Rearrange the scrambled words, one letter to a square, to form 4 real words.

RHOON

CHITH

IRSAT

CEABH

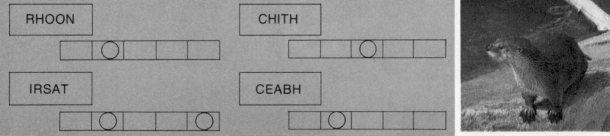

Use the circled letters to form a word that fits the picture.

Answers: 1. funny bunny, 2. swift gift, 3. new shoe, 4. stuck duck, 5. dull gull, 6. book crook, 7. treasure pleasure; honor, stair, hitch, beach, otter

261

Combining Sentences

Sentences can be combined with adjectives and appositives.

Thinking It Through

When sentences contain adjectives that describe the same nouns, the sentences can be combined.

The skier was graceful. The skier was young. The skier glided down the slopes. The slopes were sparkling.	The graceful young skier glided down the sparkling slopes.

The sentence *The skier glided down the slopes* is the main part of the combined sentence. The word *graceful* from the first sentence is an adjective that modifies *skier* in the combined sentence.

● Which word from the second sentence modifies *skier?*
● Which word from the fourth sentence modifies *slopes?*

Sometimes sentences can be combined by changing one sentence to an appositive that identifies a noun.

The skier was Amy Jordan. The skier swerved to miss a pine tree.	The skier, Amy Jordan, swerved to miss a pine tree.

● What is the appositive in the combined sentence? What noun does it identify?

Some combined sentences use adjectives **and** appositives.

The skier was Amy Jordan. The skier took off her mittens. The mittens were soggy.	The skier, Amy Jordan, took off her soggy mittens.

● Which sentence has been changed to an appositive?
● Which word from the third sentence modifies *mittens* in the combined sentence?

Working It Through

A. Combine the following groups of sentences.

1. Long ago mustangs galloped freely over the plains.
   The mustangs were wild.
2. These horses supplied power for farms and ranches.
   These horses were hardy.
   These horses were useful.
3. Bands of mustangs were a common sight in the Old West.
   The bands were large.

B. Combine these groups of sentences.

1. Jules Verne wrote tales.
   The tales were science fiction.
   Verne was a French novelist.
2. Felix Nadar was Verne's friend.
   Felix Nadar had a plan.
   The plan was exciting.
3. Nadar wanted to build a balloon.
   The balloon was huge.
   The balloon was free-floating.
4. Verne wrote a story about Dr. Fergusson.
   Dr. Fergusson was a rich man.
   Dr. Fergusson was an adventurous man.
5. Verne described Dr. Fergusson's adventures in a balloon.
   The adventures were incredible.
6. Verne also described a voyage to the moon.
   The voyage was scientific.

Trying It Out

Choose a topic that interests you.

1. Write 3 groups of sentences similar to those in
   Exercise A or B above.
2. Be sure each group of sentences can be combined,
   using adjectives or appositives or both.
3. Exchange papers with a classmate. Combine each
   other's groups of sentences. Each of you should write
   3 combined sentences.

Lesson 8 Combining Sentences

Sentences can be combined by using prepositional phrases.

Thinking It Through

Sometimes two sentences can be combined by changing one into a prepositional phrase that acts as an adjective.

That bike belongs to me. ———— That bike <u>with a flat tire</u> belongs to me.
It has a flat tire.

The underlined group of words in the combined sentence is a prepositional phrase that acts as an adjective.

● What noun does the phrase modify?
● Which sentence was changed into this phrase?

Sentences with prepositional phrases that describe the same person or thing can also be combined.

The boy in the striped shirt boarded the bus. ———— The boy in the striped shirt and corduroy slacks boarded the bus.
The boy in the corduroy slacks boarded the bus.

● Which prepositional phrases from the first two sentences were combined in the third sentence?
● What noun is modified by both phrases?

Sentences containing prepositional phrases that act as adverbs and modify the same verb can often be combined.

We left for the station. ———— We left for the station at noon.
We left at noon.

● Which prepositional phrases from the first two sentences were combined in the third sentence?
● What verb is modified by both phrases?

Working It Through

A. Combine the pairs of sentences on the next page.

1. Yesterday Dad and I walked to the supermarket.
   We walked in the rain.
2. We looked around the store.
   We looked for fifteen minutes.
3. We shopped for meat.
   We shopped for fresh vegetables.

B. Combine the following groups of sentences.

1. The stranger looked suspicious.
   He was wearing dark glasses.
   He was wearing a shapeless
   navy raincoat.
2. A boy with a blue cap saw the
   man turn down a side street.
   A boy with red gloves saw the
   man turn down a side street.
   The man was wearing a large hat.
   The man was wearing very dark
   glasses.
3. A lady in a beige dress called the
   police.
   A lady in a brown suede jacket
   called the police.
4. An officer drove a squad car.
   The officer wore a blue uniform.
   The car had flashing lights.
5. The officer found the man at an
   eye doctor's office.
   The officer found the man down
   the street.

Trying It Out

Write a detective story about a missing object.

1. Write groups of sentences to describe the owner of the
   object, the detective on the case, and any witnesses.
2. Make up groups of sentences that can be combined, as
   in Exercise B above.
3. Be sure the sentences can be combined with
   adjectives, appositives, or prepositional phrases.
4. Explain how and where the object was finally found.

Lesson 9 **Compound Subjects and Compound Predicates**

Two sentences with the same predicate or with the same subject can often be combined into one sentence.

Thinking It Through

Two sentences with the same predicate can be combined.

The coach watched the melting snow.   The coach and the skiers watched
The skiers watched the melting snow.   the melting snow.

The subjects of the first two sentences were combined to form a **compound subject** in the third sentence. Two or more subjects joined by *and* or *or* are called a compound subject.

Two sentences with the same subject can be combined.

The fans shook their heads.   The fans shook their heads and
The fans started to leave.   started to leave.

The underlined predicates in the first two sentences were combined in the third sentence to form a **compound predicate.** Two or more predicates joined by *and* or *or* are called a compound predicate.

Sometimes prepositional phrases, adjectives, or appositives can also be added to the combined sentence.

The fans were disappointed.   The disappointed fans in the
The fans were in the bleachers.   bleachers shook their heads and
The fans shook their heads.   started to leave.
The fans started to leave.

Mr. Lee was the drama coach.   Mr. Lee, the drama coach,
Mr. Lee encouraged the actors.   encouraged the young actors and
Mr. Lee gave the actors advice.   gave them advice.
The actors were young.

● In the first example, what adjective modifies *fans* in the combined sentence? What phrase modifies *fans?*

266

• In the second example, which sentence was changed to an appositive? What adjective modifies *actors*?

Working It Through

A. Combine each pair of sentences to form a third sentence with a compound subject.

1. The team boarded the bus.
   The coach boarded the bus.
2. Rain made the driving dangerous.
   Fog made the driving dangerous.
3. Photographers stood by the gates.
   Reporters stood by the gates.
4. Carol helped carry the trophy.
   I helped carry the trophy.

B. Combine each pair of sentences to form a third sentence with a compound predicate.

1. The hurricane raged.
   The hurricane howled.
2. Trees were bent by the wind.
   Trees were struck by lightning.
3. My baby brother cried.
   My baby brother yelled.
4. The lights in our house flickered.
   The lights in our house went out.
5. Finally, the storm died down.
   Finally, the storm ended.
6. The sun broke through the clouds.
   The sun glowed a warm yellow.

C. Combine these groups of sentences.

1. The store manager was Ms. Jacobs.
   The store manager put an ad in the newspaper.
   The store manager interviewed several people.
2. Ms. Jacobs hired an assistant.
   Ms. Jacobs told him to start on Monday.
   The assistant was new.
3. Ms. Jacobs walked with the assistant.
   The store detective walked with the assistant.
   They walked around the store.

Trying It Out

1. Write 2 groups of sentences that can be combined to form new sentences with compound subjects.
2. Write 2 groups of sentences that can be combined to form new sentences with compound predicates.
3. Use adjectives, appositives, and prepositional phrases.

Combining Sentences

Sentences can be combined with a conjunction or with a group of words beginning with *who*, *which*, or *that*.

Thinking It Through

Two complete sentences closely related in meaning can be joined by a conjunction such as *and*, *but*, or *or*. The combined sentence is called a **compound sentence.** Notice how the following sentences are combined.

Some engineers design spacecraft. Others design computers.	Some engineers design spacecraft, <u>and</u> others design computers.
Nurses can give medicine. They cannot prescribe it.	Nurses can give medicine, <u>but</u> they cannot prescribe it.
The actress will play the doctor. She will direct the play.	The actress will play the doctor, <u>or</u> she will direct the play.

When you write compound sentences, use *and* to show addition, use *but* to show contrast, and use *or* to express choice. Use a comma before the conjunction.

Some sentences can be combined by changing one sentence into a group of words starting with *who*, *which*, or *that. Who* refers to persons, *which* refers to things, and *that* refers to persons or things. Look at these examples.

The boy won the contest. The boy lives next door.	The boy <u>who lives next door</u> won the contest.
I opened the present. Julia gave me the present.	I opened the present <u>that</u> (or which) Julia gave me.

- In the first example, which sentence was changed into a group of words beginning with *who?* What noun does the group of words modify?
- In the second example, which sentence was changed into a phrase beginning with *that* or *which?* What noun does the group of words modify?

Working It Through

A. Combine the following pairs of sentences to form compound sentences. Use the conjunctions *and*, *but*, and *or*.

1. Some bakers bake only bread.
   Some bake only pastry.
2. Pam will go to college.
   Pam will join the army.
3. Secretaries must type fast.
   They must also type accurately.
4. Carl wants to be a park ranger.
   He must study forestry first.
5. Do you want to be an electrician?
   Do you want to be a contractor?
6. Auto mechanics repair cars.
   Many can also repair motorcycles.
7. Ben will teach in a high school.
   Ben will teach in a college.
8. Josie plans to be a pianist.
   Her sister plans to be a pilot.

B. Combine the following pairs of sentences using groups of words beginning with *who, which*, or *that*.

1. The guitar is broken.
   The guitar belongs to my brother Harold.
2. The violinist is quite famous.
   The violinist played the solo.
3. The robot is being sold at the local toy store.
   The robot was designed by Mr. Clark.
4. I finished the science project.
   I began the project two weeks ago.
5. Leo read the mystery.
   Sarah recommended the mystery.
6. The student teacher was very helpful.
   The student teacher explained our math lesson.
7. The dishes were dirty.
   The dishes were stacked in the sink.
8. We talked to a man.
   The man was feeding the pigeons.

Trying It Out

Suppose that a spaceship has just landed in your yard.

1. Write 3 sentences about the creatures <u>who</u> were in the spaceship.
2. Write 3 sentences about the noise <u>that</u> (or <u>which</u>) the spaceship made.

Lesson 11   Using Commas in Sentences

Use commas to separate a noun of address or an introductory word from the rest of a sentence. Set off an introductory prepositional phrase only when necessary for clarity.

Thinking It Through

Notice how the comma completely changes the meaning of the second sentence in the following example.

> Dr. James Frank has a headache.
> Dr. James, Frank has a headache.

In the second sentence *Dr. James* is the person spoken to or addressed. When you speak to someone and use that person's name or title, the name or title is called a **noun of address.** Separate the noun of address from the rest of the sentence with a comma or commas.

● What is the noun of address in each of these sentences?

> The violinist is Laura, Anne.
> When you stop writing, Mrs. Gomez, please see me.

Use a comma to separate an introductory word, such as *yes, no,* or *well,* from the rest of the sentence:

> Yes, I'm wearing my seat belt.

Use a comma after an introductory prepositional phrase only when it is necessary to make the meaning clear:

> In the afternoon classes were dismissed.
> In the afternoon, classes were dismissed.

> To John Howard seemed adventurous.
> To John, Howard seemed adventurous.

● Which sentence in the first example is clearer? Why?
● Which sentence in the second example makes it clear that two people are being discussed?

A. Add 18 commas to the following conversation to set off nouns of address and introductory words.

"Georgette have you seen *The 50-Foot Frog* yet?" Chuck asked.

"No I haven't Chuck. Have you seen it?"

"No I haven't, either. But Lefty has. He said it's great!"

"Well it was terrible Chuck," Sue interrupted. "Take my advice Georgette and don't go see it."

"Is it scary Sue?" Chuck asked.

"Yes it is in some parts. But mostly it's boring."

"You're wrong Sue," defended Lefty.

"No I'm not Lefty," Sue said. "You're not going to waste your money, are you Georgette?"

"No I don't think so. Well thanks Sue for the advice."

B. Write each sentence. Add a comma after an introductory prepositional phrase if it is necessary to make the meaning of a sentence clear. You should add 3 commas.

1. In our classroom activities are posted every week on the bulletin board.
2. In our classroom we have an aquarium with tropical fish.
3. To Joan Allen seemed bored.
4. At the county fair I won a blue ribbon for my delicious strawberry-rhubarb pie.
5. In our county fair days are big events.

Trying It Out

Imagine that the school paper has asked you to interview a famous person, a friend, or an imaginary creature.

1. Prepare at least 10 questions. Set them up so that several answers will begin with *yes* or *no*.
2. Several questions should contain the name of the person you are interviewing.
3. Use your name in several of the responses.
4. Write your interview. If you wish, post it on your classroom's bulletin-board newspaper.

Take Another Look Did you use commas to separate all nouns of address and introductory words?

Problem Verbs

Some pairs of verbs are confusing because they have similar meanings or because they look alike.

Thinking It Through

Study the chart below. It shows the principal parts of several regular and irregular verbs.

Simple	Past	Past Participle
lay	laid	(has/have) laid
lie	lay	(has/have) lain
set	set	(has/have) set
sit	sat	(has/have) sat
let	let	(has/have) let
leave	left	(has/have) left
lend	lent	(has/have) lent
borrow	borrowed	(has/have) borrowed
teach	taught	(has/have) taught
learn	learned	(has/have) learned
bring	brought	(has/have) brought
take	took	(has/have) taken

Choosing which one of these pairs of verbs to use in a sentence can cause problems. The following guidelines will help you choose the right verb and its correct form.

1. Use *lay* when you mean "to put or place." Use *lie* when you mean "to rest or recline."

2. Use *set* when you mean "to put something somewhere." Use *sit* when you mean "to sit down."

3. Use *let* when you mean "to allow or permit." Use *leave* when you mean "to go away."

4. Use *lend* when you mean "to give." Use *borrow* when you mean "to get."

5. Use *teach* when you mean "to show how to do." Use *learn* when you mean "to gain knowledge."

6. Use *bring* when you mean "to carry something toward." Use *take* when you mean "to carry something away."

Working It Through

A. Choose the correct verbs in the sentences below.

1. Can I (borrow, lend) your camera?
2. Sure, I'll (borrow, lend) it to you.
3. Has anyone (taught, learned) you how to use it?
4. Yes, Ms. Murphy (taught, learned) me in photography class.
5. (Let, Leave) me (bring, take) it over.
6. I'll (set, sit) on the porch and wait.
7. (Bring, Take) your slides too.
8. I've (sat, set) up the projector that you (borrowed, lent) me.
9. I also (laid, lay) out the light table so we can sort them.
10. My brother (laid, lay) down so we must (leave, let) him alone.
11. Will your parents (leave, let) me bring my dog?
12. Yes, (bring, take) him along with you.

B. Write the following, choosing the correct verbs.

Mom was the first to (**1.** teach, learn) me about photography. She used to (**2.** take, bring) me to exhibits, and we would (**3.** set, sit) and look at photographs. She'd then (**4.** teach, learn) me what made a good or bad picture.

After a while, I wanted to (**5.** borrow, lend) her camera, but she wouldn't (**6.** borrow, lend) it to me because it was a very expensive one.

"I'll (**7.** let, leave) you use my old box camera instead," she said.

Mom then wanted me to (**8.** learn, teach) how to develop film. She (**9.** took, brought) me to her darkroom which was (**10.** set, sit) up in the basement.

We had to (**11.** lay, lie) all the equipment out in order and (**12.** set, sit) out the chemicals so we could find everything in the dark.

Then I (**13.** laid, lay) the film reels in the developing tanks and (**14.** sat, set) the tanks in water to keep the chemicals at 72° F. After fixing the film, I (**15.** took, brought) out the reels and rinsed the film in water. Then I hung the film by one end and (**16.** let, left) it dry.

Trying It Out

Choose 8 of the following verb pairs. Write an original sentence using <u>both</u> verbs in each pair you choose.

1. bring, take
2. borrowed, lent
3. lay, lie
4. set, sit
5. teach, learn
6. let, left
7. laid, lay
8. brought, took
9. borrow, lend
10. sat, set
11. leave, let
12. taught, learned

Review • Conjunctions and Verbs

A. Write the following sentences. Circle all the conjunctions.
1. We'd like to go skating, but there isn't time.
2. Keiko and Nora are brushing their dogs.
3. We will either go camping or hike in the forest.
4. The wind blew and snow fell.

B. Using conjunctions, combine the following pairs of sentences to form compound sentences.
1. The favorite season of some people is summer.
   Others prefer fall.
2. Our trip to Hawaii was perfect.
   I hope we can go there again.
3. Shirley may go to college next fall.
   She may get a job instead.
4. We tried to get Allan to come with us.
   He had other plans.
5. We wanted to buy a new car.
   We decided to get a good used car.

C. Complete each sentence with one of the words in parentheses.
1. May I please ____ your bike?   (lend, borrow)
2. Will you ____ me wear your sweater?   (let, leave)
3. My dad ____ me to play the piano.   (taught, learned)
4. Let's ____ our ball and mitt along.   (take, bring)
5. The dog ____ down by the fire.   (laid, lay)
6. Mom is going to ____ down on the sofa.   (lay, lie)

For extra practice turn to pages 367 and 374.

Take Another Look   Complete the sentence with the correct word in parentheses.

   ____ car is a blue sedan.   (Their, They're, There)
Did you use *their*?
For more practice turn to Handbook pages 356–357.

Evaluation • Conjunctions and Verbs

A. Write the letter of each word that is a conjunction. If the sentence is a compound sentence, write *Yes*. If it is not, write *No*.

1. Rita wants to swim, but Joe doesn't.   Yes   No
   a   b   c   d   e   f   g

2. Jack paints and acts on TV or on the stage.   Yes   No
   a   b   c   d   e   f   g   h   i   j

3. Snow or rain is forecast for tomorrow.   Yes   No
   a   b   c   d   e   f   g

4. I'd go, but my homework isn't done yet.   Yes   No
   a b   c   d   e   f   g   h

5. You can use this door or the one on the porch.   Yes   No
   a   b   c   d   e   f   g   h   i   j   k

6. Our reports are due, but mine isn't ready.   Yes   No
   a   b   c   d   e   f   g   h

7. Be sure to wear a warm sweater or a coat.   Yes   No
   a   b   c   d   e   f   g   h   i   j

8. We flew to Arizona, and they met our plane.   Yes   No
   a   b   c   d   e   f   g   h   i

B. Write the letter of the word that completes the sentence correctly.

1. Jorge was going to ____ down.   **a.** lay   **b.** lie
2. They ____ out here in the evening.   **a.** set   **b.** sit
3. ____ Delores see the picture.   **a.** Let   **b.** Leave
4. Did your dad ____ you to swim?   **a.** learn   **b.** teach
5. She'll ____ it here Tuesday.   **a.** take   **b.** bring
6. The dog ____ at her feet.   **a.** lay   **b.** laid
7. Did you ____ this bat from Tim?   **a.** borrow   **b.** lend
8. Namiko, ____ the lamp here.   **a.** set   **b.** sit
9. He has ____ there an hour.   **a.** laid   **b.** lain
10. Did you ____ how to knit today?   **a.** learn   **b.** teach
11. She ____ her book to Nancy.   **a.** borrowed   **b.** lent
12. ____ the food over there.   **a.** Take   **b.** Bring

Spotlight • Activities to Choose

1. Begin a family newsletter. Put together a newsletter to send round robin to members of your family. Besides interesting family news, your newsletter can include the following: your own editorial, want ads describing items you would like to trade or jobs you'd like to do, crossword puzzles or other word games you make up. Invite family members to add their own newsy items to the newsletter before they send it on.

2. Have a contest. Get together with interested classmates and have a contest for the most interesting or unusual headline. Display contest entries on a bulletin board. All who took part in the contest can vote to select the best entry. The prize for the person who found the winning entry might be choosing and leading group games for a week.

3. Combine sentences. Work with a friend to do this activity. First, each of you choose one of the following nouns: *sunset, summer, rain, cities, litter, butterfly, cave, spaceship, costume, friend, vacation.* Write 3 short sentences telling something about the noun you chose. Then exchange sentences. Use conjunctions and words such as *who, that,* and *which* to combine the 3 sentences you received to make 1 sentence. Continue in this way, using other nouns from the list.

4. Get firsthand information. Plan a class visit to a local newspaper office. Or, invite a reporter or other newspaper employee to visit your classroom. Prepare a list of questions that will help you get the information you want about putting out a newspaper.

5. Make up tongue twisters. Use some of the problem verbs presented in Lesson 12 in original tongue twisters. For example, you might say, "Tim took tape to Tom," or, "Sue sat on Sheila's settee."

Spotlight • Books to Read

What Can She Be? A Film Producer
by Gloria and Esther Goldreich

This book introduces the everyday world of a film producer. It shows how a children's TV special is made—from planning, filming on location, editing, and sound mixing to videotaping the complete film.

Nellie Bly: First Woman Reporter
by Iris Noble

In 1885, young Elizabeth Cochrane became America's first woman reporter. She used the name Nellie Bly for her articles. To get information for her articles, she went into slums, toured the world, and posed as an immigrant.

The Make-It, Play-It, Show Time Book
By Roz Abisch and Boche Kaplan

How would you like to put on an old-time silent movie, a magic show, or a country-and-western music concert? This book can help make you a performer. Step-by-step directions are given for making costumes, props, scenery, and sets from ordinary objects you find around the house.

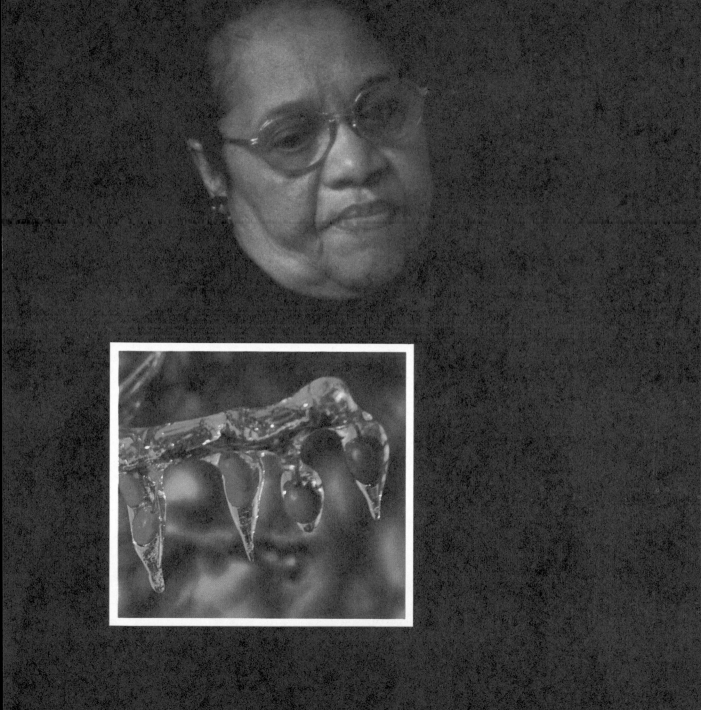

Unit Nine

Imagine an autumn flower, wind-blown and bent by a freezing rain. Why do you think the poet has chosen this kind of flower to describe a troubled woman?

Troubled Woman

She stands
In the quiet darkness
This troubled woman
Bowed by
Weariness and pain
Like an
Autumn flower
In the frozen rain,
Like a
Wind-blown autumn flower
That never lifts its head
Again.

Langston Hughes

You can almost see this troubled woman through the poet's description. Telling how someone looks, acts, and feels makes a character vivid and real. In this unit you will learn how to use details to make characters you describe seem real.

Describing How People Look

Specific details about how someone looks can create a vivid description of that person.

Thinking It Through

Read the following paragraph.

When you first meet my brother, his looks can fool you. Part of his face is hidden by his neat, rusty-red beard, though he's only nineteen. He is over six feet tall and well built. His arm and neck muscles bulge from under his faded-blue work shirt. His hands, already rough from working in the fields, still show a feeling of gentleness, as do his warm eyes.

• Which of the pictures at the left do you think the paragraph describes?

• Which specific details in the paragraph helped you pick out the picture?

When describing people, focus on the details about their looks—such as their eyes, hair, hands, and clothes. Then choose the important descriptive details to make that person seem real in your writing.

• What details could you add to the following list to describe the person in the last picture?

raven black hair   broad shoulders   white turtleneck shirt

Working It Through

A. Choose the two details from each group that will create a clearer word picture for the general description. Then write one more descriptive detail for each.

1. He looks tired.
   - **a.** half-closed eyes
   - **b.** wearing a new shirt
   - **c.** stooped shoulders

2. Our neighbor seems worried.
   - **a.** mowing the lawn
   - **b.** wringing hands
   - **c.** wrinkled forehead

3. My sister dresses neatly.
   - **a.** spotless skirt
   - **b.** crisp blouse
   - **c.** a purse

4. Henry was really angry.
   - **a.** red-flushed cheeks and ears
   - **b.** dirty fingernails
   - **c.** clenched fists

5. Estella is a beautiful baby.
   - **a.** drinks all her milk
   - **b.** tiny bunny nose
   - **c.** winter-gray eyes

B. Choose one of the following as an opening sentence for a paragraph. Then write the paragraph, using specific descriptive details to create a vivid description.

1. My brother is strong.
2. Charlene looks sad today.
3. He is quite a graceful dancer.
4. I feel awful.

Trying It Out

Imagine that you and your younger brother, sister, or friend have become separated in a large store. Write a description to give to the store's security guards. See the example at the right.

My younger sister's name is Abigail. She is three years old. She has curly black hair, a cute nose, and tiny hands the size of plums. She is wearing a yellow sweatshirt with a picture of Beethoven on it. The last time I saw her, she was clutching Rags, her teddy bear.

Describing How People Feel and Think

Describing the ways that people feel and think is another good way to make characters seem real.

Thinking It Through

Tom and his rather overweight dog, Genevieve Trueheart, have just come face to face with a Vancouver panther:

> Tom felt sick and cold, but his brain was working. I can't run, he thought, if I run he'll be on me. He'll rip Genevieve with one paw and me with the other. Tom thought, too, that if he had a match he could rip pages from one of his books and set them on fire for he knew cougars and tigers and leopards and lions were afraid of anything burning. . . . Maybe, he thought, if I had a big stone I could stun him. He looked. There were sharp, flat pieces of granite at the side of the road where somebody had blasted.

- What words and phrases tell you Tom was frightened?
- What does Tom think of doing?
- Based on what Tom feels and thinks, how would you describe him as a person?

The ways characters in stories feel and think, especially in critical situations, can reveal much about whether they are honest, generous, resourceful, brave, excited, mean, or sad.

Working It Through

A. Beside each emotion, write the sentence that best describes it.

1. Affectionate
2. Sad
3. Excited
4. Angry
5. Imaginative
6. Kind

a. She let all the neighborhood kids ride her new bike.
b. He lovingly smoothed the crying baby's hair.
c. The clown's heart was like a broken vase.
d. Throwing down her bat, she glared at the umpire.
e. Their plan was a spark of light.
f. She jumped up and down with joy as her name was announced as the winner.

B. Rewrite the following paragraph to add specific descriptions of the character's thoughts and feelings. Refer to the paragraph in Thinking It Through as an example.

Jane is coming home from school. She is feeling quite excited because it is her birthday, and a week ago, she overheard her father and mother making plans for a surprise birthday party. As she gets closer to her apartment, she hears voices saying, "Shhhhh."

Trying It Out

Imagine yourself in one of the following situations, or choose one of your own. Write a paragraph describing your thoughts and feelings. Be sure to add details that will create a vivid picture.

1. You are up to bat in the bottom of the ninth inning. The bases are loaded, and there are two outs. Your team needs two runs to win the championship.
2. You find a wallet with fifty dollars in it. The new radio you have been saving for costs forty dollars.
3. You are at an awards presentation, and the judges announce that your citizenship essay has won first prize.
4. You forgot to do a reading assignment. Your teacher announces he or she is going to give a surprise quiz.

Describing How People Act

Use specific details in your stories to describe how people act.

Thinking It Through

Read the following paragraph. Pay close attention to the specific details which describe the character's actions.

> Corinne sat waiting for the bus to arrive. Soon she would be reunited with her father whom she hadn't seen in three years. She crossed and uncrossed her legs, and her eyes darted to the clock on the wall every few seconds. Sitting on the edge of her seat, she wondered what she would say to him.
>
> Finally, she got up, and without looking, picked up a magazine from a nearby rack. She flipped the pages quickly, not really noticing the pictures she was looking at. At last, the loudspeaker blared, announcing the bus had arrived. Corinne jumped, then slowly walked to the gate.

You can tell by the way she acts that Corinne is nervous and anxious about seeing her father again.

Notice how each of the following details focuses on and helps present a clear picture of a nervous, anxious person:

> crossed and uncrossed her legs
> eyes darted to the clock
> sitting on the edge of her seat
> not noticing the pictures

Working It Through

A. List the phrases you could use to describe someone who is bored.

half-closed eyes
wringing his hands
staring into space

stifling a yawn
stretching his arms
wrinkling his forehead

B. List at least three details you would use in a paragraph to describe the actions of the people described below.

1. Billy was a very generous person.
2. Jill was quite tired.
3. Angela is the friendliest kid I know.
4. Walter panicked when he remembered that he forgot his music.
5. Meg looked so surprised.
6. I was embarrassed when she called out my name.
7. He walked absent-mindedly down the street.

C. Read the paragraphs below.

1. Pay close attention to the details that describe Jack acting in an excited, happy manner.
2. Rewrite the description using details to describe how he might have acted if he hadn't been elected captain.

Jack wanted to fly home with the news. He quickly grabbed his coat, snatched up his books, and hurriedly said good-bye to his teammates. Bounding down the stairs three at a time, Jack could hardly keep from yelling "Whoopee!" People he passed on the street stared at the strange grin bursting out on Jack's glowing face.

When he got to his house, he dashed up the sidewalk and flung open the front door. "Mom! Dad! Jennie! I won! I've been elected team captain!"

Trying It Out

Select one of the topics below, or one of your own, and write a description of what you would do in a pantomime of the character. (In a pantomime you use the actions of only your body and face to express ideas.) Later, get together with your classmates and perform your pantomimes.

1. Someone getting ready for the first day in a new school
2. Someone waiting in a long line
3. Someone very hungry sitting down to a big dinner
4. Someone about to take his or her first plane ride

Writing Conversation

Conversation can reveal much about characters' personalities. It also makes stories seem more real.

Thinking It Through

In the following conversation, Sam tries to get a baseball autographed by Jackie Robinson, a famous ballplayer with the old Brooklyn Dodgers.

"Let the kid go," Jackie Robinson said when he got to the railing. "All he wants is an autograph."

"He's a fresh kid," the usher said, but he let me go.

"Kids are supposed to be fresh," Jackie Robinson said.

I thrust my ball into Jackie Robinson's face. "Gee, thanks, Mr. Robinson," I said. "Sign it, please."

"You got a pen?" he asked.

"A pen?" I could have kicked myself. "A pen?" I'd forgotten a pen! I turned to the usher. "You got a pen?"

"If I had," the usher replied triumphantly, "I certainly wouldn't lend it to you!"

"Oh, come on," Jackie Robinson said, "don't be so vindictive. What harm did the kid do after all?"

You can tell from what he said that Jackie Robinson was a kind man and that he liked and understood young people. You can also tell that Sam was first very excited at meeting the famous ballplayer, then very disappointed for forgetting to bring a pen.

- Pick out the words Jackie Robinson said that indicate he was kind and understanding.
- Reread the usher's reply to Sam's question. What does it tell you about the usher?

We often learn what we know about people from what they say and how they say it. Conversation also makes stories and the characters in them seem more lifelike.

Here are some guidelines for punctuating conversations:

1. Begin a new paragraph each time there is a change of speaker.
2. Begin each quoted sentence with a capital letter.

3. Enclose all quoted words within quotation marks.

4. When a quoted sentence is broken up by words such as "she said" or "he asked," do not begin the remainder of the sentence with a capital letter.

5. Quotation marks almost always follow other punctuation.

Working It Through

A. Read the following conversation and answer the questions.

"Okay, Sis, where is it?" Felipe asked. "You stole it. Now give it back!"

"Cool it, Felipe," Isabel replied. "Take it easy. Stole what?"

"My new record. It's gone and you took it. I'm telling Mom and Dad."

"Aw, quit whining, Felipe," Isabel said. "I didn't steal it."

"But I left it on the floor by the stereo."

"Did you look in the record rack?" she asked. "That's where it should be."

"I never thought of that. Well, maybe you're right," Felipe said softly, leaving the room. "Thanks."

1. How would you describe Felipe from what he says early in the conversation? Which words make you think so?

2. How would you describe Felipe at the end? Which words make you think so?

3. Which words spoken by Isabel might make you think she is patient and helpful?

B. Rewrite the following conversation using the guidelines in Thinking It Through to add quotation marks correctly.

Hi, Mrs. Omachi!

Why, hello, Theresa. What brings you here so early on a Saturday?

Well, Mrs. Omachi, I wondered if you needed someone to mow the lawn and rake leaves.

I just might, replied Mrs. Omachi. How much do you charge?

What do you think is fair, Mrs. Omachi? Theresa asked. Does three dollars an hour seem all right?

That sounds fine, she replied.

C. Write what someone might say in each of the following situations.

1. A driver in a car waiting for a long train to go by
2. A volunteer collecting for a charity
3. A police officer to a lost child
4. A teacher to a pupil with an "A" spelling paper
5. A boy or girl seeing a parent who has been away for three years
6. A youngster trying to get a bigger allowance from his or her parents
7. A dentist to a patient
8. A young person to an ill relative

Trying It Out

Select one of the following situations, or choose one of your own. Write a short conversation that might occur between the two people indicated.

1. A nervous coach and a confident player before the championship game
2. An understanding neighbor and a frightened child who just broke a window
3. A parent and a child during vacation
4. The winner and the loser after class elections

Take Another Look Use these questions to improve the conversation you wrote.

1. Do the words your characters use reveal how they feel, think, and act?
2. Did you enclose all quoted words with quotation marks?
3. Did you begin each quoted sentence with a capital letter?
4. Did you begin a new paragraph each time there was a change of speaker?

Writing a Story

The looks, thoughts and feelings, actions, and conversations of characters are important in the stories you write.

Thinking It Through

In the previous four lessons, you have learned how to describe how people look, how they feel and think, how they act, and what they say. You can use all of these together when you write stories.

The following selection is from *The Search for Delicious*, by Natalie Babbitt. Pay close attention to the details the author uses to describe her characters' looks, thoughts, feelings, actions, and conversations.

Gaylen rode up to the house and called, "Gather round! Gather round! I'm here on the King's business!"

The woman on the porch peered out at the boy and the big horse in his royal draperies, and her eyes opened very wide. She put aside the bowl of potatoes she had been peeling and called in a loud voice, "Mildew! *Mildew!* Come here at once!" Then she came down the path. She was a big woman with a red face and red hands and she wore a dark jacket and a great many skirts and petticoats. The man who had been plowing loped puffing to her side and they both stood staring up at Gaylen with their mouths open.

Gaylen took out the proclamation and unrolled it, fumbling self-consciously. He read in a voice somewhat louder than necessary:

Let it be known that every single creature in my kingdom who is capable of speech shall register with my messenger the following information: name, age, home, and the foods he or she honestly believes to be the most delicious of all foods.

Then he rolled up the proclamation again and took out the notebook.

The farmer and his wife looked at each other and then looked back at Gaylen. An expression of self-satisfaction spread over the woman's red face and she reached up a hand to smooth the knot of hair at the back of her neck. "The most delicious food, is it?" she beamed. "Well, now, there's no trouble with that. My name is Whimsey Mildew and I'm fifty-nine, and I make the best fruitcake in the kingdom. It's by far the most delicious thing there is and I'm sure a great many people will agree with me." She stopped and looked expectantly at her husband.

But the farmer scratched at his knee nervously and kept his eyes on Gaylen. "Did the King say we have to be honest?"

"Absolutely," said Gaylen.

"Honest, eh?" said the farmer. He looked miserably up at the sky and swallowed. Then he looked at Gaylen again. His eyes narrowed. He shoved his hands into his pockets and drew a deep breath. "My name is Mildew," he said slowly, "and I'm sixty-one, and *I just hate fruitcake!*" His wife's jaw dropped and she stared at him, her face changing to a deeper shade of red. "I don't care, Whimsey!" he cried. "I'm glad it's out at last. For thirty years I've been eating that fruitcake of yours—*ugh!*—when all I really wanted was a simple plumcake. *Plumcake!* Do you hear?"

"Plumcake?" choked his wife, her face now quite purple. "You'd rather have a soggy plumcake than my fruitcake? I can't believe it. I can't *stand* it! *Plumcake!*"

"Now, Whimsey, don't be cross," pleaded the farmer, but it was too late. She turned on him and grabbed at his jacket. He dodged away and headed off across the yard and out into the field, the plowed earth flying up from his heels, and his wife churned after him, mighty in anger, with her skirts flapping out behind.

Gaylen sat in dismay and watched them disappear into an alder wood behind the farm. He sat until he could no longer hear them shouting. And then all of a sudden he felt very tired. "No wonder the woldweller says there will always be wars," he said to Marrow. He wished he were back in the orchard again, listening to the minstrel's songs. But the minstrel was far away. Gaylen wrote the votes in the notebook and slid it into his saddlebag. Then he touched his horse's ribs with his heel and they moved slowly off down the road.

- What details did you notice?

Working It Through

A. Think of an idea for a story and write it down in a few sentences. Look for ideas from your own life, from your imagination, and from others' experiences.

B. Use these steps to plan your story:

1. Who are the people or characters that will be in your story? Write their names.
2. Write a list of words and phrases to answer each of these questions:
   a. How does each character look?
   b. How might each character feel and think?
   c. How might each character act?
   d. What might each character say?

Trying It Out

Write a story, using the idea and characters you invented. Follow these guidelines:

1. Think of a place where these characters are and of what might happen there.
2. Write on every other line so you will have room to improve your first draft.
3. Write a beginning that will catch your readers' interest.
4. Use specific details about your characters.
5. Use conversations to make your story lively.
6. Include action in the middle of your story to keep your readers' interest.
7. Write a good ending.
8. Write a title that will interest readers.

Before handing in your story, turn to Lesson 6, "Improving Your First Draft."

Lesson 6 Improving Your First Draft

You can improve the first draft of your story by adding details about your characters and by adding conversation.

Thinking It Through

Read part of Jim's story with some of the improvements he made in it.

Proofreader's Marks

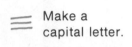

≡ Make a capital letter.

⊙ Add a period.

ℓ Take out.

∧ Put in one or more words.

⁋ Begin a new paragraph.

∧ Put in a comma.

Bobbie could hardly wait for the steer judging to begin. she had spent four long years on her project, raising Reggie a steer from a calf to a 1200-pound reserve grand champion. ⁋ Bobbie's entry was to be judged last. As she waited for the judges to reach her stall, she paced up and down and fiddled with her the scarf, around her ponytail. Then she shined the tops of her scuffed boots on the back of her stiff, new jeans. Her sweaty hands showed she was nervous. Her knees felt funny, too.

Finally, the judges came to her. One judge introduced herself, then she asked Bobbie her name and her steer's name. Another judge asked what she had been feeding him, and whether if the steer had ever been sick or injured.

- Which details did Jim add to improve the descriptions of his characters' looks? thoughts and feelings? actions?
- What marks of punctuation did Jim add?
- Where did Jim decide to start a new paragraph? Why?

Working It Through

A. Rewrite and improve Jim's story, using the details he added and answering the following questions.

    1. What else could you say about how Reggie looked?

    2. What color is Bobbie's hair? her scarf?

    3. Does the sentence "Her knees felt funny too" give a clear picture? Add more specific details.

    4. How many judges were there? What did they look like?

    5. What was Bobbie feeling and thinking as the judges came up to her?

    6. Where in Jim's story would you add conversation?

    7. What was Bobbie feeling and thinking as the judges were asking their questions?

B. Write a title and an ending for the story.

Trying It Out

    1. Improve the first draft of the story you wrote in Lesson 5 by answering these questions:

        a. Where can you add specific details to give a clearer picture of your characters' looks? thoughts and feelings? actions?

        b. Where can you add conversation to make your story more real, interesting, and lively?

        c. Did you use the guidelines for punctuating conversations on pages 286 and 287?

        d. Have you given a clear picture of where your story takes place?

        e. Are the events that happen in your story in the right order?

        f. Do you have any run-on sentences or sentence fragments?

        g. Have you checked all the punctuation and indented every paragraph?

    2. Ask a classmate to read your story and to write 2 questions to improve it.

    3. Revise your story using your classmate's questions and the questions above.

Review • Describing a Character

A. Read the following description of a story character. Then answer the questions that come after it.

Jennifer climbed briskly up the steep, rocky path, carrying her backpack. She was a tall, slender, blue-eyed girl with short brown hair. She loved to hike, and her movements were sure-footed and graceful. Suddenly a vista opened in front of her. Range after range of mountains extended as far as she could see. The twelve-year-old girl stood stock-still, her eyes filled with wonder. She breathed deeply of the pure air. The sun felt warm on her bare, tanned arms. This was what she had always wanted—to be alone in the wilderness. She felt peaceful and happy.

1. What did Jennifer look like?
2. Was she athletic? How can you tell?
3. Did she notice the sights, smells, and other things around her? How do you know?
4. What can you tell about her feelings and thoughts?

B. Write a description of a character. It can be a person you know, a character from a story you have read, or a character you make up. Include information about the person's looks, actions that are typical of him or her, and clues to the character's thoughts and feelings.

C. Reread the description you have written.
1. Did you include words and phrases that describe the physical appearance of the character?
2. Did you tell about the character's actions and movements?
3. Did you tell about the character's thoughts and feelings?

Evaluation • Describing a Character

A. Use the facts given in the following paragraph to write a vivid description of the character.

1. Include details that will give a better idea of what you think Jeff looks like.
2. Tell about Jeff's actions and the way he moves.
3. Tell what kind of person you think Jeff is.
4. Include a description of what some of Jeff's thoughts and feelings may be.

Jeff is eleven years old and in the sixth grade. He lives with his mother in an apartment in a big city. He likes sports. Most of all he likes to go to the library and get books about dogs. He has read nearly all the dog stories in the library. Jeff has never had a dog of his own.

B. Write a description of a character. You can use one of the suggestions below, make up a character, or describe one you have read about.

1. A shy eleven-year-old girl living on a farm
2. A clever orphan left with the care of younger brothers and sisters
3. An awkward ten-year-old boy with an older brother who can do everything well

Your description will be evaluated on your use of the following:

    details that tell how the character looks
    words and phrases describing the character's actions and movements
    words and phrases that tell what kind of person the character is
    details describing the character's thoughts and feelings

Which is the *platypus* at play?

Can you identify the platypus in these pictures? If you knew some Greek, you would easily be able to choose the correct one. In Greek *platys* (pla tus') means "flat." Does that help your detective work?

Many other English words have come from the Greek word *platys*. Here are some of them:

plate	platform
plaza	plateau
place	platter

What do a platter and a plate have in common?
How is a platform like a plateau?

There are many groups of words in English that are related because they come from the same source. Can you find the words in the following sentences that are related? They all come from the Greek word *hydor* (hù'dōr), meaning "water."

The firefighters attached a hose to the hydrant.
Sugar is a carbohydrate.
That large blue flower is a hydrangea.
Wandering in the desert sun caused the lost prospector
  to dehydrate.
Sylvia Habib, a hydraulic engineer, designed Silver
  Creek Dam.

Spotlight · TV Talk

You understand the conversation shown because you know some of the language of television. This special television talk, or jargon, has developed to describe the variety of TV programs and the technical skills needed to make TV work. Each year more words are added to people's vocabularies as television expands or changes.

New words have been coined and others borrowed to describe the different kinds of programs we watch. Can you think of at least 2 different programs for each category? Share your favorites with classmates.

What's on the tube?

Oh, not much now-- just a rerun. Next is a soap, or we could switch to a quiz show.

Fantasy

Situation comedy

Quiz show

Variety show

Documentary

TV drama

Soap opera

News/weather

Talk show

Have you ever wanted to get behind the cameras and tape a program for TV? If you have, you will be interested in the language of TV crews. Note the special TV terms, or jargon, in italics in the comments below.

"Now, let's *replay* that scene."

"Begin with a *fade-in* and then let the camera move in for a *close-up*."

"After the *close-up* of the conversation, we want to *pan* around the room to pick up the expressions of the rest of the family."

"Are the *cue cards* in place?"

"We need some *canned laughter* during that comment!"

"Everything ready? Let's *roll*."

Lesson 7   # The How-to Paper

A how-to paper explains how to make or do something.

Thinking It Through
Read the following directions on how to make and play
"Hoop Loops," a game for 2 or more players.

Things You Will Need
hoop (old tire, lampshade frame,   watch
   bike wheel, or hula hoop)   (with second hand)
short stick   masking tape
4 round oatmeal cartons   chalk

Before You Play
Find a sidewalk, driveway, or other hard, flat place to play.
Mark a starting line with chalk. Make 2 goals. Make each
goal by taping one oatmeal carton on top of another. Put
one goal about 20 steps away from the starting line. Put
the other goal about 30 steps away.

How to Play
Start behind the line. Roll the hoop with your hand to
start it. Keep it rolling by hitting the rim with the stick. See
if you can roll the hoop in a "Figure 8" around the goals.

If you knock a goal down, you must start again. Have a friend time you by counting seconds. The winner is the player who can roll the hoop around the goal in a "Figure 8" in the shortest time.

- What kind of information is given about the game?
- Why do you think the directions are broken into parts?
- What helps you know in what order to do things?
- How do the directions make it easy for you to learn how to set up and play the game?

Every explanation of how to make or do something should include all the necessary information. Any unnecessary information should be left out. Any materials, equipment, or ingredients required should be listed and, if necessary, explained. The steps to be followed should be stated clearly and arranged in the order in which they take place.

A how-to paper can be organized in many ways. Steps can be listed in order and numbered, or related steps can be grouped in paragraphs. Information can also be grouped under headings, as in the example.

A topic for a how-to paper must be one that can be presented in ordered steps. Besides directions for making and playing games, recipes and instructions for putting together or using things are good topics for how-to papers.

- Which of the following topics would be suitable for a how-to paper: riding a bike, my dreams, flying a model plane? Why?

Working It Through

A. Choose and list the 5 topics that could be developed into a how-to paper. Then add 5 topics of your own to the list.

1. my allowance	**6.** loading a camera
2. flying a kite	**7.** reading is fun
3. changing a bicycle tire	**8.** winter vacations
4. my favorite movie	**9.** learning to use chopsticks
5. making a sandwich	**10.** my best birthday

B. Read both sets of directions that follow. Decide which would be useful and which would not. List 4 reasons that explain why you decided as you did.

Peanut-butter Popcorn Balls

Pop 1/2 cup popping corn and season with salt and butter. Then, in a small saucepan, combine 1/3 cup honey with 1/2 cup brown sugar. Heat honey mixture over medium heat until it is hot and bubbly. Next, add 1/2 cup peanut butter to the bubbly mixture and cook over low heat. After mixture is well blended, pour it over popcorn in a large bowl and mix well. Finally, with well-buttered hands, form the popcorn mixture into balls.

Riding a Bicycle

Well, first you need to find a bike, which may be hard to do. Then you put your feet on the pedals and hold onto the handlebars. Riding a bike is a good way to get to school. By the way, don't forget to put up the kick-stand. After you point the bike in the direction you want to go, try to balance yourself. When you feel you might fall, look for a soft patch of grass to land on. Be sure to adjust the seat on the bike. Usually, you have to adjust the handlebars too. If you have trouble, just keep trying. The hardest part is keeping your balance.

C. The following recipe for icepops was written by a kindergarten-aged child. This and similar "recipes" were collected in a book called *Smashed Potatoes*. The actual ingredients for icepops should be a 16-ounce can of fruit juice, an icecube tray, and 12 sticks.

Shake up the juice for some hours. Be sure to put the sticks in upside down, else you won't have handles, and maybe you could never get the icepops out.

Now it has to freeze good—or— oh boy!—when you open it, it will spill all over, and the floor gets all sticky, and bad ants come.

Usually it takes till lunch time, but not always.

1. Discuss the recipe with a group of your classmates. Decide what needs to be changed, added, or taken out.
2. Work together to rewrite the recipe. Group your directions under the headings, Things You Need and What to Do.

Trying It Out

Look for examples of directions that explain how to make or do something. You might check children's magazines and how-to books, newspaper food sections, and directions for putting together toys and playing games. Compare the examples, noticing how they are alike and how they are different.

Listing Steps in Order

The steps in any how-to directions should be arranged in order, with all necessary information provided.

Thinking It Through

Notice the order of steps as you read the directions below.

How to Draw a Circle

Things You Will Need:
    pencil, paper, string

What to Do
    1. Tie one end of a string to a pencil.
    2. Hold the free end of the string in the middle of the paper with the finger of one hand.
    3. With the other hand pull the string straight and rotate pencil, making a circle.

- Why are the steps for making a circle arranged as they are?
- What would happen if the directions began with Step 2?
- What would happen if Step 3 were left out?

When you explain how to make or do something, it is important to put the steps in their proper order. Here are some guidelines to help you do so.

1. Before you begin, go through the process in your mind. Think about and list any equipment, materials, or ingredients needed.
2. Begin with the first step. Then list additional steps in the order in which they take place.
3. Check to make sure you have not put too much information into one step.
4. Check to make sure you have not omitted any steps.
5. Decide whether to group directions under headings to make them easier to follow.

Working it Through

A. The following scrambled steps describe a trick in which you can make confetti (small bits of paper) come out of an egg. Rewrite the steps to show their correct order.

1. Hold the egg with your thumb and index finger over the holes.
2. With a small nail, poke a hole in each end of a raw egg. Make one hole larger than the other.
3. Blow the contents of the egg through the larger hole into a cup or glass.
4. Holding the egg, stand before your audience and explain what you will do.
5. Move your free hand mysteriously over the egg. As you do so, squeeze the egg with your thumb and index finger to break it and release a shower of confetti.
6. Put confetti into the egg through the larger hole.

B. Unscramble the order of the pictures and use them as a guide to write a simple set of directions for making a pencil holder. You should list 4 steps. If you feel it would be helpful, group the materials and steps under appropriate headings.

Trying It Out

Using the guidelines in Thinking It Through, list and number directions for one of the following topics.

1. making a peanut-butter-and-honey sandwich
2. folding a paper airplane
3. performing a card trick
4. brushing your teeth
5. climbing a tree
6. rowing a boat

Lesson 9 Organizing Steps in a Paragraph

Words such as *first, next, then,* and *finally* can be used to show the order of steps in a paragraph.

Thinking It Through
Notice how the steps are given in the directions below.

How to Remove Chewing Gum from Clothing
First, harden the gum by rubbing it with ice. Then, scrape the hardened gum as much as possible without damaging the fabric. Next, sponge the gum spot with a spot remover. Now, rinse the article of clothing. Finally, launder as usual.

- What is the first thing you do? What is the second thing?
- What is the final step?
- What words help make the order of the steps in the paragraph clear?

Words such as *first, then, next, now,* and *finally* can act as signal words. These words help make the order of steps clear when directions are written in paragraph form. Other signal words include *secondly, thirdly,* and *lastly.*

Signal words also make directions in paragraph form easier to read. They help join together related steps in a paragraph.

- Read aloud the paragraph showing how to remove chewing gum, omitting the signal words. How does the paragraph sound?

Working It Through
A. The following steps for planting a seed are mixed up. Decide what the order of the steps should be, and then rewrite them in paragraph form. Use signal words to make the order clear.

How to Plant a Seed
Water daily until seed sprouts.
Fill a flowerpot with fine soil.
Cover the seed with soil.
Make a hollow 1 inch deep in soil.
Place seed in hollow.

B. In the following directions for making a candle, the steps have been scrambled. Rewrite the directions in their proper order in paragraph form. Use the signal words as clues to help you.

Then, pour the melted wax into your mold.

Finally, after wax has cooled and hardened, peel off the mold.

Secondly, tie one end of an ordinary cotton string (or regular candle wicking) to a thumbtack.

First, find an empty milk carton to use as a mold.

Next, tie the other end of string or wick to a stick or pencil laid across the top of mold (so that thumbtack is suspended in the mold).

Once the wick is in place, melt candle wax in a tin can placed in a saucepan of hot water on the stove.

C. Write a paragraph telling how you would do one of the following. Use signal words to show the order.

1. learning a new song
2. performing a magic trick
3. making a stick
4. making a mask
5. climbing a tree
6. scrubbing a floor
7. playing hockey
8. learning to skate

Trying It Out

Get together with 2 or 3 of your classmates. Choose one of the topics below and write a fanciful how-to paragraph that includes at least 4 steps and signal words. Share your how-to description with your class.

1. how to prevent nightmares
2. how to turn into a monster
3. how to ruin a beautiful day
4. how to cure hiccups

Lesson 10 Using Illustrations with Directions

Some directions can be made clearer with illustrations.

Thinking It Through

Some directions are easier to understand when they include illustrations. An illustration may be in the form of a picture, chart, or diagram. Illustrations can prevent confusion as well as identify unfamiliar terms.

Read the following directions for making a bird feeder.

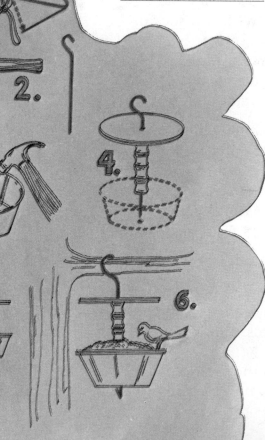

You Need   soft, plastic bowl   thin nail
            plastic lid for bowl   wire cutters
            wire clothes hanger   pliers and hammer
            3 or 4 large, empty spools tape

To Make the Feeder

1. With wire cutters or pliers, cut clothes hanger close to hook and at the center of crosspiece. Straighten the hook half of hanger to form a long piece of wire with hook at one end.
2. With the nail and hammer, punch a hole in center of lid. Make another hole in bottom of bowl, also in center.
3. Make 3 or 4 more holes in bottom of bowl for drainage.
4. Thread straight end of hanger through hole in lid, then through spools, and finally through center hole of bowl.
5. Bend end of wire beneath bowl so that it can't pull out.
6. Fill bowl with sunflower seeds, bread crumbs, or any dry bird food. Then hang feeder by its own hook.

- Why do you think illustrations were included with the written directions?
- What steps are clearer because of the illustrations?
- How do the illustrations make the meaning of *crosspiece* clear?

Working It Through

A. List the 5 topics below that could best be explained if illustrations were included with the written steps.

1. how to give a haircut
2. babysitting made easy
3. how to improve your memory
4. making shadow pictures
5. tying a square knot
6. how to study for a test
7. folding paper animals
8. learning to use a typewriter

B. Choose 1 of the following to do.

1. Write a set of directions for a game that you know. Include a picture, chart, or diagram to make your directions clearer.
2. Select 1 of the topics you listed for Exercise A. Write a description of the illustrations you would include in a how-to paper about the topic.
3. Write a paragraph explaining how to use a gadget or appliance in your home. Include any illustration that will make your directions clearer.

Trying It Out

Choose 1 of the topics below or one of your own to use for a how-to paper. Select a topic you know about. Think about illustrations you might include to make your directions clearer.

1. making a clay animal
2. painting a mural
3. building a campfire
4. putting together a model plane
5. learning how to float
6. setting up a tent

Take Another Look When you wrote directions did you include all necessary information? Are the steps in order?

Improving Your First Draft

Using a checklist can help you improve the first draft of your how-to paper.

Thinking It Through

Roger wrote instructions for making a sand castle. Then he used the following checklist to help him decide if his directions could be improved. Read the checklist and Roger's instructions.

1. Have you included all necessary information and omitted any unnecessary information?
2. Have you listed the necessary materials, ingredients, or equipment?
3. Are your steps arranged in the proper order?
4. When helpful, have you grouped together related steps into one paragraph or listed them under headings such as Before You Begin or How to Play?
5. Have you used signal words such as *then*, *next*, and *finally* to make the order of your steps easier to follow?
6. Are your directions clear? Have you used illustrations when you felt they would be helpful?

> ### How to Make a Sand Castle
> Well, you take a giant mound of sand for the body of the castle, but first you have to wet the sand. You can make a tower at both ends of the castle by packing wet sand into a bucket and tipping the bucket upside down so the sand comes out in the shape of a bucket. Unmold another bucket of wet sand on top of the first one to make a sort of tower. Like I said, make a tower at both ends of the castle. You can use your hands or a knife to shape the body of the castle and the towers, and you can dig around the whole castle to make a moat and use a small piece of wood for a drawbridge. Add a flag or banner if you want.

- What materials does Roger need to build his sand castle?
- What do you think should be the first step in his directions?
- What unnecessary information has Roger included?
- What terms seem unfamiliar?
- Where could he have added signal words to make his steps clearer?
- Which sentences could be broken down into several steps?

Working It Through

A. Apply the suggestions from the checklist in Thinking It Through to improve Roger's first draft.

1. List the necessary materials under <u>Things You Will Need</u>.
2. Rewrite the first draft, paying special attention to making the instructions clear and putting the steps in order. Make the order easy to follow by using signal words. For example, the first step might be, "First, get and wet the sand."

B. Look at the first draft of your own how-to paper from Lesson 10. Use the checklist to help you make changes that will improve your paper. Then rewrite your paper.

Trying It Out

Exchange your how-to paper with those of your classmates so that you can read each other's directions. Then collect all the how-to papers and combine them in a class booklet. This booklet may be used as a reference source for students who wish to try out different how-to projects.

Making an Oral Presentation

Giving a demonstration can make an oral presentation of a how-to process clearer and more interesting.

Thinking It Through

Laurie showed her class how to make a crayon-resist painting. The following describes her presentation.

Laurie began by stating her topic and telling what materials she needed. She explained that first she used crayons to draw the objects she wanted in the picture. She pointed out that she made her crayon marks very heavy. Then she showed how she mixed water with liquid paint to make the paint thin enough to spread quickly. Next, she showed how she painted over the entire picture with the thinned paint. Finally, she explained that the paint resisted, or would not stick to, the crayon areas of the picture, and because of this, the picture was called a crayon-resist painting.

Laurie's presentation was a success. The following guidelines helped her and can help you make an effective presentation of a how-to process.

1. Review the process carefully so you will be able to explain it easily.

2. Gather and organize all materials you need for your presentation.

3. Begin your presentation by stating your purpose.

4. Present and demonstrate each step in sequence.

5. Always speak clearly, distinctly, and directly to your audience.

Working It Through

A. Work with a partner to do this activity, each of you following the steps given.

1. Choose one of the how-to topics listed below.

   sharpening a pencil   tying a bow
   cleaning a chalkboard   braiding hair
   lacing a shoe   addressing an envelope

2. Explain to your partner what you would do to make an oral presentation of the topic. Show how you would demonstrate the steps.
3. Discuss your presentation with your partner. Decide what would be good and what might be improved.

B. Work in groups of 4 or 5 to do this activity.

1. Choose one of the following topics or one of your own.
   how to do a dance
   how to introduce one person to another
   how to play an indoor game
   how to conduct a telephone call to get information
      about a dog for sale

2. Prepare a presentation of the topic that includes a demonstration.
3. Make your presentation to the group.
4. After everyone has made a presentation, use the guidelines in Thinking It Through to help the group discuss things in general that were good or that need to be improved.

Trying It Out

Plan a class "How-to Fair." Invite another class in your school to see and hear presentations of some of the how-to papers members of your class have written. You might display all of the how-to papers and any completed projects.

Review • Writing Directions

A. Read the set of directions. Then answer the questions that follow.

Making Applesauce

First, wash 6 large apples and cut each into quarters. Put the apples into a heavy pot, add ½ cup of water, and cook over high heat. When the water boils, turn the heat down and simmer the apples for about 25 minutes. Then turn the heat off and let them cool for about 20 minutes. Next, pour the mixture through a strainer into a large bowl. Throw away the skins and pits left in the strainer. Finally, add ½ cup of honey or brown sugar to the apples.

1. In what order are the steps in the directions given?
2. What signal words are used?
3. How do the signal words help make the directions clear?

B. Write directions for one of the topics below or for a another topic you choose. Put the directions in the form of a paragraph. Use signal words to make the order clear.
1. making a finger puppet
2. how to make popcorn
3. how to make a collage
4. making a clown face
5. how to make lemonade
6. how to cover a book

C. Think about the questions that follow.
1. Did you give the steps in the order in which they should take place?
2. Did you use signal words to make the order easier to follow?
3. Did you include all the necessary information and omit any unnecessary information?

Evaluation • Writing Directions

A. Improve and rewrite the directions for making a false nose. Use the following guidelines to help you.

1. The steps should be in order.
2. Signal words should be used to help make the order clear.
3. All the necessary information should be given and the unnecessary information left out.

> *How to Make a False Nose*
> Once a boy used a false nose as a part of a disguise. You can too. Paint one of the egg holders from a cardboard egg carton. But first you will have to cut the egg holder apart from the others in the carton. You can get cardboard egg cartons from most grocery stores or supermarkets. Make a small hole on two opposite sides of the painted holder. Thread string through the holes. Place the false nose over your own nose and tie the ends of the string together in back of your head to hold the nose in place. Having a false nose might be fun.

B. Write directions for one of the topics below or for another topic you choose.

1. how to hang a picture
2. making a get-well card
3. making a disguise
4. how to wash a car
5. how to eat spaghetti
6. playing stickball

You will be evaluated on the following:
    order of steps
    use of signal words
    type of information included (providing all necessary
        information, omitting unnecessary information)

Spotlight • Activities to Choose

1. Make a collage. Work with a friend to make a collage showing interesting faces. You can look in magazines, newspapers, catalogs, and on posters for pictures to use in the collage. Develop a list of words and phrases to describe the characters in your collage. Then present your collage and list to the class.

2. List your qualifications. Describe yourself by listing your qualifications for one of the following: cheerleader, team captain, class officer, class entertainer, teacher for a day, class mascot. Explain why you think you are suited for the job or position, what you would do, and how you would feel if you were elected or appointed.

3. Show and tell. Choose one of the topics that follows and prepare an amusing how-to presentation for your class.
  How to Get Lost
  How to Spend a Backwards Day
  How to Be a Genius for One Day
  How to Cure Crying
  How to Become Invisible

4. Describe a character. Imagine this: a crime has been committed and both the hero and the villain appear at the scene of the crime. Describe how the villain and hero look, act, and feel, and what each says.

5. Guess who. Put yourself in one of the following situations: waiting for an exam to begin, being very hungry, scoring a point for your team, being very angry. Write 3 sentences describing how you would look, feel, or react, or what you would say in the situation. Then get together with others who did this activity and exchange descriptions. Read aloud the description you receive and see if the others can guess who wrote it. Continue in this way with the other descriptions.

Naturecraft
by Carol Inouye

This book explains how to make charming and useful gifts, using objects from nature such as shells, flowers, fruit, and herbs. All the materials you need are listed, and the directions are given in clear, illustrated steps.

Latin American Crafts and Their Cultural Backgrounds
by Jeremy Comins

Many of the crafts of ancient and modern Latin American artists are explained in this book. Sculpture, jewelry, string design, and carvings are among the crafts described. Photographs of original works and copies made by students are included with the directions.

Zeely
by Virginia Hamilton

Zeely Taylor is dark, stately, and mysterious. Eleven-year-old Geeder Perry imagines that Zeely is an African queen. Geeder spreads that fantasy to other children in her village. Only Zeely herself can bring Geeder back to reality.

Unit Ten

An open door may mean many things to different people.
What does it mean to you?

With
the
Door
Open

Something I want to communicate to you,
I keep my door open between us.
I am unable to say it,
I am happy only
with the door open between us.

David Ignatow

In this final unit, you will review many of the things you have
learned. Once you know how to make language serve you,
the doors of communication will always be open to you.

Sentences

Look at the underlined subjects and verbs in sentences 1, 2, and 3. In sentences 4 and 5, notice the sentence fragments and see how they are corrected in sentence 6.

1. <u>Both Pat and Louis</u> <u>are</u> ready.
2. <u>Either books or my lunch</u> is in the bag.
3. <u>Neither Luis nor Ramon</u> <u>works</u> here.
4. A marvelous gift.
5. Was my surprise.
6. A marvelous gift was my surprise.

If you need help with subject-verb agreement, see pages 54–57 or 346–347. For help with sentence fragments, see pages 50–51 or 333–334.

A. Complete each sentence with the correct verb form.
  1. Jean and Jack (make, makes) sculptures.
  2. Neither Jean nor Jack (is, are) an artist.
  3. Rocks and a large shell (decorate, decorates) Jean's favorite work.
  4. Either rope, wood, or sticks (is, are) a part of Jack's lastest creation.
  5. Jean's cousins or her sister (work, works) with her.
  6. "Dawn" and "Twilight" (was, were) the names of Jean's first sculptures.
  7. Both her family and Jack's family (want, wants) to display the sculptures.

B. Read each item below. Correct and write each that is a sentence fragment. You should find 6 fragments.
  1. We saw an incredible bicycle race.
  2. Over thirty riders, each one over fifty years old.
  3. When all the riders had lined up.
  4. Huge red balloons marked the starting point.
  5. Whenever there were bumps on the road.
  6. Over a hundred people came to cheer the group.
  7. Stopped to fix her tire.
  8. And finished first.
  9. Served delicious refreshments and had entertainment.

Plural and Possessive Nouns

Notice the underlined nouns in each set of sentences.

Plural Nouns: Another leaf fell on the pile of <u>leaves.</u>
   I need one dish to complete my set of <u>dishes.</u>
Singular Possessive Nouns: <u>John's</u> book is over there.
   <u>Frances's</u> mom just graduated from medical school.
Plural Possessive Nouns: The <u>children's</u> park was ruined.
   The <u>boys'</u> clubhouse was completed last week.
Plural and Possessive Nouns: The <u>dresses</u> are red.
   Your <u>dress's</u> zipper is broken.

If you need help with regular and irregular plural nouns,
see pages 82–83 or 339–340. For help with possessive
nouns, see pages 84–87 or 340.

A. Write the plural of each noun below. Then use 8 of the
plurals in sentences that tell about the picture.

1. glass	**5.** leaf	**9.** loaf	**13.** radio
2. tree	**6.** dish	**10.** deer	**14.** coat
3. moose	**7.** child	**11.** orange	**15.** wolf
4. fork	**8.** berry	**12.** cabin	**16.** monkey

B. Write each phrase below, using the correct possessive form of each underlined noun.

1. the <u>girls</u> team
2. my <u>pet</u> bed
3. <u>Chris</u> hat
4. the <u>wolves</u> noise
5. our <u>class</u> party
6. the <u>Johnsons</u> reunion
7. the <u>witness</u> story
8. the <u>radio</u> cabinet
9. <u>Ms. Jones</u> garage
10. the <u>wind</u> howl
11. your <u>wagon</u> handle
12. the <u>bushes</u> blooms

C. Rewrite the following paragraph, adding apostrophes where they are needed. You should add 8 apostrophes.

All of the boys and girls from our block met yesterday at Alices house. We discussed the citys plan to make our street a main travel route. Charlottes dad spoke to us about action we might take against the plan. Annas cousin told how her brother Bobs youth group spoke out against a similar plan for their families neighborhood. The groups action was successful. Wilburs mom said that she would help us organize our own youth group.

D. In each sentence there is a missing, misplaced, or unnecessary apostrophe. Rewrite each sentence correctly.

1. Kims' hobby is ventriloquism.
2. She learned the art from her best friends father.
3. Kim has an act that she performs at childrens' parties.
4. Her dummies' name's are Chuckles and Buzzy.
5. Chuckles' has a silly but cute grin.
6. Kim makes Buzzys voice sound like high, buzzing sounds.
7. All of her friends and neighbors' like to watch Kim perform.
8. Once in her classroom, Kim used her talent to make her teachers desk "talk."

320

Review 3 Verb Tenses and Principal Parts

Look at the underlined verbs in the following sentences and notice the tenses and principal parts.

Tense:

Present   I <u>help</u> with the cooking.

Past   Marty <u>helped</u> Dad fix the car.

Future   We <u>will help</u> you with your assignment.

Principal Parts:

Present   I <u>swim</u> every weekend.

Past   We <u>swam</u> in the relays.

Past Participle   He <u>has swum</u> daily.

If you need help with the tense forms of regular and irregular verbs, see pages 118–119 or 342–346. For help with principal parts, see pages 122–125 or 344–346.

A. Complete each sentence with the correct form of the verb in parentheses.

1. Centuries ago people in India (practice) yoga.
2. They (imitate) the movements of animals.
3. This ancient system (last) to this day.
4. Modern Americans (recognize) yoga as a way to increase physical and mental alertness.
5. Today acrobats (use) yoga to improve their skills.
6. People (practice) yoga in the future.

B. Use the present, past, or past participle form of the verb in parentheses in each of the following.

1. Yesterday we (learn) about Frankenstein, a doctor who (create) a monster.
2. Until then, I had (think) that Frankenstein was the name of the monster.
3. Tony has (go) to the movie twice. He has (explain) that the monster has green skin and a square skull.
4. Our teacher has (say) that although many Frankenstein movies have been (make), the 1931 film is best.

Review 4   Adjectives and Adverbs

Look at the underlined adjectives and adverbs in the following sentences and notice their labels.

Regular Adjectives:

Positive	I like living in a <u>large</u> house.
Comparative	That house is <u>larger</u> than mine.
Superlative	It is the <u>largest</u> I've ever seen.

Irregular Adjectives:

Positive	She makes <u>good</u> soup.
Comparative	She uses <u>better</u> cuts of meat.
Superlative:	It was the <u>best</u> I've ever eaten.

Regular Adverbs:

Positive	Sara walks <u>fast</u>.
Comparative	She walks <u>faster</u> on cold days.
Superlative	She walks <u>fastest</u> on payday.

Irregular Adverbs:

Positive	Ramon plays the piano <u>badly</u>.
Comparative	But he played <u>worse</u> before.
Superlative	Of the four, he played <u>worst</u>.

If you need help with regular and irregular adjectives, see pages 156–159 or 347–349. For help with regular and irregular adverbs, see pages 194–197 or 350–351.

A. Read the following paragraph and tell whether each underlined word is an adjective or an adverb. Remember that adjectives modify nouns and adverbs modify verbs.

Mosquitoes, gnats, and bugs in general have <u>always</u> considered me a <u>tasty</u> treat. But <u>these</u> creatures <u>carefully</u> avoid my father. I was <u>nearly</u> twelve before I discovered that his <u>secret</u> weapon was the <u>old</u> pipe he <u>often</u> smoked. Tobacco is one of the <u>best</u> repellents for insects. Another <u>good</u> repellent is mud, but this can be <u>messy</u>. A <u>common</u> and <u>easy</u> way to frighten off mosquitoes is with smoke from a campfire.

B. Use the correct form of the adjective in parentheses in each of the following sentences.

1. When Cindy graduated from veterinary school, she was the (young) person in her class.
2. Her grades were (high) than most of her classmates.
3. She wanted to work for another veterinarian until she saved (much) money than she already had.
4. But she knew she would be (happy) of all with her own private practice in a rural area.
5. She felt a farm would be the (wonderful) place of all.
6. She moved into an apartment over a clinic—the (tiny) apartment she had ever seen.
7. At first, she had (little) business than she wanted.
8. But things got (busy) after several months.

C. Write the following sentences, correcting the forms of the underlined adverbs.

1. I baby-sit <u>more oftener</u> than I used to.
2. I try to arrive a few minutes <u>more earlier</u> than required.
3. <u>Oftenest</u> I learn the names of the children beforehand.
4. Mrs. Jamison says I play <u>most patiently</u> with the children than she does.
5. She says the kids behave <u>well</u> than usual with me.
6. I told her they are the <u>bestest</u> behaved kids around.

D. Complete the following paragraph by supplying the proper forms of the words in parentheses. Be ready to tell whether each word is an adjective or an adverb.

I think codes are the (good) way of making secret communications. Some codes are (easy) than others, but the (simple) one I found is substituting a number for each letter of the alphabet. Some codes take (much) time to decipher than others, but all codes must be done (carefully). The (hard) code I ever did had to be read backwards. The (bad) code was written in invisible ink.

Objects, Predicate Nouns, and Adjectives

Look at the underlined words in the following sentences.

Direct Object: I saw two <u>monkeys</u> at the zoo.
Predicate Noun: Mr. Grasso is the <u>zookeeper</u>.
Predicate Adjective: I am <u>eager</u> to go there again.

If you need help with direct objects, predicate nouns, or predicate adjectives, see pages 226–231 or 340–341, 349–350.

A. List the underlined words in the following paragraph. Beside each write DO for direct object, PN for predicate noun, or PA for predicate adjective.

We did an <u>experiment</u> with roots today A carrot is a big <u>root</u> I was <u>eager</u> to see how the carrot gets water to its stem and leaves. First we cut off the bottom <u>tip</u> of the carrot. Then we put the <u>carrot</u> in a glass of water. The water became <u>green</u> after we added green ink. We set the <u>glass</u> in bright sunlight for four hours. Then we cut the <u>carrot</u> in half. We could see the <u>ink</u> in tiny tubes that feed the carrot.

Look at the following underlined pronouns.
Pronoun as a subject: <u>I</u> enjoy talking with friends.
Pronouns as objects: Yoko called <u>us</u> from Boston.
She talked with <u>us</u> for an hour.
Possessive pronoun: <u>Her</u> bill will be huge.

If you need help with pronouns, see pages 232–236 or 372–373.

B. Complete the paragraph with pronouns and tell whether each is a subject, object, or possessive pronoun.

_____ was a strange-looking woman with a purple hat perched on _____ head. _____ couldn't help staring. She smiled at _____ from across the street, but _____ wasn't sure if _____ smile was sincere. As _____ approached _____ , I heard her say: "City folks! _____ are so unfriendly."

Review 6 Combining Sentences

Look at each pair of sentences and the underlined word,
words, or phrases in the combined sentence for each pair.

Chess is a great game.
Sometimes it moves slowly.

> Chess is a great game, <u>but</u>
> sometimes it moves slowly.

The boy ran for an hour.
He ran in the rain.

> The boy ran <u>in the rain</u> for an hour.

Takako designs cars.
She rebuilds engines.

> Takako designs cars <u>and rebuilds
> engines.</u>

The dancer was graceful.
She twirled across the stage.

> The <u>graceful dancer</u> twirled across
> the stage.

If you need help with combining sentences, see page
262–269 or 336–337.

A. Combine the sentences. Then see if you can provide an
answer for each riddle-sentence you have written.

1. This kind of bean is in stores.
   Farmers don't grow this bean.
2. This object is white when dirty.
   It's black when clean.
3. This room has no doors. It has no
   windows. It has no walls.
4. You put this on a table. Then you
   cut it. You never eat it.

Answers: 1. jellybean; 2. blackboard; 3. mushroom; 4. deck of cards

B. Use adjectives, prepositional phrases, conjunctions, or
appositives to combine the following sentences.

1. The lion was fierce.
   The lion was proud.
   The lion stalked in its cage.
   The cage was dark.
2. My favorite sport is tennis.
   It has become a popular game.
3. I ate too much meat.
   I ate too much salad.
   These are my favorite foods.
4. My teacher is Ms. Borski.
   She likes to cook.
   She teaches French.
5. Leo exercises each day.
   He does it in the morning.
   He exercises in the basement.
6. I see my sister.
   She is walking across the street.
   She is younger than I am.

Punctuation and Capitalization

Look at the punctuation in the following sentences.

Commas with nouns of address: Please come in, Dr. Burgos.
Commas with introductory words: No, I can't go.
Commas with compound sentences: Irene can leave, but I'll stay.
Quotation marks with conversation: "What do you want?" asked Sara.
Commas with quotation marks: Kenji called, "I'm ready."

For help with punctuation, see pages 268–271 and 286–288 or pages 359–361.

A. Rewrite each sentence, providing the necessary punctuation.

1. I was late but I saw the play.
2. Yes the star was terrific.
3. Dad asked, Was she believable?
4. I met her and I got her autograph.
5. You must see her Katie.
6. Ned will see the play Sunday or he'll go next week.
7. Mrs. Silva will you go?
8. She said "It'll be a treat."
9. Go with Mrs. Silva Margaret.

Notice the underlined words in the sentences below.
Capital letters for proper nouns: I wrote to Terry in Mexico.
Capital letters in direct quotes: She said, "It was a good trip."

For help with capitalization, see pages 80–81 and 286–288 or pages 358–359.

B. Rewrite each sentence and supply the necessary capital letters.

1. Did mrs. Beane visit jamaica?
2. Phyllis said, "yes, I did."
3. I took anita and jon with me.
4. The tops travel agency made travel arrangements for the beanes.
5. The west indies is beautiful.
6. I asked, "what did you like most?"
7. Jon said, "we enjoyed kingston."
8. Next year the beane family plans to tour hawaii.

Review 8   The Character Sketch

Read the paragraph below and notice the underlined details that describe the character.

   Meeting Paula for the first time was like greeting an old friend. Her <u>wide, brown eyes sparkled warmly</u> as she extended a <u>soft, chubby hand</u> to me. <u>Dimples in her fat cheeks</u> deepened as she spoke, and her <u>short, dark curls bounced</u> with every move she made. <u>Barely five feet tall, she seemed more round than anything else.</u> Everything about her was <u>lively</u>. Even her <u>slight limp</u> gave a certain <u>spring to her walk.</u>

If you need help in describing how a person looks, see pages 280–281.

A. List details that will create a clear word picture of the character shown. You should list at least 6 details.

B. Write 3 specific details that will create a vivid word picture of each character listed below.

1. a tired worker
2. a cranky baby
3. a nervous passenger
4. an angry customer
5. an excited child
6. a shy newcomer
7. a happy grandmother
8. a bored visitor

C. Choose one of the following characters and write a paragraph to describe him or her. Include at least 4 descriptive details in your paragraph.

1. a person who has impressed you greatly
2. an actor you have seen on television or in movies
3. a person you fear
4. a person you enjoy being with
5. a person you would like to have as a friend
6. a person you think is silly or foolish

Evaluation

A. Some of the following sentences contain mistakes. Write the letter of any word in a sentence that is wrong.

1. Both Josh and Chiyo want to read this book.
     a   b   c   d   e   f   g   h   i

2. Shoes and a box was under the bed.
     a   b c d   e   f   g   h

3. Neither Juan nor Amy run fast enough.
     a   b   c   d   e   f   g

4. Either Angela or Isao go to the state spelling finals.
     a   b   c   d   e f   g   h   i   j

B. Write the letter of the word that correctly completes the sentence.

1. The _____ leader was a majestic animal.
   a. wolves'   **b.** wolfs'   **c.** wolves

2. Did you pick enough _____ for supper?
   a. berrys   **b.** berry's   **c.** berries

3. People with their _____ were at the beach.
   a. radio's   **b.** radios   **c.** radioes

4. The _____ calf was standing in the water beside her.
   a. mooses   **b.** moose's   **c.** mooses'

C. Write the letter of the verb that correctly completes the sentence.

1. The trees have _____ a lot this summer.
   a. grow   **b.** grew   **c.** grown

2. Shirley _____ an interesting picture yesterday.
   a. draw   **b.** drew   **c.** drawn

3. Patrick has _____ us his collection several times.
   a. show   **b.** showed   **c.** shown

4. I _____ many birds in the dunes whenever I go there.
   a. see   **b.** saw   **c.** seen

5. Pedro _____ a lot of work on his train set yesterday.
   a. does   **b.** did   **c.** done

D. Write the letter of the word or words that correctly completes the sentence.

1. Tom goes camping _____ than I do.
   a. most often   **b.** more often   **c.** more oftener

2. This mess is the _____ of all to clean up.
   a. worst   **b.** most worse   **c.** worse

3. Michiko plays the piano _____ than Jim.
   a. more better   **b.** best   **c.** better

4. He was the _____ person in town.
   a. most stingiest   **b.** stingier   **c.** stingiest

5. Ellen had saved _____ money than Anne.
   a. much   **b.** more   **c.** most

E. Write the letter that tells which of the following the underlined word in each sentence is.

a. direct object   **b.** predicate noun   **c.** predicate adjective

1. Noriko is <u>excited</u> about going to Hawaii.
2. Sam bought <u>bread</u> for our sandwiches.
3. Lois is an <u>engineer</u> with that company.
4. Lorenzo drove the <u>truck</u> to our house.
5. The sky seems extremely <u>clear</u> tonight.

F. Write the letter of the pronoun that completes the sentence correctly.

1. She and _____ explored the cave.
   a. I   **b.** me   **c.** my

2. The trees were all around _____.
   a. they   **b.** them   **c.** their

3. Joe gave the box to _____ uncle.
   a. he   **b.** him   **c.** his

4. It was _____ car that Joan drove in the parade.
   a. we   **b.** us   **c.** our

5. They invited Norio and _____ to lunch.
   a. I   **b.** me   **c.** my

6. _____ garden is filled with vegetables.
   a. They   **b.** Their   **c.** Them

G. Write the letter of the punctuation mark that is missing after the underlined word in each sentence.

1. How can we help <u>you</u> Mrs. Omachi?

    a. ⊙   **b.** ⊚

2. "Is this your <u>dog</u>? asked Bill.

    a. ⊙   **b.** ⊚

3. <u>Yes</u> Francisca, I'll gladly go with you.

    a. ⊙   **b.** ⊚

4. Mrs. Silva <u>fished</u> but Mr. Silva read a book.

    a. ⊙   **b.** ⊚

5. "What an unusual <u>bird</u>! said Mark.

    a. ⊙   **b.** ⊚

H. Write the letter of each word that should start with a capital letter.

1. To reach hawaii we flew over the pacific ocean.
    a   b   c   d   e   f   g   h   i

2. The eaton book store is on royal oak drive in tampa.
    a   b   c   d e   f   g   h   i   j   k

3. Tatsuo exclaimed, "yes, of course I do!"
    a   b   c   d   e   f g

4. From the atlas space center, the craft sped to mars.
    a   b   c   d   e   f   g   h   i   j

I. Write a description of how you think one of the following characters might look.

1. an active, alert grandmother

2. a mischievous three-year-old

3. a ten-year-old who is a careless dresser

4. a bus driver with a bad temper

5. a busy supermarket manager

6. a high-school football star

Your description will be evaluated on your use of vivid descriptive words and details that tell about the character's appearance and movements.

Handbook

Sentences

A sentence may be a statement, a question, a request or a command, or an exclamation. A sentence always begins with a capital letter and has end punctuation.

> The fireworks display was fantastic.

Kinds of Sentences

A statement tells something and ends with a period.

> The night was dark and clear.

A question asks something and ends with a question mark.

> How many people were in the stadium?

An exclamation is a statement or command made with emotion or strong feeling. It ends with an exclamation mark.

> That was a fantastic race!

A request or command asks for or orders something. It has an understood subject—*you.* It ends with a period or exclamation mark.

> Give me the equipment.

Practice

Change each sentence below into the kind given in parentheses.

1. Isn't this basketball game exciting?   (exclamation)
2. The score is tied.   (question)
3. Can you make a free throw?   (command)
4. Did Ken make a foul?   (statement)
5. He told me the score.   (request)
6. Did we win the game?   (exclamation)
7. We are in first place in our league!   (question)
8. Did Pam congratulate the players?   (statement)

A sentence has two parts—a subject and a predicate. The complete subject is all the words in the subject. The complete predicate is all the words in the predicate.

The clumsy boy|tripped over his own feet.

The simple subject is the noun or pronoun that tells who or what the sentence is about.
The simple predicate is the verb.

The clumsy <u>boy</u>|<u>tripped</u> over his own feet.

One word can be both the simple and complete subject.
One word can be both the simple and complete predicate.

<u>He</u>|<u>dropped</u> a carton of eggs.
All the eggs in the <u>carton</u>|<u>broke</u>.

Write each sentence below. Draw a line between the complete subject and complete predicate. Then draw one line under the simple subject and two lines under the simple predicate.
1. Arthur built a canoe.
2. His older sister helped him.
3. His family canoed down the White River.
4. They traveled swiftly through the rapids.
5. A large branch blocked part of the river.
6. The weary people rested.

A part of a sentence punctuated as if it were a complete sentence is called a sentence fragment. A sentence fragment doesn't make sense or sound complete by itself.

Mr. Alvarez likes to cook. <u>And try new recipes.</u>
He cooks Mexican dishes. <u>Such as tacos and beans.</u>

Practice

Write each item below. If it is a fragment, add a word or words of your own to make a complete sentence.
1. Paula bought a rabbit from a pet store.
2. And built a cage for it.
3. She feeds it raw vegetables.

Run-on Sentences

A run-on sentence is two ideas run together as though they were one sentence. Run-on sentences should be separated with a period or a comma and a connecting word.

> Ken has a telescope he studies the stars.
> Ken has a telescope. He studies the stars.

Practice

Write the items below, correcting those that are run-ons.
1. Our family has a large garden we grow many vegetables.
2. Setsuo waters the garden and pulls the weeds.
3. Can I pick this watermelon, can I eat a piece of it?

Compound Subjects

Two or more subjects joined together by *and* or *or* are called a compound subject.

The students applauded.
The teachers applauded.   >   The students and teachers applauded.

Practice

Combine each pair of sentences to form a sentence with a compound subject.
1. The bands practiced. The baton twirlers practiced.
2. Cars were decorated. Bicycles were decorated.
3. The mayor will ride in the parade. The governor will ride in the parade.

| Compound Predicates | Two or more predicates joined by *and* or *or* are called a compound predicate. |

The professor spoke.
The professor showed slides. > The professor spoke and showed slides.

| Practice | Combine each pair of sentences below to form one sentence with a compound predicate. |

1. Sarah bought a camera. She took a photography course.
2. She saw a blue jay. She took a picture of it.
3. The picture was developed. The picture was framed.
4. Sarah could keep the picture. Sarah could give it to a relative.

| Compound Sentences | Two sentences closely related in meaning can be joined by a conjunction such as *and, but,* or *or.* The combined sentence is called a compound sentence. |

Maude sent a telegram.
Les made a phone call. > Maude sent a telegram, and Les made a phone call.

| Practice | Combine the following pairs of sentences to form compound sentences. Use a comma before *and, but,* and *or.* |

1. Bald eagles are an endangered species. They should be protected.
2. These birds could be saved. They could become extinct.
3. Once buffaloes roamed the plains. Now there are few left.
4. The government has passed laws. It has set aside protected areas for animals.
5. We must not pollute our environment. Many animals will die.

Combining Sentences

When sentences contain adjectives that describe the same nouns, they can be combined.

The gymnast was talented.
The gymnast was young.
The gymnast did a flip.

> The talented, young gymnast did a flip.

Sometimes sentences can be combined by changing one sentence to an appositive that identifies a noun.

The gymnast was Cathy Rigby.
The gymnast placed first in her event.

> The gymnast, Cathy Rigby, placed first in her event.

Some combined sentences use adjectives and appositives.

The gymnast was Cathy Rigby.
The gymnast waved to the crowd.
The crowd was enthusiastic.

> The gymnast, Cathy Rigby, waved to the enthusiastic crowd.

Sometimes two sentences can be combined by changing one into a prepositional phrase that acts as an adjective.

A bird lives in that nest.
It has red feathers.

> A bird with red feathers lives in that nest.

Sentences with prepositional phrases that describe the same person or thing can be combined.

A skunk with a white stripe walked through my yard.
A skunk with a long tail walked through my yard.

> A skunk with a white stripe and long tail walked through my yard.

Sentences containing prepositional phrases that act as adverbs and modify the same verb can be combined.

We went to the art fair.   We went to the art fair
We went on Saturday.   on Saturday.

Some sentences can be combined by changing one
sentence into a group of words starting with *who, which,* or
that. Who refers to persons, *which* refers to things, and *that*
refers to persons or things.

The boy sent away for   The boy who sits next to
   some flower seeds.   me in class sent away
The boy sits next to me   for some flower seeds.
   in class.

Practice   Combine each pair or group of sentences into one
sentence.
1. We visited a house with an old-fashioned stove.
   We visited a house with antique furniture.
2. The bus driver took us to the museum.
   The bus driver was Lenny Schultz.
   The museum was interesting.
3. That bus tour was exciting.
   That bus tour included visiting a lighthouse.
   The lighthouse was very old.
4. This exhibit is rare.
   This exhibit is fascinating.
   This exhibit is crowded with visitors.
5. I enjoyed listening to the guide.
   The guide talked to us about old tools.
6. Many students took pictures of this display.
   Many students had cameras.
7. We ate lunch at noon.
   We ate lunch in the museum cafeteria.
8. I bought a postcard.
   The postcard showed my favorite exhibit.

Nouns

A noun is a word that names a person, place, or thing.
A noun marker signals that a noun will soon follow.
A, an, and *the* are noun markers.

For the <u>stew</u> we need an <u>onion</u> and a large <u>carrot</u>.

Practice

Write the sentences below. Draw a line under each noun marker. Circle the noun that follows it.
1. The boy built a large model of a railroad.
2. He repaired an engine and rebuilt a boxcar.
3. A friend made a station for the trains.
4. The caboose was painted a red color.
5. The completed project was set up in the basement.

Common and
Proper Nouns

A proper noun names a particular person, place, or thing and begins with a capital letter. All other nouns are called common nouns.

Common Nouns	Proper Nouns
friend	Peter Klein
relative	Aunt Rosa
coach	Mr. Robertson
city	San Diego
state	Indiana
region	Northeast
continent	Europe
planet	Jupiter
river	Ohio River
building	Empire State Building
holiday	Memorial Day
school	Willow School
organization	Camp Fire Girls
company	Smith Tool Company

Copy the list below, capitalizing the proper nouns.

1. teacher	4. three states
2. dayton, ohio	5. mars
3. mountain	6. hudson river

A singular noun names one person, place, or thing and a plural noun names more than one.

Plural nouns are formed by

adding -*s* to some nouns

street   streets

adding -*es* to nouns ending in *ch, sh, s, ss,* or *x*

business   businesses

changing *y* to *i* and adding -*es* to nouns that end in *y* preceded by a consonant

penny   pennies

adding -*s* to nouns that end in *y* preceded by a vowel

monkey   monkeys

changing the *f* or *fe* to *v* and adding -*es* to some nouns that end in *f* or *fe*

knife   knives

adding -*s* to some nouns that end in *f*

roof   roofs

adding -*es* to most nouns that end in *o* preceded by a consonant

tomato   tomatoes

adding -*s* to some nouns that end in *o*

rodeo   rodeos

changing some of the letters within a noun

goose   geese

using the same spelling as the singular

deer   deer

Practice

Make the following nouns plural.

1. potato   4. mouse   7. turkey
2. life   5. bunch   8. sheep
3. baby   6. box   9. radio

Possessive Nouns

A possessive noun shows ownership or possession.
An apostrophe and the letter *s* (*'s*) are added to singular nouns to form the possessive.

bird's nest   Charles's truck

Only an apostrophe is added to a plural noun that ends in *s* to form the possessive.

two cats' kittens

An apostrophe and the letter *s* (*'s*) are added to plural nouns that do not end in *s* to form the possessive.

children's books

Practice

Rewrite each phrase below. Use the correct possessive form of each noun in parentheses.

1. (Chris) hammer   6. my (cousin) letter
2. the (men) jackets   7. (Mrs. Stevens) car
3. two (bears) tracks   8. our (families) picnic
4. the (geese) feathers   9. the (building) tenants
5. the (tree) leaves   10. two (trout) fins

Nouns Used as Direct Objects

A direct object is the noun or pronoun that follows an action verb and tells who or what was the object of the action. A direct object is in the predicate of the sentence.

Andrea brushed her <u>dog</u>.

Practice

Write each sentence. Underline the verb and circle the direct object.
1. Samantha arranged the books on the shelf.
2. Tim erased the chalkboards.
3. Two students washed the desks thoroughly.
4. Pedro put the students' pictures on the bulletin board.
5. Greg helped Pedro with the bulletin board.

Predicate Nouns

A predicate noun follows a linking verb and tells about or means the same thing as the subject of the sentence.

My mother is an <u>engineer</u>.

Practice

Write the three sentences below that have a linking verb and a predicate noun. Circle the predicate noun in each.
1. My father is a gardener.
2. He takes care of people's lawns and gardens.
3. These people are his assistants.
4. These yellow flowers are tulips.
5. My father owns two trucks.

Nouns Used as Appositives

An appositive is a noun or phrase that follows a noun and identifies or explains it.
If the appositive appears in the middle of a sentence, it is set off by two commas.

My favorite cousin, <u>Sheryl</u>, is coming for a visit.

If the appositive appears at the end of a sentence, it is set off by only one comma.

This letter is from Sam, <u>my older brother</u>.

341

Practice

Rewrite the sentences below. Use commas to set off the appositives.

1. Last week I read *The Black Stallion* an excellent book.
2. The author Walter Farley has written many books.
3. Ms. Carlsen the librarian suggested the book.
4. I wrote a book report and gave it to Mr. Chen my teacher.

Verbs

Words that show action in a sentence are called action verbs. Words that join, or link, the subject to a word in the predicate are called linking verbs. Every sentence has a verb.

> The athletes <u>raced</u> down the track.   (action verb)
> This girl <u>is</u> the winner.   (linking verb)
> That girl <u>seems</u> disappointed.   (linking verb)

Practice

Write the sentences below. Underline the action verb or linking verb in each sentence.

1. Mr. King plays in a jazz band.
2. He is a music teacher at the high school.
3. I am a student of his.
4. I practice on the trombone every day.
5. My dog covers its ears with its paws.
6. These instruments are flutes.

Tenses of Action Verbs

The tense of a verb tells whether something happens in the present, past, or future.

> I <u>paint</u> the table now.
> Yesterday I <u>painted</u> the table.
> Tomorrow I <u>will paint</u> the table.

Regular verbs, like *paint,* end in *-ed* to show action that happened in the past. Irregular verbs do not end in *-ed* to show action that happened in the past.

Present	Past	Future
ring	rang	will ring
throw	threw	will throw
buy	bought	will buy
eat	ate	will eat
ride	rode	will ride
run	ran	will run
sell	sold	will sell
choose	chose	will choose
speak	spoke	will speak

Practice

Write the sentences below and underline the verb in each. Write *present, past,* or *future* beside each sentence to show the tense of the verb.

1. Mr. Steinberg sells cars for this company.
2. Ms. Ruiz bought a new car yesterday.
3. We will ride in it tomorrow.
4. My dog runs after cars.

Tenses of Linking Verbs

Linking verbs can change to show present, past, and future tense.

Subjects	Linking Verbs		
	Present	**Past**	**Future**
I	am	was	will be
you	are	were	will be
he, she, it	is	was	will be
we	are	were	will be
they	are	were	will be

Practice

Complete the sentences below by writing a subject (S) and a linking verb (LV) in the tense given.

1. Today _S_ _LV_ (present) sick and in bed.
2. Yesterday _S_ _LV_ (past) very tired.
3. _S_ _LV_ (past) their family doctor years ago.
4. _S_ _LV_ (future) better tomorrow.

Auxiliary Verbs

Sometimes the verb in a sentence is made up of more than one word. The main verb expresses the action. The other verb or verbs used with the main verb are called helping, or auxiliary verbs. The main verb and one or more auxiliary verbs together make up the verb phrase.

Glen is painting a fence.
Will he be working for more than two hours?

Practice

Write each sentence below. Draw a line under each auxiliary verb. Circle the main verb.

1. Fran is considered a champion ice skater.
2. She has been practicing for years.
3. She can spin expertly.
4. Fran will be competing in the Olympics.
5. She did win this trophy last year.

Principal Parts of Verbs

The principal parts of a verb are the present, past, and past participle forms. The past participle form of a verb is the past form that is used with an auxiliary verb.

	Present	Past	Past Participle
	clean	cleaned	(has/have) cleaned
Regular	move	moved	(has/have) moved
	want	wanted	(has/have) wanted

	Present	Past	Past Participle
	do	did	(has/have) done
	go	went	(has/have) gone
	see	saw	(has/have) seen
Irregular	tell	told	(has/have) told
	begin	began	(has/have) begun
	know	knew	(has/have) known
	choose	chose	(has/have) chosen

Practice

Rewrite the following sentences, supplying the correct form of the verb in parentheses.

1. I have (go) to the city a few times with my father.
2. Yesterday I (go) to the city with my cousins.
3. I have never (see) these buildings.
4. I (know) more about the city now.

Problem Verbs

The verbs in the chart below are often confused.

Present	Past	Past Participle
lay	laid	(has/have) laid
lie	lay	(has/have) lain
set	set	(has/have) set
sit	sat	(has/have) sat
let	let	(has/have) let
leave	left	(has/have) left
lend	lent	(has/have) lent
borrow	borrowed	(has/have) borrowed
teach	taught	(has/have) taught
learn	learned	(has/have) learned

Present	Past	Past Participle
bring	brought	brought
take	took	taken

Lay means "to put or to place." *Lie* means "to rest or recline."

Set means "to put something somewhere." *Sit* means "to sit down."

Let means "to allow or permit." *Leave* means "to go away."

Lend means "to give." *Borrow* means "to get."

Teach means "to show how to do." *Learn* means "to gain knowledge."

Bring means "to carry something toward." *Take* means "to carry something away."

Practice

Choose the correct verbs in the sentences below.
1. Mae and Bruce (teach, learn) a cooking class.
2. They (brought, took) a delicious dish last night.
3. They (laid, lay) their prize soufflé on the table.
4. I (set, sat) in the front row and listened to their recipe.
5. I tasted the soufflé and then (let, left) the class.
6. I've (lent, borrowed) my neighbor's soufflé dish, and I'll make my own soufflé tonight.

Subject-Verb Agreement

The subject and verb in a sentence must agree with each other. A singular subject takes a singular verb. A plural subject takes a plural verb. Two or more subjects joined with *and* take a plural verb.

The grasshopper jumps.
The grasshoppers jump.
Both the frog and grasshopper jump.

When a compound subject is joined by *or, either . . . or,* or *neither . . . nor,* the verb agrees with the subject closer to it.

The beans or the potato is included in the meal.
Neither I nor they eat dessert.

Practice

Write each sentence, choosing the correct verb form in parentheses.

1. Dogs and cats (are, is) mammals.
2. Neither dolphins nor whales (is, are) fish.
3. The porpoises or the dolphin (swim, swims) in this tank.
4. The largest animals (live, lives) in the ocean.

Adjectives

Adjectives modify, or describe, nouns. They tell what kind, how many, or which one.

Allison is a good swimmer.   (what kind)
She practices for several hours daily.   (how many)
She took first place in this meet.   (which one)

Practice

Add at least one adjective to the underlined nouns in the sentences. The words after each sentence will help you.

1. Ramon is packing his suitcase.   (what kind)
2. He has pamphlets that tell about Oregon.   (how many)
3. Ramon is taking shirts and pants with him.   (how many)
4. He needs a roll of film for his camera.   (which one)

This, That, These, Those

The adjectives *this* and *these* tell what is near in time and place. The adjectives *that* and *those* tell what is further away in time and place.

This shell in my hand is cracked.
I bought these shells at a hobby store.
We found that starfish on the wall at the beach.
Those shells in the case belong to my father.

Do not say or write *this here, that there, these here,* or *those there. This* and *these* refer to something "right here," and *that* and *those* refer to something "over there."

Practice

Complete the sentences with *this, that, these,* or *those.*
1. _____ dog licking my hand is very friendly.
2. His dog is _____ spaniel chasing the squirrel.
3. _____ puppies in the pet store were cute.
4. _____ pictures I am showing you are of my beagle.

Using Adjectives
to Compare

Adjectives can be used in the following ways to compare things.

Positive	Comparative	Superlative
large	larger	largest
different	more different	most different
good	better	best
bad	worse	worst
much	more	most
little	less	least
far	farther	farthest

The comparative form of an adjective is used to compare two people or things. The superlative form is used to compare more than two people or things.

Do not use *more* or *most* with adjectives ending in *-er* and *-est* or with *good, bad,* and their forms. For example, it is incorrect to say or write *more prettier, most best.*

Write the correct form of the adjectives given. Then write a sentence for each adjective.

1. old (superlative)
2. much (comparative)
3. famous (positive)
4. good (comparative)
5. bad (superlative)
6. graceful (comparative)

Proper Adjectives

An adjective formed from a proper noun is a proper adjective. Proper adjectives are always capitalized.

Proper Nouns	**Proper Adjectives**
Africa	African
Poland	Polish

Proper nouns can also be used as adjectives. The common nouns modified by proper nouns are not capitalized.

Proper Noun	**Proper Noun as Adjective**
Thanksgiving	Thanksgiving dinner

Practice

Write the following sentences, capitalizing the proper adjectives and proper nouns used as adjectives.

1. We ate at a french restaurant over labor day weekend.
2. Do you like german food better than chinese food?
3. This dessert is made with florida oranges.

Predicate Adjectives

A predicate adjective is an adjective that follows a linking verb and modifies the subject of a sentence.

My new boots are <u>brown</u>.

Complete the sentence with a predicate adjective that modifies the subject.

1. The carnival yesterday was ＿＿＿ .

2. The clowns were ___.
3. After that ride I felt ___.

Adverbs

Adverbs modify verbs by telling how, when, or where. Some adverbs are formed by adding *-ly* to an adjective, for example, *graceful, gracefully; quiet, quietly.*

> Harlan sings <u>beautifully</u>.   (how)
> He <u>always</u> has enjoyed music.   (when)
> He is singing <u>downstairs</u>.   (where)

Some adverbs, such as *very, really, extremely,* and *too,* can modify adjectives and other adverbs.

> He moves <u>very</u> slowly.

Practice

Write the sentences below and underline the 5 adverbs.
1. The night was extremely dark.
2. The moon shone dimly.
3. Tonight ghosts might suddenly appear.
4. Most people stayed inside.

Using Adverbs to Compare

Adverbs can be used in the following ways to compare things.

Positive	Comparative	Superlative
soon	sooner	soonest
quickly	more quickly	most quickly
well	better	best
badly	worse	worst

Ken dances <u>well</u>.
Marlene dances <u>better</u> than Ken.
Juan dances the <u>best</u> of the three.

Do not use *more* or *most* with adverbs ending in *-er* and *-est* or with *well, badly,* and their forms. For example, it is incorrect to say or write *more higher, most best.*

Practice

Write the following sentences, using the correct form of the adverbs in parentheses.
1. Sumi plants her bulbs (neatly) than I do.
2. Her bulbs came up (soon) than mine.
3. Sumi's tulips bloom the (early) of everyone's.
4. She also weeds her garden (well) than I.

Pronouns

Pronouns are words that stand for nouns.

Gretchen made Arnie a tie.
She made him a purple tie.

Pronouns as Subjects and Predicate Pronouns

Some pronouns can be used as the subject of a sentence.

Subject Pronouns	
Singular	**Plural**
I	we
you	you
he, she, it	they

Anna squeezed the oranges.
She made orange juice.

Subject pronouns can also take the place of a predicate noun. When a pronoun follows a linking verb and means the same thing as the subject of a sentence, it is called a predicate pronoun.

The teacher is Mr. Greenberg.
The teacher is he.

Practice

Rewrite the sentences below. Substitute a pronoun for each underlined word or group of words.
1. Luis needed some books.
2. The books were at the library.
3. The librarian is Mrs. Wong.

Pronouns as Objects

Object pronouns are used as direct objects in the predicate part of the sentence.

Object Pronouns	
Singular	**Plural**
me	us
you	you
him, her, it	them

Harriet visited Rita.
Harriet visited her.

The noun or pronoun that follows the preposition is the object of the preposition. Object pronouns are used as objects of the prepositions.

Sharon will wait with the children.
Sharon will wait with them.

Practice

Rewrite the sentences below. Substitute a pronoun for each underlined word or group of words.
1. Masami took Cheryl to the circus.
2. We sat beside Masami and Cheryl.
3. The clowns amused Cheryl and me.
4. This popcorn is for my brother.

Possessive Pronouns

A possessive pronoun shows possession or ownership.

Possessive Pronouns	I bought this bike.
mine, yours, his, hers, its, theirs, ours	This bike is mine.

Practice

Complete each sentence with a possessive pronoun.

1. This red pencil is ———.
2. Frank, is this pencil ———?
3. The girls are sharpening ———.

Ending with *Self* and *Selves*

Pronouns that end in *self* are singular pronouns. Pronouns that end in *selves* are plural pronouns.

Singular Pronouns	Plural Pronouns
myself	ourselves
yourself	yourselves
himself	themselves
herself	
itself	

Avoid mistakes in using pronouns ending in *self* and *selves*.

Do not say:	Do say:
hisself	himself
theirselves	themselves
ourself	ourselves

Practice

Fill in the blanks with a pronoun ending in *self* or *selves*.

1. Ken built this treehouse by ———.
2. His friends carried all this wood by ———.
3. His younger sister can climb this ladder by ———.

Conjunctions

A conjunction is a word that is used to combine words, phrases, or sentences. *And, but,* and *or* are commonly used conjunctions. A comma is placed before a conjunction that is used in a series of words or in a compound sentence.

Angelo makes pizza, spaghetti, <u>and</u> lasagna.
His pizza is good, <u>but</u> I like his lasagna better.

Practice

Use the conjunctions in parentheses to combine the sentences below.
1. Harriet went skiing. Bob went skiing. Jo went skiing.   (and)
2. Bob fell down the hill. He didn't hurt himself.   (but)
3. Should I try the beginner's slope? Should I try this steeper slope?   (or)

Prepositions

A preposition is a word such as *on, at, to, of, from, with,* and *around.*
A prepositional phrase is a phrase made up of a preposition and a noun or pronoun. Sometimes modifiers and noun markers come between the preposition and the noun or pronoun. Prepositional phrases can act as adjectives by telling which one or what kind or as adverbs by telling how, when, or where.

The tree <u>in the yard</u> has no leaves.   (adjective)
The leaves fell <u>to the ground</u>.   (adverb)

Practice

Write each prepositional phrase and tell whether it is acting as an adjective or as an adverb.
1. The ball was hit over the fence.

2. The player ran around the bases.
3. The crowd in the stands cheered.
4. The coach of the losing team looked unhappy.

Contractions

A contraction is one word made up of two words. An apostrophe is used to show that a letter or letters have been left out.

Verb + Not	Contraction	Pronoun + Verb	Contraction
is not	isn't	we will	we'll
will not	won't	I am	I'm
could not	couldn't	he is, has	he's
		you are	you're
		we have	we've

Practice

Write contractions for the words below. Then use the contractions in sentences.

1. are not   3. she will   5. I have
2. they are   4. would not   6. will not

Noun-making Suffixes

A suffix is an ending that is added to a word to change the word's meaning.

The suffixes *-er, -or, -ment, -ance,* and *-ness* can change certain words into nouns.

Words	Suffixes	Nouns
write	er	writer
conduct	or	conductor
entertain	ment	entertainment
assure	ance	assurance
sad	ness	sadness

Practice

Change each of the words below to a noun by adding one of the noun-making suffixes. Then write a sentence for each noun.

1. instruct   3. sing   5. assist
2. assign   4. bold   6. govern

Adjective-making Suffixes

The suffixes -*ful*, -*less*, -*ish*, and -*able* can change some nouns and verbs into adjectives.

Noun	Verb	Suffix	Adjective
care		ful	careful
	wash	able	washable
home		less	homeless
fool		ish	foolish

Practice

Complete each sentence below by adding an adjective-making suffix to each underlined word.

1. We had a <u>wonder</u> time at the zoo.
2. You were <u>fool</u> not to come with us.
3. Giraffes are <u>remark</u> animals.
4. It was <u>use</u> to try to see all the animals.

Problem Words

Homophones

These words are often confused because they sound alike. Notice their meanings and how they are used in sentences.

your, you're	You're finished with your chores now.
its, it's	It's too bad the cat hurt its paw.
there, their, they're	They're working on their projects over there.

Choose the correct word in parentheses to complete each sentence.
1. (Its, It's) a nice day for a picnic.
2. Put (you're, your) lunch over (there, their, they're).
3. (There, their, they're) starting a softball game.

Good, Well

The word *good* is an adjective. It modifies nouns.
The word *well* is an adverb and it modifies verbs.

Bob is a good soccer player.
He played well the last game.

Practice

Fill in the blanks with *good* or *well*.
1. This is a ＿＿ report.
2. You researched the topic ＿＿.
3. I'm sure you will get a ＿＿ grade.

Negative Words

A negative word means "no." Only one negative word is used to make a statement mean "no."

Incorrect—Two Negatives	Correct—One Negative
There isn't nothing here.	There isn't anything here.
	There is nothing here.
I haven't never seen them.	I haven't ever seen them.
	I have never seen them.

Practice

Complete each sentence by choosing the correct word in parentheses.
1. I haven't (ever, never) been to this museum.
2. There are (any, no) dinosaurs like these alive today.
3. I don't know (anything, nothing) about these animals.

Handbook • Mechanics

Abbreviations

An abbreviation is a shortened form of a word. An abbreviation often begins with a capital letter and ends with a period.

Monday	Mon.	doctor	Dr.
November	Nov.	Oak Street	Oak St.

Practice

Rewrite the sentences below, writing each abbreviation correctly.

1. Will pres Jenkins speak at the university tomorrow?
2. He will speak on fri, dec 2.
3. You can buy tickets from mr chen at 34 Meadow ave.
4. Was dr. Sanders at the meeting?

Apostrophes

An apostrophe is used in contractions and with nouns to show possession. See pages 340 and 355.

Capital Letters

Capital letters are used for the following:

proper nouns	See page 338.
proper adjectives	See page 349.
title of a person	Governor Danberg
first word of a greeting in a letter	Dear Jill and Jan,
first word of a closing in a letter	Your cousin,
first word in a direct quotation	Al said, "The bus is coming."
first word, last word, and all important words in a title	*A Wrinkle in Time*

Rewrite the sentences below, adding capital letters where necessary.

1. My friend has a pen pal who lives in tucson, arizona.
2. Her family visited the southwest over labor day.
3. She sent a postcard to her uncle howie.
4. He has written a book on saturn called *the rings of saturn.*

Colons

A colon is used in the following ways:

after the greeting in a business letter	Dear Ms. Park:
between the hour and minutes when the time is written in numbers	4.30
after a speaker's name in a play	Narrator:

Commas

Commas are used in the following ways:

between the name of a city and the state or country	Dallas, Texas Athens, Greece
between the day and the year	June 3, 1981
after the greeting in a friendly letter	Dear Wally,
after the closing in a letter	Yours truly,
to separate a quotation from the rest of the sentence	Kate said, "Here's your book."
after a noun of address	Gina, speak louder.
after an introductory *yes, no,* or *well*	Yes, that is mine.
between the words in a series	Gail, Arturo, and Sam helped me.
before a conjunction in a compound sentence	Sue kicked the ball, and Joe caught it.

after some introductory prepositional phrases	To Paco, Frank looked tired.
with an appositive	Pokey, my turtle, has disappeared.

Practice

Rewrite the following items, adding colons and commas where necessary.

1. 534 Madison Avenue
   Chicago Illinois 60611
   July 9 1980
2. The plane will arrive at 7 31 in the morning.
3. Yes this is Renzo my younger brother.
4. Dear Sir
5. Bill can I borrow your red green and black markers?
6. Sincerely yours
7. Maria said "The cheerleaders will practice today."
8. Pete Allen my neighbor sent this postcard from Madrid Spain.

End Punctuation

A sentence ends with a period, a question mark, or an exclamation mark. See page 332.

Proofreader's Marks

The following marks are used by writers all over the country when they improve their writing.

≡	Make a capital letter.
⊙	Add a period.
℮	Take out.
∧	Put in one or more words.
¶	Begin a new paragraph.
⌄	Put in a comma.

Rewrite the paragraph below, making the changes that are marked.

> Wyoming is a beautiful state. The Rocky mountains tower over the land, and there are sparkling lakes, streams, and waterfalls and many kinds of animals live in this state. Yellowstone National Park is in Wyoming. It is the nation's oldest national park. The park has many spectacular attractions.

Quotation Marks

Quotation marks are used to show the exact words of a speaker.

The coach said, "Watch that player."

Titles of Books

Underline the title of a book.

<u>Charlie and the Glass Elevator</u>

Rewrite the following sentences. Place quotation marks before and after the exact words of a speaker. Underline the titles of books.

1. Pete said, My report is on the book Ramona the Brave.
2. The author, Beverly Cleary, also wrote Henry and Ribsy.
3. Cynthia asked, Did she write the book Runaway Ralph?

Extra Practice

Sentences

Sentence Fragments

Write each item, correcting the fragments. You should correct 6 items.

1. The *Iliad* is a famous story. About a war between the Greeks and the Trojans.
2. The Trojans kept the Greeks outside the city walls. For ten years.
3. Ulysses was the Greek leader. He had a clever idea.
4. He and his men built a wooden horse. As tall as the walls.
5. Ulysses and his brave men hid inside the horse. The Trojans did not know this.
6. The Greeks pretended to sail away. They left the horse behind.
7. The Trojans came to look at the strange horse. After the Greek ships sailed away.
8. The Trojans took the horse. Inside the walls of their city.
9. The Trojans felt certain. That the Greeks had gone for good.
10. The Trojans went to sleep. The Greeks left the horse and captured the city.

Run-on Sentences

Correct the following items to eliminate all run-ons.

1. Jim hit the ball Nancy raced to catch it.
2. She threw the ball quickly to first base, the crowd roared.
3. Mike dashed back to first Julia tagged him out.
4. The third batter up was Kenji he got a fast ball.
5. Kenji hit the ball into left field, it was almost caught.
6. Kenji raced toward second the outfielder fumbled the ball.

Write each item. Correct any run-on sentences.

1. George Washington was the first President of the United States, he was born in 1732.
2. He always celebrated his birthday on February 11.
3. When Washington was born, a different calendar was in use.
4. This calendar was created by Julius Caesar, it was used for over 1500 years.

5. The calendar was not accurate it was off by about eleven minutes a year.
6. Scientists made a new calendar we use this calendar today.
7. Washington's birthday would be on February 22 according to this new calendar.
8. Washington was twenty he did not change his birthday.

Choose the correct form of the verb to complete each sentence.
1. Jim and Alice (is, are) doing their homework.
2. Jim (think, thinks) his problems are difficult.
3. Jim or Alice (check, checks) answers with Mae.
4. Neither the third problem nor the last one (seem, seems) hard.
5. Either the first or the fifth (is, are) the hardest.
6. Alice and Jim (understand, understands) what to do.

Complete each sentence with the correct verb in parentheses.
1. The television and the radio (has, have) news programs.
2. The football and baseball scores (interest, interests) me.
3. The weatherman often (tell, tells) jokes.
4. The most interesting feature (is, are) the local news.
5. Either sports or a feature (end, ends) the broadcast.
6. My dad or my sisters (turn, turns) the TV off.

Nouns

Capitalize all the proper nouns in the following sentences. You should capitalize 28 words.
1. I went to the smithsonian museum in washington.
2. It was founded by james smithson, a scientist.
3. It is located between constitution avenue and independence avenue.
4. I saw charles lindbergh's famous plane.

5. Lindbergh flew his plane across the atlantic ocean.
6. I met my cousins, luis and ramona, in the hall.
7. They had been to a store called woody's.
8. We all went to the national gallery of art.
9. Everyone wanted to see the posters by norman rockwell.
10. Then we climbed to the top of the washington monument.
11. Later, uncle peter took us to a restaurant.
12. On friday we will visit the lincoln memorial.

Singular and Plural Nouns

Rewrite the following sentences, using the plural form of each underlined noun.

1. Zoo are entertaining places to spend an afternoon.
2. My little brother always wants to see the monkey.
3. I like the four buffalo at our local zoo.
4. One has horn that span a distance of at least thirty foot.
5. The baby calf were only a few week old.
6. They like to stand in the shade of large bush.
7. They switch their tail trying to keep the fly away.
8. There aren't any fox in our small zoo.
9. There were wolf at one time, but they have been sent away.
10. Most large city have one or more zoos.

Rewrite the paragraph, using the plural form of each numbered noun.

One hot day, several (1) family on our block decided to have a potluck supper. Dan offered to help me fix several small (2) dish instead of one large one. I gathered the (3) ingredient, and he got out two (4) knife. It took almost an hour to clean, slice, and arrange the (5) tomato, (6) carrot, (7) celery, and (8) clump of fresh cauliflower. I thought we could use (9) mix for dip, but Dan insisted that we make it from scratch. After we finished our work, both of us had several (10) glass of lemonade and some (11) pretzel.

Possessive Nouns

Rewrite each sentence, using the correct possessive form of each underlined noun.

1. The flash flood left the Boy <u>Scouts</u> campsite in a mess.
2. Fortunately, everyone was away on a <u>campers</u> hike.
3. Only the <u>boys</u> gear was damaged.
4. One of <u>Ramon</u> shoes was washed away.
5. The Kelly <u>brothers</u> food was ruined.
6. <u>Mr. Lopez</u> wildlife collection floated away too.
7. <u>Tim</u> tent had been knocked over.
8. <u>Jess</u> tent was never found.
9. The <u>children</u> parents were relieved to hear that no one was hurt.
10. They heard the <u>radio</u> report that night.

Rewrite the paragraphs, using the correct possessive form of each numbered word.

The Meirs were just able to fit into the (1) family van with one extra item each. (2) Pete bat and ball fit under one of the (3) car seats. (4) Cass book could be easily carried. The (5) babies rattles were tied to their car seats. (6) Father thermos and (7) Mother maps fit in the front seat. But (8) Irena biggest problem was where she could fit her dog, Fluff. The (9) parents decision was that Fluff could go if he stayed on the (10) children laps.

Verbs

Tenses of Verbs

Complete each sentence with the verb and verb tense given in parentheses.

1. Most raccoons ____ in North America.   (live, present)
2. You usually ____ a raccoon in a woods near water.   (find, future)
3. Sometimes you ____ wild raccoons in city parks.   (see, future)
4. The raccoons in the zoo ____ like bandits.   (look, past)
5. The patches around their eyes ____ like masks.   (seem, past)
6. Raccoons always ____ everything they eat.   (wash, present)

Complete each sentence with the correct form of the verb.

1. I just (hear, heard) the weather report.
2. It (will rain, rain) again this afternoon.
3. But it (is, will be) clear tomorrow.
4. This weather (remind, reminds) me of my trip to England.
5. It (rain, rained) every day.
6. I almost (wear, wore) out my umbrella.
7. I (become, became) grateful to Samuel Fox.
8. He (invented, will invent) the first collapsible umbrella.

Principle Parts of Regular Verbs

Rewrite the paragraph, using the past or past participle form of each numbered verb.

One evening the winds (1) pound against her house so fiercely that Meg (2) decide to go down to the kitchen for a cup of cocoa. She had (3) ask her little brother Charles to wait there for her. Before long, the two of them had (4) start on an adventure that Meg (5) hope would lead them to their father. He had (6) disappear two years before. At that time his work (7) concentrate on experiments with time travel. The search for their father (8) involve the Murray children, their friend Cal, and three unusual ladies. The ladies were named Mrs. Which, Mrs. Who, and Mrs. Whatsit. To find out how their story (9) end, read *A Wrinkle in Time.*

Complete each sentence with the present, past, or past participle form of the verb in parentheses.

1. Pelé has (retire) from playing professional soccer.
2. As a small boy, Pelé (live) in Bauru, Brazil.
3. His father had (play) soccer whenever he could.
4. Pelé (stuff) his father's socks with newspaper.
5. He (use) these stuffed socks as soccer balls.
6. By age 11, Pelé had (join) a league team.
7. Pelé has (inspire) many soccer players.
8. I (watch) reruns of Pelé's games on television.

Principal Parts of Irregular Verbs

Rewrite the paragraph, using the past or past participle form of each underlined verb.

The other day I <u>find</u> out that the word *school* originally <u>come</u> from the Greek word *schole*. That word first <u>mean</u> "rest or vacation." In ancient Greece, private tutors <u>teach</u> the schoolboys. The boys <u>take</u> lessons in reading, writing, math, music, and gym. But, many <u>feel</u> that the boys were not learning enough. So, the boys <u>give</u> much of their leisure, or *schole,* to listening to the discussions of the wise men. In time, the discussions themselves <u>become</u> known as *schole.* Later, the place to which people <u>go</u> to hear the discussions was called *schole.*

Complete each sentence with the past or past participle form of the verb in parentheses.

1. A fire had _____ out on the southwest side.   (break)
2. Strong winds _____ the flames in every direction.   (blow)
3. Very little rain had _____ that year.   (fall)
4. As the fire spread, people _____ from their homes.   (run)
5. Many had been _____ with only a few of their belongings.   (leave)
6. Thousands of people had _____ homeless.   (become)

Problem Verbs

Rewrite the paragraphs, choosing the correct words in parentheses.

It wasn't such a good idea to (borrow, lend) Jody's dog, Spark. Jody wasn't really eager to (borrow, lend) Spark to me. So I (took, brought) him away without explaining my plans. Jody did yell after me that I shouldn't (let, leave) Spark get near any cats.

I needed Spark because I wanted to (teach, learn) him to pull my brother's wagon. I had to (bring, take) a batch of papers to the community collection center. I had Spark (sit, set) down and nap while I loaded the wagon. I had just (set, sit) a weight on the papers when our cat walked by Spark. In no time at all, the wagon was broken, the cat was in the tree, and papers were (laying, lying) everywhere.

367

Choose the correct word in parentheses to complete each sentence.

1. My uncle promised to (lend, borrow) me his video game.
2. He wanted to (learn, teach) me how to use it first.
3. Last month he (took, brought) everything over to my house.
4. I looked over the material I would have to (learn, teach).
5. We (sat, set) on the couch and went over the instructions.
6. He said he would (let, leave) it for two weeks.
7. I promised not to (lend, borrow) it to any of my friends.
8. I hope he'll forget to (take, bring) the game back home.

Adjectives

Using Adjectives to Compare

Rewrite the paragraph, using the correct form of each underlined adjective.

Nkeka and Jon like to play the superlative house game. They pretend that they will buy a house with the thick walls and high ceilings you have ever seen. Their living room will be ugly than one they saw in a horror movie. They plan to have three chairs in the room. One would be the large they could find, another the beautiful, and the third chair the expensive. They want the large one to be comfortable than the expensive one. Whenever Nkeka and Jon plan their house, Jon's sister says, "Your plans and your game are the silly I've heard of."

Complete each sentence with the correct form of the adjective in parentheses.

1. Lately, there's been ____ interest than ever in black holes.   (much)
2. The ____ way to describe them is as the vacuum cleaners of the universe.   (good)
3. Some black holes are ____ than a golf ball.   (small)
4. One that size would still be ____ than our solar system.   (heavy)
5. Anything, even the ____ space station, can be sucked into a black hole.   (large)
6. Its gravity is ____ than any other force.   (strong)

Adjectives Used as Prepositional Phrases

Write the sentences. Underline the prepositional phrase in each, and circle the noun each phrase modifies.

1. Cabbies in London need more than a driver's license.
2. They must know every street in the city.
3. They must identify the shortest route between two locations.
4. They must also know the fastest way through the busy streets.
5. Cabbies must study and memorize the streets of London.
6. They must pass a written and an oral test of their knowledge.
7. This is the most important test of their lives.
8. The rewards for passing the test are great.

Proper Adjectives

Rewrite the following paragraph, capitalizing all the proper adjectives. You should capitalize 17 words.

Last summer we went to the second international Folk Fair. We watched dancers do irish jigs, russian sword dances, and sioux rain dances. There were tables and tables of german streusel, greek pastries, chinese rice candy, and african fruits to snack on. In one area we saw lovely polish, turkish, and caribbean handicrafts. A jamaican craftsman was also there. We are looking forward to going to the third international folk Fair. Many american families will attend it.

Rewrite the following sentences, correcting all errors in capitalization. You should capitalize 11 words.

1. I like to watch the olympic events on television.
2. I would like to be on the american ski team.
3. It would be thrilling to compete with japanese, french, and russian skiers.
4. The european competitors are usually tough to beat.
5. Many skiers train on the steep swiss slopes.
6. Of course, it would also be great to match skills with dutch and austrian skaters.
7. Last year a yugoslavian couple won the competition.
8. A canadian skating pair was my pick.

Adverbs

Adjectives or Adverbs
Tell whether the underlined word or phrase in each
sentence is used as an adjective or adverb.

1. Miyoko walked quickly down the
   street.
2. She was following a man with a
   tan briefcase.
3. Miyoko wondered what was going
   on and waited impatiently.
4. Finally the man appeared, but he
   no longer had the tan briefcase.
5. The man nervously looked around
   to see if he was being followed.
6. Then he started up the steps of an
   old brown house.
7. Miyoko now had a clue to the
   mystery.
8. The thief was not planning to keep
   the stolen jewels himself.

Tell whether each underlined word or phrase in the
paragraph below is used as an adjective or adverb.

The cheetah is a large cat of the
plains of Africa and Asia. Because of
its long body and slender legs, the
cheetah can run faster than most
animals. It is the fastest animal
known for running short distances.

The cheetah moves through the grass
quietly. Then it swiftly rushes after its
prey. Hunters in India have tamed
and trained cheetahs. The number of
cheetahs is declining. The species is
nearly extinct in Asia.

Using Adverbs to Compare
Choose the correct positive, comparative, or superlative
form of the adverb in each sentence below.

1. Pedro arrived at the pool the
   (earliest, earlier) of anyone.
2. He (nervous, nervously) changed
   into his trunks.
3. He had trained (more harder,
   harder) for this meet than the
   last meet.
4. Also, the coach had worked
   (patient, patiently) with him.
5. He expected Pedro to do (good,
   better) with the crawl than with
   the butterfly.
6. Pedro did (better, best) of all in
   the freestyle.

Write the following sentences, using the correct form of
the adverbs in parentheses.

1. "Two weeks from now is the (soon) I can offer you more work," said Mrs. Grey regretfully.
2. "You have worked (reliably) than our other errand runner."
3. Tanya nodded her head (sadly).
4. It seemed (hard) than ever to pay for her horse, Thunder.
5. Thunder was growing (fast) than ever before.
6. He ate the (eagerly) of any horse she had ever seen.

Using *Good* and *Well*

Use *good* or *well* to complete each sentence.

1. My friend Fran can't cook very
   .
2. In fact, even her plain, boiled eggs don't taste very ____.
3. I planned to give her a ____ cookbook for her birthday.
4. I decided that a cookbook would not be such a ____ gift.
5. I know of a cookbook that sells quite ____.
6. Fran's brother, George, is a ____ cook.
7. He prepares plain and fancy dishes ____.
8. George especially makes ____ desserts.
9. No one wants to tell Fran that she's not a ____ cook.
10. She should stick to doing things she does ____.

Using Negative Words

Complete each sentence with the correct word in
parentheses.

1. "Haven't (any, none) of you ever been to France?" asked Mr. Star.
2. (Any, No) pupils had been there.
3. Emile said that he was born in England, but he had been to (any, no) other country.
4. "Do you know (anything, nothing) about England?" asked Mr. Star.
5. "I didn't live there (any, no) longer than four years."
6. "I couldn't really learn (anything, nothing) much."
7. "Even worse, I don't remember (anything, nothing) I learned."
8. "My family hasn't (any, no) good pictures of England."

Direct Objects, Predicate Adjectives, Predicate Nouns

Write these sentences and identify each underlined word.
Put DO above each direct object, PA above each predicate
adjective, and PN above each predicate noun.

1. King Arthur is a popular British folk <u>hero</u>.
2. He was an important Celtic <u>chief</u>.
3. Camelot, his castle, was <u>well-run</u> and <u>secure</u>.
4. Arthur was <u>skillful</u> and <u>successful</u> in war.
5. He fought and defeated the Germanic <u>invaders</u>.
6. He was the last Celtic <u>chief</u> to do so.
7. Perhaps King Arthur was not his real <u>name</u>.
8. Perhaps Camelot was not a real <u>castle</u> either.
9. But scientists have discovered an ancient Celtic <u>camp</u>.
10. According to some scholars, this camp was <u>Camelot</u>.

Write these sentences. Underline each direct object, put
two lines under each predicate adjective, and circle each
predicate noun.

1. James Thomas Brudenell was the seventh Earl of Cardigan.
2. He commanded a cavalry troop in the Crimean War.
3. He ordered the Light Brigade into a fatal ambush.
4. But Cardigan is famous for something else as well.
5. The weather was terribly cold in the Crimea.
6. Cardigan wore a knitted woolen vest to keep himself warm.
7. His officers copied the style of his vest.
8. Soon the cardigan sweater became popular.

Pronouns

Pronouns as Subjects, Objects, and Predicate
Pronouns

Complete each sentence with the correct pronoun.

1. You and (I, me) probably eat cereal for breakfast often.
2. It was news to (I, me) that cereal was named for Ceres.

3. It was (she, her) who was the goddess of cereal grains.
4. The Greeks made sacrifices to (she, her).
5. Modern farmers no longer believe in (she, her).
6. Science helps (they, them) with their crops.

Rewrite the paragraph below, choosing the correct pronouns in parentheses.

When Thomas Edison was a boy, (he, him) asked many questions. His mother, a teacher, couldn't answer (they, them) all. It was (she, her) who taught (he, him) at home. (She, Her) gave (he, him) books to read. (He, Him) tried every experiment in (they, them). Sometimes (he, him) had accidents with (they, them). (We, Us) now have electric lights because of (he, him). If ever there was a genius, it was (he, him).

Possessive Pronouns and Problem Words

Complete each sentence with the correct word in parentheses.

1. That red jacket with the gold buttons is (my, mine.)
2. It looks very much like (your, you're) jacket.
3. But (their, there) is a navy stripe on (my, mine) collar.
4. (Our, Are) jackets are similar to Bill's and Tom's.
5. Both of (their, there) jackets are down-filled.
6. (There, They're) extremely warm jackets, even in cold weather.
7. We have name labels in the pockets of (our, are) jackets.
8. (Your, You're) careful not to lose (your, you're) jacket.

Rewrite the paragraph below, choosing the correct words in parentheses.

Tom picked out a robot for (your, you're) birthday. All of (its, it's) special features were chosen by Tom. (Their, There) were many kinds of robots at the factory. (Their, There) features were all different. I know which robot would be (your, you're) first choice. You would want one that would keep (your, you're) room clean. The robot over (their, there) washes dishes. (Its, It's) a very popular machine.

Conjunctions and Compound Sentences

Conjunctions

Write the sentences and circle the conjunction in each.

1. Both American Indians and Egyptians built pyramids.
2. Pyramids were used as temples, or they were used as tombs.
3. Egyptians mummified their kings' bodies and hid them in tombs in secret chambers.
4. Gold and precious objects were placed with the king's tomb.
5. The king's relatives and servants were buried nearby.
6. Spanish conquerors destroyed many pyramids in Mexico, but there are still some standing.

Write the conjunction in each sentence. Then tell whether it joins subjects, predicates, or sentences.

1. The kite may have been invented by a Greek, or the Chinese may have invented it.
2. Dragons or butterflies make beautiful designs for kites.
3. Paper can be used as a covering, but cloth is stronger.
4. Benjamin Franklin flew a kite during a storm and made an important discovery.
5. Weather bureaus and armies have used kites for various purposes.
6. Many communities conduct kite tournaments and give prizes.

Compound Sentences

Use a conjunction to combine each pair of sentences into one compound sentence.

1. Mario trains his dog Howie. He teaches Howie tricks.
2. Howie can shake hands and roll over. He will not play dead.
3. After each trick, Mario pets Howie. He gives Howie a treat.
4. Sometimes Howie chases cats. He barks to scare them away.
5. Mario entered Howie in a local dog show. Howie did not win.
6. Howie fetches the newspaper every morning. He drops it at the back door.
7. Howie is a gentle dog. He is a good watchdog.
8. Howie is playful. He is smart.

Punctuation and Capitalization

Rewrite the thank-you note below, correcting the mistakes in capitalization and punctuation.

217 grove street
houston texas 77020
May 3. 19__

dear aunt mary:
   Thank you for the backpack you sent me for my birthday. It seems durable, and it's just the right size. I will enjoy using it on bicycle and hiking trips.

your nephew
Dryan

Rewrite the friendly letter below, correcting the mistakes in capitalization and punctuation.

39 meadow road
atlanta. georgia 31314
February 3 19__

dear margo
   I enjoyed your last letter very much. Congratulations on getting the lead in your school play. Write and tell me what your costume is like.
   A few weeks ago Midnight had five kittens. They're all cute, but they're a lot of work. That's why this letter is so short.

your friend.
Carolyn

Rewrite the business letter below, correcting the mistakes in capitalization and punctuation.

419 8th street
whittier. california 90605
september 4 19___

allen sporting goods company
416 mountain drive
denver colorado 80224

dear Ms or Mrs,
Please send me your most recent catalog of camping and hiking equipment. I have seen some of your products advertised in your company's magazine.
If there is any cost, please notify me. I will send the money promptly.

yours truly
Kimiko Tanaka

Address an envelope to go with the business letter above. Be sure to use capital letters and punctuation correctly in the following parts of the envelope.

1. return address
2. mailing addresss

Index